BLOOD
OF THE
TIGER

BLOOD
OF THE
TIGER

A Story of Conspiracy,
Greed, and the Battle to Save
a Magnificent Species

J. A. MILLS

BEACON PRESS, BOSTON

Beacon Press
Boston, Massachusetts
www.beacon.org

Beacon Press books
are published under the auspices of
the Unitarian Universalist Association of Congregations.

18 17 16 15   8 7 6 5 4 3 2 1

This book is printed on acid-free paper that meets
the uncoated paper ANSI/NISO specifications for
permanence as revised in 1992.

Text design by Wilsted & Taylor Publishing Services

Library of Congress Cataloging-in-Publication Data
Mills, Judy A., author.
Blood of the tiger : a story of conspiracy, greed, and the battle to save a magnificent
species / J.A. Mills.
    pages cm
Provided by publisher.
 Includes bibliographical references and index.
 ISBN 978-0-8070-7496-1 (hardcover) — ISBN 978-0-8070-7497-8 (ebook)
 1. Tiger trade—China. I. Title.
 SK593.T54M55 2015
 639.97'9756—dc23   2014015760

For tigers,
the Croc Farm bear,
and Mingma Norbu Sherpa,
who died in service to wildness

The most alive is the wildest.
Not yet subdued to man,
its presence refreshes him.

HENRY DAVID THOREAU, "WALKING"

He who rides the tiger
is afraid to dismount.

CHINESE PROVERB

CONTENTS

1

THE THRALL OF THE WILD

For fifty-seven years after "the Crown of the Continent" became Montana's Glacier National Park, there was not a single documented case of a grizzly killing a human. Then, between midnight and dawn on August 13, 1967, two grizzlies killed two nineteen-year-old women at two different backcountry campsites nine mountainous miles apart.

While nestled in for my first-ever overnight in the backcountry, deep within Canada's side of what is now Waterton-Glacier International Peace Park, I was gripped by the details of that gruesome night, as chronicled by Jack Olson in *Night of the Grizzlies*.[1] In a small orange tent, inside my blue sleeping bag with a red down jacket rolled under my head, I shined the flashlight in my right hand on the paperback in my left. I joked with my wilderness-savvy boyfriend Larry Slonaker about feeling like we were in that *Far Side* cartoon in which two bears behind trees peer at three people in sleeping bags and declare, "Sandwiches!"

"Are you sure we won't become bear sandwiches tonight?" I said, flashing a smile I didn't feel.

"You'll be fine," Larry said, kissing my forehead as if I were a child afraid of ghosts.

I read on.

"You know, I really *am* worried about becoming a bear sandwich."

Larry didn't respond. He didn't hear my fear unfurl because he had floated serenely into his dreams.

What haunted me most about Olson's account was Julie Helgeson's cry for her mother, who was hundreds of impossible miles away when a grizzly pulled the slim Minnesota coed from the warmth of her sleeping bag into the chilly blackness below the towering spires of the Continental Divide. And how another grizzly, nine miles across the park's astonishing vertical contours, dragged away delicate California beauty Michele Koons from a circle of campers bedded down beside an alpine lakeshore.

Larry and I had camped just above six thousand feet, four and a half miles up a steep, rocky path from a trailhead on a narrow strip of Waterton Lake's long, mountain-rimmed shoreline accessible only by boat. Our tent was thirty paces from a trail that was little more than a ledge that clawed its way along a cliff face and into a round of turquoise water cupped by soaring rock. *How apt it's called Crypt Lake*, I thought. If a grizzly did attack us, no one would hear our cries. And we had no means to call in help.

I lay awake all night, straining to listen and imagining in detail. *Was that a bear? Was THAT?* I tried to grasp how alone those young women must have felt as they were pulled over plants, rocks, and fallen trees in the death clamp of creatures they could barely see. *What was it like for them? What was it really like?*

Halfway to dawn, I could no longer ignore my nagging bladder. But my mind saw the menace in wait. His dished forehead above close-set dark eyes, his humped back, his shimmering silver-tipped fur. His long snout with yellow fangs set in a steel-trap jaw. If I stepped outside to relieve my growing discomfort, he would surely carry me off by my bare bottom, ankles tangled in jeans. Then again, what defense was a bubble of orange nylon against four-inch switchblade claws? I had never spent a longer night or known such unremitting fear.

I rejoiced at first light and made my loo just inches from the back of the tent. Immediately after our breakfast of instant coffee and oatmeal, we packed up and I led a speed-trudge down miles of switchbacks. Larry tried to calm me with facts. The main causes of death in Glacier were drowning, heart attack, car accidents, and falling from high places. Did I know I was exponentially more likely to get hit by lightning than mauled by a grizzly?

"C'mon, Heart," he said, "we're going to be fine."

Yes, he called me Heart. And wrote me love poems. As assistant city editor at the newspaper where I worked in Washington State, he massaged my stories from the cop beat into better reads. But I didn't think he could knock out a grizzly.

After a three-hour forced march, accompanied by an unbroken stream of my anxious babbling, off-key singing, and clapping of hands to scare off bears, we reached the trailhead. I plopped down, backpack still affixed, at the far end of the dock to await the water taxi that would motor us back to the tourist bustle of Waterton Township.

As it turned out, safe ground was far less transcendent than I had so desperately anticipated. Instead of feeling heady with relief when we checked into the storied Prince of Wales Hotel on its panoramic bluff above the lake, I felt deflated. Let down. Less alive. Something wondrous had gone missing. I thought it was the vertiginous dazzle of Glacier's backcountry. But it wasn't.

Shortly after I started a new job at another daily newspaper, a large male grizzly entered a campground near Yellowstone National Park on a moonlit summer night, tore open a tent with two Wisconsin men inside, yanked one out, and dragged him into the woods. When rescuers found twenty-three-year-old Roger May an hour later, he was dead and missing some seventy pounds of flesh and blood.[2] I begged my editors to dispatch me to write about killer bears.

As I neared the site of the attack in my burgundy Honda Civic, I began to feel what had slipped my grasp after escaping my imagined Night of the Grizzlies near Crypt Lake. I call it the Man-Eater Effect.

It wasn't the threat of being eaten alive that energized me. It was the firing on all primal cylinders to *avoid* being eaten. Cylinders most of us rarely, if ever, activate. The primordial cocktail of chemicals that floods the human brain on alert for man-eaters brings a person sublimely, electrically, and wholly to life. Every detail of every second becomes acutely vivid. The color of wildflowers and whether any favored by man-eaters have been nibbled. A slight movement on a hillside. A muddy spot that could have registered a massive paw passing by. An abrupt change in birdsong or the flick of a deer's ears that could signal alarm. The snap of a twig in forest shadows.

This heightened state was better than the morphine bliss that once made me sit up on a gurney leaving an operating room and ask, "Can we do that again?" It's the full-on mindful state our brains were wired for, before guns and wheels gave us dominion over all other creatures and the leisure to let our most arousing instincts atrophy. There are modern-day facsimiles. Like the opiates our brains generate when we fall in love, exercise into a "runner's high," parachute out of perfectly good airplanes, reach orgasm, or eat dark chocolate. The Man-Eater Effect is more akin to the high that compels war veterans to seek repeated stints in combat. There's just no brain chemistry like that triggered by the possibility of becoming prey.

In reality, wild animals capable of killing us rarely do. Except in desperation or fear—when they're unable to hunt quicker, less-dangerous game or when their young seem at risk. Otherwise, humans are to be avoided. We come with trouble that is often deadly—a threat now encoded in the instincts of most wild animals that could eat us. In normal circumstances, *we* are the ones who seek exhilaration in proximity to *them*. Entire industries are built on our desire to get as close as safely possible to wild tigers, lions, bears, and many other species that could kill us at whim. Their wildness unleashes our own.

Before discovering man-eaters, I held no romantic notions about wild places and their inhabitants. I was a mall-rat child of Federal Way, Washington, a strip development cemented on either side of what was once the main highway between Seattle and Tacoma. I grew up with zero affinity for zoos, the pictures in *National Geographic*, or wildlife documentaries. The only predator I could name was Ted Bundy. My formative hobbies were thinking and talking about boys and clothes. My mother and I bonded while combing the racks at Nordstrom, then communing afterward over Starbucks and a shared piece of carrot cake. It was only by serendipity that I came to be a newspaper reporter in the thrall of wildness rather than the pie-baking fashionista wife Mom raised me to be.

Once I felt it, the Man-Eater Effect redefined me. This drug-better-than-any-other compelled me to elope with a bear specialist, move to bear country, go to grad school, and leave journalism for investigating wildlife trade. I later divorced and moved halfway across the world for it. One day I would risk nearly everything for it, but only after my new vocation delivered me into the remains of a maharaja's hunting palace in the dry forests of northwestern India, where I fell under the spell of the King of the Jungle. (Yes, the tiger is the jungle king; the lion reigns over the savanna.)

My colleague Ashok Kumar, an elegantly bald businessman turned full-time conservationist, arranged my enchantment. He booked us overnight via vintage sleeper car on a train from New Delhi to Sawai Madhopur, the stop for Ranthambore Tiger Reserve in the heart of the arid state of Rajasthan. I could hardly believe the domes and archways of the Arabian Nights architecture and the parade of epochs that passed by every few moments on the two-lane road to the park. A man walking a camel from a biblical age was followed by a turbaned Sikh at the wheel of a dusty white 1950s Ambassador taxi followed by a uniformed driver ferrying a VIP in a shiny new black Mercedes. Women walking beside the road wore airy saris of tomato red, saffron, and every shade of the desert sky at sunset. Semi-precious stones sparkled from the pierced ears of men and women.

The driver of our topless India-made jeep barely stopped at Ranthambore's guard post because of our boisterous, barrel-chested host Fateh Singh Rathore, the park's retired field director. With a graying handlebar mustache and thick sideburns, a khaki Stetson, aviator sunglasses, and a tiger-print ascot tucked in his safari shirt, Fateh may have looked like a Bollywood caricature, but he had once been beaten nearly to death by attackers for his bold initiatives to protect the reserve's tigers.[3] A decade later, he enjoyed the run of the place as if it were his private estate.

Our jeep passed under a stone arch overgrown with thick vines from a monster banyan tree and into a woodland oasis ringed by red hills that was more fanciful than any movie set. At the side of the dirt road, pilgrims draped with marigold garlands streamed toward a temple for the elephant-headed god Ganesha inside a medieval fortress at the park's highest vantage. Below Ranthambore Fort stretched a plain dotted with blue lakes and the remains of stone arches, domes, and steps from an ancient palace complex surrounded by what were once the private hunting forests of Rajput kings. With hunters long gone, tigers sometimes napped, even gave birth, on the ruins.

Families of langur monkeys crossed the road, their undulating tails longer than their lithe bodies, or sat in trees, staring from black faces framed in platinum fur. Groups of spotted deer grazed in the spare shade of scrubby dhok trees not far from clusters of larger, meatier sambar deer. Peacocks flaunted arrays of eyes with their splayed tail feathers. The only sound besides birdsong and the occasional yip of a deer or langur announcing a passing predator came from our driver gunning the gas.

Fateh and Ashok were what Indians call tiger wallahs—experts in the ways of India's elusive and revered national animal. Fateh was legendary for knowing every tiger by its stripes and for sensing where tigers could be found at any moment. The park rule of keeping to the road did not apply to us. His driver took us speeding through forest, across meadows, and up streambeds.

When we spotted the tigress in the tall, golden grass on a hill above a large pond, there was something familiar about her. She was a cat, after all, and I'd lived with house cats all my life. But I'd never seen a living creature so vivid and perfectly drawn. Her burnt orange was much deeper than I'd imagined and the black of her stripes much bolder. I hadn't anticipated the stark white of her belly fur or the white spots flashing at the backs of her rounded ears. Her paws were as big as my face. She was a sleek, muscled eight feet from heart-shaped pink nose to black-tipped tail. The same weight as a grizzly but 100 percent carnivorous. No berries or wildflowers in this one's diet. Another animal—on four legs or two—would have to die for her to eat.

We watched as she lay in hiding, ears rotating to pick up threats and opportunities. Now and then she raised her nose to sample the warm breeze coming from the direction of a sambar group languidly munching plants in the pond's shallows thirty yards downhill.

"Let's go," Ashok said. "I think she's settled in for a rest."

"No," I said. "She's about to go after those deer."

Afterward, Ashok asked me how I had known what her next move would be when I'd never seen a wild tiger before that week. "Because my cats are just like her," I told him. I recognized the ears and whiskers shifting forward in preparation to pounce. Her body tensed, golden eyes fixed on the grazing sambar. A minute later, she rose slowly into a deep crouch and began to inch her way downhill, muscles taut to keep her footfalls silent. One massive forepaw advanced past the other, belly low to the ground, mighty back held below the tops of the swaying grass. The deer carried on dining at water's edge as the sun arced toward dusk. No langurs were perched in the scattering of nearby trees to call out the killer's approach.

I held my breath as she stood to her full height and leaped into a sprint. The sambar herd panicked, bolting in two groups around the jeeps that had clustered with ours. A lone adult female deer ran directly toward us. The tigress closed the gap in seconds. She released a quick roar as her powerful back legs propelled her airborne, mouth open, landing with teeth sunk deep in the deer's neck, only a foot from our front tires. The deer's legs frantically pedaled the air before relaxing into death. The tigress, mouth still locked on neck, dragged the limp body up the hill between her splayed legs. Three cubs with teenage appetites lay hidden safe from our sight.

As the tigress disappeared over the hill, I felt something in me go with her. A giant creature so familiar, so deadly, so artfully detailed seemed impossible. The intimacy of witnessing her wildly take a life so she could live made me feel anointed. I had seen magnificence embodied. The only thing I yearned for more than seeing it again was to protect it.

I saw five wild tigers in five days—one for each of the remaining subspecies identified at that time—and took this as a directive from the Great Mystery to pivot my passions toward tigers. Valmik Thapar, a brooding, bearish man who is arguably India's most fervent tiger wallah, would tell you that I'd been bewitched into the Cult of the Tiger.[4]

• • •

Biologists call the tiger an apex species because it eats from the top of the food chain. Microbes in the soil nourish the plants and trees that feed and shelter the boar and deer that sustain the tiger. Protecting tigers protects them all, along with the many goods and services humans enjoy from intact forests.

I call the tiger an apex species because it sits at the center of an extraordinary international drama. Since I first fell under the tiger's spell, I have watched the jungle king enthrall many people. Whether they were drawn to save or exploit the monarch, they were all on fire with it.

Human reason and moderation seem to evaporate in proximity to tigers. This may be an innate response. Besides their well-reasoned fear of tigers, humans throughout history have found reflected glory in the beast's dominance and allure. Ancient Chinese saw the character for "king" written in the stripes on the tiger's forehead. For centuries, China maintained a tradition of "rulers establishing their legitimacy by demonstrating their dominion over wild, disorderly things—tigers in particular," according to historian Robert Marks.[5] Chinese warlords sat on tiger skins to manifest their power. In Southeast Asia and on the Indian subcontinent, nobles over centuries hunted or ordered the killing of tigers to demonstrate their entitlement to rule—kings killing "kings" to prove their kingliness. In modern times, the tiger's name and image are ubiquitous, invoked to convey superiority in everything from gasoline to sports teams to national economies—even a style of parenting. A 2004 survey of *Animal Planet* viewers in seventy-three countries named the tiger the world's favorite animal, ahead of "man's best friend" and also the dolphin, horse, lion, elephant, and whale.[6]

What most people don't know is that there are businessmen working to capture the tiger's intoxicating essence, mass-produce it, and sell it globally in the form of luxury consumer goods. Bears led me to tigers, and tigers led me to this scheme to make billions of dollars for a handful of backers—a conspiracy so treacherous that it threatens to take out the world's last wild tigers and a growing list of other invaluable species.

You might ask how such a thing could happen in our linked-in,

Google-searched, viral-videoed, tiger-loving global village, where even the Taliban and NATO forces communicate via Twitter and the NSA can't keep its secrets. The major driver is an old-school Communist Party mandate brought to fruition by a small group of Chinese entrepreneurs in league with a cadre of government bureaucrats. Many in the international community who might intervene have had their hands and tongues tied by threats from the wild tiger's archenemies. Meanwhile, the United States, once the wild tiger's most aggressive defender, has dirty tiger secrets of its own—a fact little known among Americans that is closely watched by Chinese officials.

My fervent, sometimes inelegant efforts to stop this menace to the King of the Jungle have led me on a thrilling journey of intrigue, triumph, and heartbreak, via transport ranging from elephant back to tuk-tuk to presidential motorcade. I enlisted help from the industry that nearly doomed wild tigers in the 1990s, assembled an alliance with more than a million voices to say no to the insanity, and brought the president of the World Bank and a Hollywood legend into the fray, which then took me to a tsar's gilded palace on the Baltic Sea with hope that world leaders would intercede. All of this led me to you.

As I write, the King of the Jungle cannot outrun death much longer. No Asian forest is deep enough. No protected area can be fortified enough. Not even the United Nations holds sway. And when the last wild tiger takes a bullet, its blood will stain China's hands forever. Other hands too. Hands you would not suspect. The hands of poachers, of course. And smugglers. But also of biologists, conservation groups, civil servants, World Bank officials, at least one army, and several world leaders. My hands as well. I could have done more. Mistakes were made. Betrayals were many.

In telling you what I've seen and heard, I'll name some names, but none in spite. I've witnessed more than a little outlandishness along my unlikely path. I promise to tell only those indelicacies that may help wild tigers. Some people will say I shouldn't be telling you this. But how can I not? While there's still time.

2

THE PROMISE

They were both in small cages, miles apart, sitting on their rumps in the sauna that is Bangkok at midday. One was homeless; the other surrounded by crocodiles. These two bears led me to other bears, across America and the world, turning up dead, with nothing but their gall bladders and paws missing. While tracking them, I stumbled upon tigers, who were in even greater peril from the same threat.

The Bangkok bears gave me the story that changed my life. They inspired me to do more than I otherwise would have had courage to do. They diverted me from making a home and babies in Montana so that I could fight a twenty-year war against an ominous subterfuge inside the country that invented *The Art of War.*

And it all happened because of bear barbecue.[1]

I met the first of the Bangkok bears in January 1989 while en route to Taiwan with the trim, mustachioed biologist I had recently married. Many people knew me then as "the wife of" Dr. Christopher Servheen, US grizzly bear recovery coordinator. Chris had been the main source for my story on killer bears in the Rocky Mountains, which grew into a nine-part series and, nine months later, our elopement to the US Virgin Islands.

"Don't tell anyone you're a journalist," Chris told me once I was his missus. He thought journalists were professional bottom-feeders because they published "news" that lacked statistically proven hypotheses and painstaking peer review. He was ashamed of the occupation I loved. His reproach was a red flag, but there were many of those, which both of us were too in lust to notice at the time. We should have heeded the fortune-cookie wisdom pinned to the dashboard of Chris's Ford pickup: "In youth and beauty, wisdom is rare."

I had quit my newspaper job in Washington to freelance for magazines from Chris's small, picket-fenced home in Missoula, Montana, a college town cradled at one end of a Rocky Mountain valley. Despite assignments from *Outside, Smithsonian,* and other respected magazines, it wasn't long before I began to feel like a wild trout confined to a bathtub—a feeling I shared with Chris after I started having paralyzing panic attacks. So when Taiwan's government invited Chris to advise on its bear problems, we scrimped enough for me to tag along.

This mountainous, potato-shaped island slightly smaller than Switzerland, where the government of the Republic of China fled from Mao Zedong's new People's Republic of China in 1949, seemed an unlikely place for wild bears. But bears are tenaciously widespread, ranging from Arctic ice to equatorial jungle, as far south as the Andes. In 1989, an estimated one hundred thousand of eight distinct varieties roamed the wilds of four continents. Asia's five species—Asiatic black, brown (cousins to grizzlies), sloth, sun, and panda—were all under threat from overhunting and shrinking forests. Taiwan had only Asiatic black bears, which look like American black bears but with longer fur and a wide, blond crescent across their chests.

Our routing to Taipei had a stopover in Bangkok, so we stayed a couple days to call on local bear specialists. The calm of our first morning touring golden-spired Buddhist temples quickly vanished as we foolishly traversed the city on foot, dodging speeding taxis, tuk-tuks, and motorcycles, all spewing fumes that made my lungs itch. We finally found sanctuary inside the quiet, two-story building that housed Wildlife Fund Thailand, where we paid our respects to Secretary General Pisit na Patalung.

"I'm honored to meet you, Kuhn Pisit," I said, using the Thai term for mister. His wire-rimmed glasses made him appear the wise elder, but standing next to him I felt like an Amazon.

He bowed with his palms joined in front of his heart. "*Sawatdee-krab*," he said with a serene smile. "Please call me Pisit."

He invited us to take tea under the ceiling fans in his second-floor office. But before we could sit, his phone rang. He excused himself and spoke for several minutes. When he was done, it rang again. Again he took the call.

While Pisit talked in what sounded like one long singsong word, I looked down into the building's courtyard framed by a crush of tropical plants. In the center sat a small iron cage that contained a creature not much bigger than a medium-sized dog, sitting up as if it too were about to have tea.

"Chris, come look at this," I said.

"That's a sun bear," he said.

Sun bears are the smallest of all bears. They have crew-cut fur, blond snouts, and a blond "U" marking their narrow chests. Tiny rounded ears give them a Mickey Mouse quality that belies their killer jaw and irascible nature. They inhabit the tangled jungles of Southeast Asia and are sometimes called honey bears because they use their long, sickle-shaped claws to climb high into rainforest canopies to raid sticky sweets from beehives.

"The calls are about that bear," Pisit said, when he finally joined us. The bear's owners had given him to the king, who had given him to Wildlife Fund Thailand. "None of the zoos can take him," Pisit said. "They're all full." The only adoption offer had come from a Korean willing to pay $1,600. "Probably for a restaurant," Pisit said.

"A restaurant?" I said.

"Koreans come here to eat bears," he said. "They eat the meat and paws, then take the gall bladder home to use as medicine."

"Is that legal?" I said. Chris tensed. I was slipping into journalist mode.

Eating bears was illegal, but keeping them as pets was not. The bear in the courtyard had been someone's pet. The law allowed two wild pets per person, and Thai Buddhists believed taking in wild animals was a good deed rewarded in the afterlife. So it wasn't unusual to see bears caged or chained in people's homes, at gas stations, in department stores, even outside brothels. The combination of good karma and legality was driving a steady stream of hunters into Indochina's forests to bag baby bears to sell to well-meaning Thai city folk.

A single bear cub was worth several months' salary to a working-class Thai and far more to the rural villagers catching them. A mother bear had to be captured or killed before anyone could get near her cubs, but middlemen also wanted adult bears to sell directly to restaurants. A mother and cub together could bring a poacher the equivalent of nearly half a year's wage. Wildlife brokers provided traps to villagers near forests, offering money in advance and promising to buy every bear caught. If a broker received a special order for a bear, he needed only to send word to his village network. The cumulative effect was hammering the region's bear populations.

Within a few months, cuddly sun bear cubs developed formidable muscles, teeth, and claws, leaving owners in residence with dangerous wild animals. "People who grow tired of these bears are usually very happy to let them go for a few thousand baht," Pisit said. About $100—less than half of what they usually paid. Animal brokers promised placement in good homes. Relieved owners didn't realize "a good home" likely meant a Korean restaurant.

As more unwitting Thais adopted and grew weary of pet bears, more Koreans were flying to Bangkok to savor bear banquets and smuggle home gall bladders. During the 1988 Summer Olympics, thirty bears were shipped from Bangkok to Seoul to fortify South Korea's athletes.

I grew up with teddy bears in my bed, Smokey Bear trying to prevent forest fires, and Yogi Bear yabba-dabba-dooing in Jellystone Park. I had only just discovered the magic of wild bears in the real Yellowstone and had fallen in love with their federally appointed savior. What Pisit was explaining was as inconceivable to me then as people flying airliners into New York's World Trade Center.

"How do the restaurants kill them?" I asked.

Pisit hesitated. "They club them to death."

•   •   •

A gridlocked crawl past gilded temples, glass high-rises, and weathered shanties lining canals crowded with boats selling fresh produce brought our taxi to the campus of the Royal Forest Department. Along the way, I proposed to Chris ways we might save Southeast Asia's bears from the grill, while he implored me to stop "interrogating" people.

"Bears are dying because of some backward belief in voodoo aphrodisiacs," I said. "They're dying because a bunch of middle-aged barbarians in Korea can't get it up. We *have* to do something."

"Relax," he said. "We need more information." To write the dissertation on dietary habits of Montana's grizzlies that earned Chris the PhD after his name, he had to collect and analyze bear scat for years. As a cub reporter, I sometimes wrote three stories before 9:00 a.m. After meeting with Pisit, I thought I had a story for the next news cycle. The way I saw it, bears were dying for barbecue, and we had to alert the world ASAP.

Chris and I had barely finished bowing our hellos to reed-thin Boonlerd Angsirijinda, chief of law enforcement for the Wildlife Conservation Division, when I asked about Koreans eating bears. Chris wasn't happy, but I kept imagining that little sun bear at Wildlife Fund Thailand walking on coals while his paws cooked. Boonlerd was gracious despite my directness, which surely violated the Thai mantra *mai pen rai* (roughly "no problem, relax, it's all good").

"Hunting, buying, selling, or eating bears is illegal," he said. "But we must catch people while they're doing these things. Otherwise we cannot arrest them."

Boonlerd had only seven officers to police wildlife crime among fifty-four million Thais across the kingdom's nearly two hundred thousand square miles, and wildlife traffickers were usually tipped off before police raids. "We park—and everything disappears," he said.

Officer Jang Dobias had nabbed more than her share of traffickers. But finding places that cook bears to order had become more difficult after the arrest of a woman with ten live bears in her home, which doubled as a Korean restaurant. The arrest followed a tip from

a neighbor who had called Dobias to complain about the bears crying. During her investigation, Dobias witnessed it firsthand. "The
bears know they're going to be killed, so they cry," she said. "It lingers
on and on."

Dobias became less inclined to track down bear barbecues after
receiving threats from traffickers. "They told me if I didn't stop, they
would cut my face."

I cajoled Chris into shopping for live bears among the thousands
of tent stalls at Bangkok's sprawling Chatuchak Weekend Market.
Chatuchak sold a flustering array of goods, from hardware to under-
wear. It was also infamous for illicit wildlife trade. I wanted to see
if we could find what police said they no longer could. Our young
female guide said she didn't think it was possible.

We passed a veritable potted jungle in the garden section. The
book area had shelves and tables crammed with volumes in what
looked like every language of every tourist who had ever passed
through Bangkok. The pet section displayed a confusion of bunnies,
puppies, koi, iguanas, snakes, and parakeets, all legal, plus illegal
African gray parrots and scarlet macaws.

I kept prodding our guide to ask stall-keepers where we could
buy a bear. A grandfatherly man selling Chinese herbs from glass
jars cocked his head like he didn't understand. A brisk woman selling Buddha statues threw up her hands and shook her head. "Some
animals the seller must hide," the guide said.

Finally, a punky guy hawking bootlegged music and movies
pointed to a woman selling fresh juice made from watermelons, pine-
apples, papayas, and midget bananas. She was younger than me but
had that worn look that comes from scrappy living.

"Do you sell bears?" I said.

"We don't have here," she said.

"Can you get them?"

"Yes. We can get."

To prove it, she sent off a boy, who returned minutes later with
a small picnic basket. She lifted the cover to reveal the tiny heart-

shaped face of a bug-eyed baby gibbon—endangered and illegal. Her opening price: $120.

"How much for sun bear?" I asked.

A cub would cost $400, she said. She would need two to three weeks to order one from neighboring Laos. But she had an adult Asiatic black bear stashed in the city that she could sell us immediately.

"My sister and I sell about two hundred bears a year," she said.

Taiwan was as grim as Bangkok in terms of wildlife trade. In Taipei's bustling traditional Chinese medicine district, the sparkling glass displays featured whole rhino horns and tiger bones tied with red ribbons. One man walked his bear through the city on a thick chain leash. Selling a bear could earn a Taiwanese poacher the equivalent of half a year's salary. Gall bladders from Taiwan's bears also were finding their way to South Korea.

I flew back to Montana desperate to expose Korea's bear-eaters. Before I even unpacked my suitcase, I called Jon Fisher, my editor at *International Wildlife*, to convince him to put me on a plane back to Thailand. This is how I came to meet the second Bangkok bear.

Back on those jarring streets on assignment for Jon, I was armed with my reporter's notebook, a grainy photocopied picture of a sun bear, and the Thai term for sun bear—*mee maa*—written in Thai script. I targeted pricey restaurants specializing in exotic menu items. Especially those with tanks of live reef fish like the coveted humphead wrasse, distinctive for its big lips, knobby forehead, and iridescent blues and greens. A place that killed rare fish to order seemed like the logical place to book a bear barbecue.

"Do you sell *mee maa*?" I asked a dozen places each day. Smiling faces answered with shaking heads. "*Mai.*" No. "*Mai mee.*" No have. I began to worry I'd talked Jon into paying hefty travel expenses for a story I couldn't deliver.

Late on a broiling day five, I finally heard a "*krab.*" A yes. Huge fish tanks were built into the walls in Pantip Restaurant's dark interior. The maître d' was taller and bigger-boned than most Thais, probably of northern Chinese lineage. He bowed deep at the waist in welcome. I bowed back, then popped my standard question.

"*Krab*," he replied.

"Sun bear?" I said. "I want to eat sun bear—*mee maa.*"

"Yes!" he said, his excitement mirroring mine.

I pulled the crumpled sun bear picture out of my back pocket. "This?"

The man's eyes widened. "No, no, no!" He shook his head while scowling and motioning me toward the exit.

Back in the frigid air conditioning of my budget hotel, I asked the concierge if I had the right words for sun bear. The written words were correct, he said, but they could mean different things depending on their pronunciation. This was my first lesson in tonal languages like Thai, Vietnamese, Lao, and Chinese. Until then, I didn't know they communicated meaning via how each syllable was sung up, down, dipped, or flat. I learned that I'd been roaming the streets of Bangkok for the better part of a week asking for yellow noodles.

In desperation, I pulled Bangkok's English-language Yellow Pages from the drawer beside my bed and looked under "Pets." Then "Restaurants." Then "Medicine" and "Traditional Chinese Medicine." Nothing. Finally, under "Animals," I found "Brokers and Dealers." I called "Suchino Corp. Ltd." and felt blessed when a deep male voice answered my hello in Thai-accented English.

"I would like to buy a sun bear," I said.

"It's illegal," the man said.

"But it can be done?" I said.

"Yes," he said.

"How much will it cost?" I said.

"Not too expensive," he said. "You keep bear in Bangkok or take out?"

"Is it possible to take it out of the country?" I said.

"Very difficult, but possible," he said. He began to sound wary. "How many head do you want?"

"Only one," I said. "Do you sell many sun bears?"

"Twenty or thirty a year."

A lead. At last.

My taxi driver found Suchino's warehouse on a shady block at the end of an isolated suburban lane. I rang the buzzer of the windowless office and was greeted by a young Thai woman who led me to a tall man named Suchin Vongngam, the company's owner. He walked me through his inventory, kept in rows of cages sized to fit everything from a squirrel to an elephant.

We stopped at one cage in which delicate white-handed gibbons huddled together. Illegal. There were slow lorises, tiny possum-like primates with bulging brown eyes and miniature human hands. Another popular pet, increasingly rare. Also civets, with their weasel heads and leopard-cat bodies—a popular entrée in Bangkok's Chinese restaurants. A large wooden bin held hundreds of snakes of several different species slithering over, under, and around one another.

"Where are your bears?" I asked.

"No bears," Suchin said. "We used to sell bears." After the law banned commercial trade, government officials pressured them to stop, he said. He looked apologetic and offered me tea. He lamented the change in the law. He showed me his company's 1985 offerings, which listed sun bears and Asiatic black bears. The current price list did not include bears.

"Where did you get bears when it was legal to sell them?" I asked.

"Lao," he said.

I thanked him for his time and the tea, explaining I had a taxi waiting. As I stood, he said, "How many do you want?"

"How many what?"

"Sun bears."

Blood rushed to my face. It suddenly occurred to me that this man might immediately dispatch poachers to fill my fake order from the forests of Laos.

"I don't think I can afford one," I said. "Let me think about it and get back to you."

•   •   •

I next visited Samutprakarn Crocodile Farm on Bangkok's rural out-
skirts because Korean tour groups went there. I thought the staff
might be able to recommend a place to eat bears.

Hundreds of Siamese crocodiles floated motionless in shallow
cement pools or lounged en masse on concrete in the scorching sun
with their long snouts wide open, showing off the sixty-some ivory
spikes that made their jaws so deadly. Hourly croc-wrestling shows
featured a boy placing his head in the mouth of an overfed croc
otherwise capable of eating him.

I wandered away from the crowds, past a clawless, defanged tigress kept on a short chain for photo opportunities, and eventually
came upon a bear. She was a sun bear, unprotected from the relentless afternoon sun, in a small, rusting cage. With nothing but an
empty water dish and a chicken neck covered in flies, she sat upright,
belly exposed. She turned her head to look at me, probably because I
was the only living thing she had seen all day. I circled her, considering her options and mine. I felt sick and sad and helpless as sweat
slid down my spine.

I hunted down some staff to give her water, knowing her bowl
would be dry the next day. Then I circled her some more. No tourists
came to see her. What was the point of the farm having her? Was she
awaiting execution by VIP banquet?

After thirty minutes, I stepped in closer. I began to cry. "Look," I
said, "I'm *really* sorry. There's just nothing I can do for you." I wiped
my cheeks and nose with the back of a salty hand. "But I promise you
I'll do what*ever* I can to help your kind."

That vow rearranged my life.

My editor was never going to run this story without confirmation of
bear barbecues. I was out of ideas about where else to look when a
break finally came thanks to John Everingham, the Bangkok-based
Aussie photographer assigned to shoot pictures for the story. His
friend, a woman I'll call Ms. Park, was a Korean who shared Thais'
disdain for the habits of her bear-eating compatriots, and she was
willing to help me.

Ms. Park phoned Koreans who phoned other Koreans. Eventually, someone referred us to the Thai-Han Travel Service, which specialized in Korean group tours. She called the agency's president, a Korean named Won Sung Ung, and told him she knew an American who wanted to attend a bear banquet. He told her eating bears was illegal but agreed to meet us anyway.

Won's office in a dingy cement-block office building had just enough space for a few desks. The walls were decorated with fading posters of Bangkok's floating market and landmark temples.

"How may I help you?" Won asked me through Ms. Park's interpretation. He was a graying gentleman who had adopted the Thai art of smiling while talking.

I didn't want to send anyone on a bear hunt, so I told him I was exploring whether I could afford to eat bear. He and Ms. Park chatted in Korean. Finally, she turned to me and said Won insisted that eating bear was illegal and that the government was cracking down on such activities. I gave her a pleading look.

I don't know what she said, but after a lengthy exchange Won glanced up at a wall calendar and said he just happened to have a group coming from Korea at the end of the month to eat bear.

"He arranges these tours all the time," she said. He needed about a month to order a bear and make the arrangements. The price for a large bear was around $30,000.

"What would it cost to join the next group and eat bear paw?" I asked Ms. Park while smiling at Mr. Won.

"He says one bear paw would cost between $500 and $600."

I acted startled. "Oh my goodness," I said. "Mr. Won, that's *so* expensive! I'm afraid it's more than I can afford."

He was gracious but did not lower his price. Everyone in Bangkok bargained. Bear barbecue clearly enjoyed a seller's market.

"I Want to Eat Sun Bear" was my story's headline in the January/February 1991 issue of *International Wildlife*. One of John Everingham's photos showed three boy monks in orange robes and one in yellow watching a sun bear they had raised from a cub tear apart a coconut. The same monastery, a half-day's drive through the rice paddies north of Bangkok, had adopted the Wildlife Fund Thailand bear. The monks named him Bobo. His quarters weren't huge but they were spacious compared to the cage he'd been in when I first saw him. He dined on fruit, eggs, and rice, and enjoyed a daily wrestle with his favorite nun. Word came later that he had a mate. Good news for Bobo, but yet another bear had been denied the joys of wildness.

I felt bewildered when the story didn't prompt reader outrage or demands that the eating and eviscerating of bears in Bangkok be stopped. Instead, readers complained to my editors about *their* distress in reading about such things

I had failed the Croc Farm Bear.

I soon learned that no bear anywhere was safe. Not even the bears in my own backyard.

An eight-hundred-pound bear in Canada was found poached, with nothing but its gall bladder taken. A Korean American was stabbed to death in his New York City apartment, apparently for the stash of bear gall bladders in his freezer. Law enforcement officials were arresting people in Alaska, California, Connecticut, Florida, Georgia, Illinois, Maine, New Hampshire, New York, North Carolina, and Tennessee for trafficking in bear parts. One sting operation nabbed nearly one hundred California hunting guides selling bear gall bladders. Networks of hunters, middlemen, retailers, and buyers were involved. Some purveyors were peddling gall bladders for up to $600 apiece in North America's Chinatowns or flying to Seoul and Taipei and selling them for $3,000.

Worried about the increasing value of dead bears over live ones and wanting to appease a restless wife, Chris agreed to help me get back to Asia to try again to make good on my promise to the Croc Farm Bear. Fortunately for me, he wasn't just leading the federal effort to save grizzlies in the Lower 48. He was also cochairman of the preeminent organization of world bear experts—the Bear Specialist Group of the International Union for Conservation of Nature (IUCN). So when he proposed investigating Asia's bear trade to

TRAFFIC, the wildlife-trade monitoring program of World Wildlife Fund (WWF) and IUCN, a contract and funding quickly followed.[2] TRAFFIC thought it was commissioning Chris to do the work. In reality, it had hired me. Eyebrows would be raised over this bait and switch, but not until after I had investigated the bear trade in China, Hong Kong, Japan, Laos, Macau, Malaysia, Nepal, Singapore, South Korea, Taiwan, and Thailand.

Sometimes I posed as a buyer. Other times, traders assumed I was selling—perhaps a hunter's wife or broker. Most of the time I introduced myself as a student researching the use of bear gall bladders in traditional Chinese medicine, or TCM as they called it. Chris joined me when he could, but dealing with errant grizzlies and their friends and enemies in the Rocky Mountain West was more than a full-time job.

My family imagined me skulking around Asia like an undercover cop, infiltrating criminal networks and setting up illicit buys down dark alleys in the middle of the night. In reality, I mostly shopped in apothecaries, nearly every one with a wall of small wooden drawers carved with Chinese characters to identify the dried bits of plants, animals, and insects that are the mainstays of TCM prescriptions. And I asked a lot of questions about a lot of items that looked a lot like dried figs.

Fresh from the gut, a bear's gall bladder looks like a deflated, brown balloon half full of water. In my shopping spree across eleven countries and territories, I encountered only one shop with wet gall bladders drying in a back room. The rest were all in dried-fig form. In some cases, the sac was cut open so the crystalline bile that looked like crushed, brown glass could be sold a gram at a time.

The mostly men who bought, sold, and prescribed bear bile were generous with their time, explaining where they bought bear gall bladders and from whom, who bought them and why, and for how much. Sometimes they gave me a taste, which reminded me of the smell of the putrefying meat that Chris used to entice problem grizzlies into traps.

I saw hundreds of gall bladders alleged to have come from every bear species and from every country with wild bears—including polar bears from Canada's arctic and spectacled bears from the cloud forests of Peru. The doctors and pharmacists I met recommended bear bile for curing everything from hangovers and dandruff to heart disease and liver failure. The higher the price—which ranged from $28 an ounce to eighteen times the price of gold—the greater the likelihood the gall bladder was actually from a bear rather than a pig, cow, ox, or dog. Demand was so high and fakes had become so pervasive that many buyers were skeptical of authenticity no matter the price point.

"When I'm sick, I go to the US for bear and watch them kill it myself," the president of South Korea's Seoryung Trading Company told me.

US wildlife and law enforcement agents confirmed that more Korean buyers were asking to go along on bear hunts or watch them on video. The only recorded hunt I watched showed several men in hunting gear releasing a pack of yelping hounds into a thick, leafy forest to sniff out an American black bear and chase it fifty feet up a tree. The tape cut to a hunter firing his rifle upward, followed by the bear plummeting to the forest floor. The final clip showed the dead bear splayed on its back while the hunter sliced open its belly to claim his bloody prize.

Koreans were paying $15,000 and more for gall bladders proven to come from wild bears. That made the gall bladder of a single wild bear worth a year's wage in some parts of US bear country. Ounce per ounce, trafficking in bear gall bladders had become more lucrative than narcotics but without the risk of prison because judges and juries didn't see wildlife crime as serious crime.

The most chilling fact I learned during my eighteen-month investigation was that bear bile wasn't snake oil. In truth, I owed an apology to the Korean tourists in Bangkok whom I'd labeled sexually challenged barbarians.

Bear gall bladders *do* contain medicine that cures diseases. Ursodeoxycholic acid (UDCA) is found in significant quantities only in the gall bladders of the bear's Ursidae family. It's used by Western doctors in synthetic form—under such trade names as Ursodiol, Actigall, and Ursofalk—to dissolve gallstones without surgery and treat liver disease. Despite an abundance of inexpensive man-made UDCA, however, many Asians still preferred bile from bears. One Chinese medicine specialist I interviewed summed it up best: "We use Chinese herbs, not Western herbs." Synthetic equaled Western.

Through trial and error over centuries, doctors serving China's emperors discovered healing elements in thousands of wild plants and animals. Bear bile was deemed invaluable around three thousand years ago. Contemporary TCM—practiced under varying names, such as *kampō* in Japan and *hanyak* in Korea—recommends bear bile from nature's source because it's perfectly balanced and buffered to restore the human body to health. The isolated active ingredient manufactured in a laboratory is regarded as too pure and too strong.

Informants told me that bear bile was so essential to TCM manufacturers in China and that the decline of China's wild bear populations had become so severe that the Communist Party had mandated that bears be farmed. Rumor had it that these farmed bears weren't slaughtered for their gall bladders but rather "milked" of bile while they were alive. If that were true, I felt sure that exposing it would catalyze the world to bring an end to it and the trade in bear gall bladders.

Two years after the world watched pro-democracy demonstrators gunned down for occupying Beijing's Tiananmen Square, Chris wrote to Chinese bear specialists asking for an invitation to come and learn about their bear issues. They swiftly responded, inviting us both. For the first time, I was happy to comply with my husband's insistence that I not tell anyone I was a journalist because international coverage of the Tiananmen massacre had nearly closed China's just-opening door to foreign media.

When we arrived in April 1991, most of what we saw of Beijing was gritty and gray, except for the mammoth painting of Chairman Mao hanging on the redbrick entrance to the Forbidden City. Many people on the streets still wore the dark blue workers' jackets favored during the Cultural Revolution. Bicyclists ruled the wide boulevards of provincial capitals. Pedaled rickshaws were more common than cars. Shenzhen, the southern fishing village chosen to become an overnight industrial giant, was said to be building one high-rise a day and a new boulevard every three days. The number of privately owned cars on China's roadways had just topped ten thousand. Careers and housing were assigned to the people we met through work units led by Communist Party designees, and few wanted to be alone with us for fear of attracting attention from security agents.

We were never without government escorts except at bedtime. I was sure our hotel rooms were bugged, which I found thrilling. Chris didn't believe me, so one night I tested my theory. "I'm dying without coffee," I said loudly. "Tea just doesn't work for me. Tomorrow I'm going to ask if we can go someplace to buy coffee." The next morning, our minders arrived with a gift for me. A box of three-in-ones—packets of premixed instant coffee, milk, and sugar. I thanked them profusely and said, "You read my mind!"

After that Chris agreed to use pen and paper at night to discuss our strategy for finagling a glimpse of bile milking. China's scientific journals had published thirty-eight articles about extracting bile from live bears, but the methods remained secret.

Our hope of being the first foreigners to see bile milking rose when our Beijing minders put us on a plane bound for the capital of Sichuan Province, famous for its hot-pepper cuisine, the world's only wild pandas, and China's largest bear farm.

We were met at Chengdu's airport by Gong Jien, a junior wildlife biologist from the Sichuan Forestry Department. He was as slender as a boy, spoke English better than some Americans, and treated Chris with the Confucian deference used for elders and teachers.

As the driver of our white government van wove through rivers of bicyclists, Gong briefed us. China's wild bear populations were down to worrying levels, he said, but selling their parts had been outlawed in 1989 and was under strict control. "They are very difficult to find now."

Except across from our hotel, as it turned out. Looking for handicrafts, I wandered into a shop while Chris and Gong unloaded our bags. Three hairy paws were displayed in the front window. The likeness of their pads to human feet made them unmistakable.

After we checked in, I led the men back to my find. Gong showed no surprise or embarrassment at the evidence contradicting what he'd told us. I would soon learn that truth in China was something to be ascertained, between the lines of official declarations.

"Are those bear paws?" I asked Gong to ask the shopkeeper.

"*Dui.*" Yes.

"What are they used for?" I asked.

"They are medicine. For strength."

"How are they prepared?"

"They are best for stew." This was an unappetizing prospect given that they looked as if they hadn't been washed since the bear last used them.

"How much do they cost?"

The shopkeeper wanted the equivalent of $24 each.

"Do you have bear gall bladders?" I asked.

"Yes."

"How much?"

He wanted $9.50 a gram—$270 an ounce. The average per capita annual income in China was around $350.[3]

I assumed farmed bears lived somewhat like dairy cows, ambling around open spaces until it was their turn for milking. But the only animals roaming the twelve-acre Deer Farm of the Sichuan Chinese Medicine Corporation were humans and Sika deer.

We were welcomed as VIPs by Tian Techeng, the farm's leader, and his management team of chain-smoking, middle-aged men in polyester golf shirts and windbreakers. Our host smiled, smoked, and talked simultaneously. We strolled past scores of spotted deer in brick courtyards. The males' antlers would be cut, sliced, and ground to make products good for "strength," favored as wedding gifts "for the groom," we were told. I knew nothing about deer husbandry, but the deer seemed relaxed despite their crowded stalls.

I was blindsided by what came next.

We rounded a corner and walked toward several corrugated-metal warehouses. After we stepped inside the first of the window-less buildings, it took my eyes a few seconds to adjust to the spare lighting. The place was filled with rows of small iron cages elevated on legs about three feet off the cement floor. Each cage contained an Asiatic black bear. Some were so large and their cages so small that they could only sit in a slouched position. Others rocked their heads back and forth or repeatedly threw their bodies against the bars. A two-year-old jumped up and down, banging her head on the top of her cage. Several extended their front paws through bars in our direction as if begging for help.

I busied myself snapping photographs to tamp down my revulsion and despair. I felt like I did the day my mother drove around a bend just as my best friend and her family, all covered in blood, were being loaded into ambulances after a head-on crash.

"Oh, my God," I whispered to Chris. "This is Dachau for bears."

The journalist in me screamed that this story must get out. The bear lover in me asked how these icons of wildness had been turned into battery animals without the world noticing.

An old woman in cloth shoes poured steaming water over the loose Jasmine tea inside each lidded cup around the long table. While I sipped and tried to surreptitiously remove the tea leaves from my teeth, Tian regaled us with his work unit's accomplishments.

The farm's bear operation began with thirty animals taken from the wild. Bile milking began in 1984. The process involved cutting open a bear's abdomen and surgically implanting a tube into the gall bladder, through which bile was drained. Infections were a problem at first. Many bears died. Since then the surgery and bile milking had been perfected, he said, and deaths were rare.

Of the 450 Asiatic black bears on the farm, only 150 were milked at any given time, Tian said. The others "rested" and bred. Bears were tapped at age three and lived to be as old as twenty. Milking took about two minutes a day, and each bear produced an average of six pounds of bile a year. Owned by the government of Sichuan Province, the farm produced 1,100 pounds of bile annually. At full capacity, it could generate four times that amount, according to Tian.

"One farm bear can produce more bile than one hundred wild bears killed for their gall bladders," he said.

But at what cost to that bear? And if this is true, then why are wild bears still being poached? I didn't ask because I wanted to see the process so I could describe it to the world.

In the farm's gift shop, Tian led us past long tables draped in red cloth displaying deer antlers, assorted medicines made from various deer parts, and glass vials filled with brown chunks of dried bear bile offered at a bargain price of $5 per gram. About thirty thousand tourists, most from Japan and Taiwan, passed through the farm each year, he said. "Some buy as many as fifty vials each. There is no limit."

Either our host didn't know or he thought Chris and I didn't know that taking the bile of endangered Asiatic black bears from any source out of China, and into the destinations he named, broke laws at home and abroad.

I repeatedly and politely asked to see bile milking and was repeatedly and politely ignored. Near the end of our visit, I asked one last time. After lengthy discussion in Chinese with his lieutenants, Tian finally said, "I am very sorry. The workers with the keys are not here."

We couldn't wait for the keys. We had an early-morning flight to Northeast China.

Where Sichuan Province had been blooming with spring, Heilongjiang Province was still in winter's raw grip. A delegation of senior bear and wolf specialists from Northeast Forestry University received us at Harbin's airport.

The sofas in the lobby of the Swan Hotel were full of Chinese men smoking and shouting conversationally when we arrived. The place was just as author Paul Theroux had described it in *Riding the Iron Rooster*. The rock garden and ornamental pool were still there, but the fish and plants that were frozen upon Theroux's Christmas Eve arrival in the mid-1980s were alive and well for our April visit.[4] Still, like nearly everyone else, we did not take off our winter coats because the temperature inside was only a few degrees warmer than outside.

Our dapper English-speaking host was Professor Ma Jianzhang, venerated founder of China's first and, at that time, only school of wildlife management. His fluency, his tweed driving cap, and the sweater vest he wore over a dress shirt gave him a Western air.

"More Korean businessmen are coming here to set up joint ventures," Ma told us during a welcome dinner of too many courses and a steady resupply of tepid beer. "There is a tendency for people from South Korea to want to carry their bear gall bladders home," he said. Despite threat of a hefty fine and possible jail time for smuggling bear parts, Koreans still were being caught trying to leave the country with gall bladders hidden inside specially made belts under their clothing.

Paul Theroux also had written about the grilled bear paw on menus in Harbin, and the *Economist* had reported that Harbin diners consumed two tons of bear paws annually. I mentioned these reports to our host.

"This is no longer the case," Ma said. "It stopped when the 1989 law against bear hunting came into effect."

The next morning as we left the breakfast room with our entourage, we passed a restaurant display case featuring the snapshot of an uncooked bear paw on a white plate with a note that read: "Fresh from Heilongjiang Province." The adjacent hotel gift shop sold vials of bile crystals from bear farms and a limited selection of tiger- and leopard-fur coats of questionable legality. No one in our party seemed alarmed or contrite.

•   •   •

We set off into the still-frozen countryside in a white government van full of Chinese wildlife experts and an interpreter from the university's foreign affairs department. The latter, a cocksure young watchdog, spoke fluent English with an American accent, although he said his only travel abroad had been for schooling in Russia. He wore his thick hair in a pompadour and called Chris "Christ."

Our driver drove and then drove some more. For days. We may have driven in circles for all Chris and I knew. The landscape was the same winterkill brown under leaden skies. Professor Gao Zhongxin, a lanky wolf expert with graying temples, was the most gregarious during our many hours of chatting, snoozing, and listening to tinny Chinese pop music in the overheated van.

"More than one hundred people are serving jail time for illegally hunting bears," he said in English that was often corrected by our watchdog. "Two have been executed for selling panda pelts."

While China shared bear species with other countries—Asiatic black bears, brown bears, and sun bears—pandas belonged exclusively to China. They were the country's national animal, considered a national treasure and a potent diplomatic tool when given as gifts to other nations. Panda poaching was punishable by death, after which families of the deceased reportedly would be billed for the executioner's bullet.[5]

"The number one reason for illegal hunting of bears is to get gall bladders for commercial use," Gao said. "Another reason is the paw of the bear, which is very delicious to the Chinese people." Reports of marauding bears had become much more frequent since the government began granting farmers permission to kill "nuisance" bears and sell their gall bladders, paws, and meat. Even police had been enticed into the bear trade. Officers in the southern city of Guangzhou were caught selling live Asiatic black bears to fine-dining establishments after one of the animals escaped from a restaurant and fled into adjacent residential streets. Around the same time, authorities intercepted an illicit shipment of 1,800 pounds of bear paws, representing perhaps one thousand dead bears, just before it departed the Chinese port of Dalian for Japan and South Korea.

"If nobody came from South Korea and Japan to offer so much

money, they wouldn't kill so many bears," Gao said. Meanwhile, the attention of Chinese wildlife biologists had been diverted from the well-being of wild bear populations to the production capacity of farmed bears. "The bear-farm managers ask us to increase bile and babies—from the *same* bears," he said. He thought the stress of life in their small cages was making both requests untenable. But his pride was obvious when he said, "We now have eight thousand bears on farms."

"I'm sorry," I said. "Will you repeat that number?" *The number I thought I heard could not be possible. Not yet. Not without the world knowing.*

"This number is right," our watchdog said. It was slated to rise to forty thousand. "Our goal is to farm bears like cows and pigs."

We drove hours in the rain to see a closed lake resort once visited by Mao's successor, Deng Xiaoping. We spent one night in a well-worn hotel with full spittoons outside every door, and a second night in what once had been an orientation center for "capitalist roaders," "intellectuals," and others with "bourgeois" tendencies sent to the countryside during the Cultural Revolution for "reeducation" by peasant masters.

On the third day, we finally saw animals. Our Van of Perpetual Motion stopped near the edge of a pine forest at a tattered fur farm that raised mink and raccoon dogs. I had never heard of raccoon dogs. Chris said that while they looked like raccoons, they actually descended from canines. Their fur was most often seen around the hoods of winter jackets increasingly made for the world in China.

"Where are the bears?" I said.

"There are no bears here," our watchdog said.

The place was raising another endangered species for the medicine market, however. Perhaps a dozen tigers stared at us from behind the rusting bars of old-school zoo cells. The farm's leader took us to the office to show off a handwritten ledger where staff were recording orders for tiger bones from pharmaceutical companies. It was a startup—China's first tiger farm.

Tigers were on a list of dozens of wild animals slated for farming that Chris and I had been shown in Beijing—species TCM factories were finding increasingly difficult to source from the wild. Musk deer, civets, armadillo-like pangolins, flying squirrels, scorpions, and seahorses. I didn't realize the scope and significance of that list at the time. I thought it was just a weird Mao-era leftover that would be put aside like the Cultural Revolution, once China fully reentered the modern world. I was laser-focused on bile milking and dismissive of any diversions. These tigers and their descendents would soon become my obsession, but on that day I only had eyes for bears.

After days of breathing stale, sweaty air inside the no-longer-white van, our driver turned up a winding driveway and passed under an arch flanked by two cement bears. The Bear Class Test Farm of Heilongjiang Shanhe Forest Farm covered a knoll with sweeping views across miles of thawing farmland. We arrived just before noon on a cloudless day.

"You can almost see Harbin from here," our watchdog said.

"Really?" I said.

"Yes, it's only an hour away."

What? I didn't ask why we hadn't driven here directly. I feared I already knew why.

We were enthusiastically met by farm leader Wang Dong, a tall man who wore a traditional blue workers' jacket, and shorter Vice Chief Li Jinghua, in a golf shirt and windbreaker.

The research farm was established in 1984 with nineteen wild bears as a joint venture of a medicine company and two municipal forest bureaus. It housed twenty-two Asiatic black bears, thirty-seven brown bears, and one hybrid.

Our hosts showed us a spacious concrete enclosure where adult bears were sent to breed and rooms where pregnant mothers were given stress-free privacy to give birth and nurse their cubs on beds of fresh straw. Newly weaned cubs played together in a large pen, and adolescent Asiatic black bears climbed on a jungle gym in a separate grotto.

"The bears like sweets," Li said, as he filled my hand with candy. He opened the door, motioned for me to enter, then closed the door behind me. Having met a man with only half a face after a close encounter with a bear, I wasn't amused. But I smiled and let the bears eat out of my hands. Anything to see bile extraction.

Afterward, I asked when we would see the bile milking.

"It's still in the experimental stage," Li said.

I assured him that Chris and I didn't mind seeing it before it was perfected.

"So many people will upset the bears," Li said.

"In that case, just one of us will go in," I said.

We were shepherded to lunch. Li inhaled a succession of cigarettes and exhaled an explanation of how China's bear farms had built the capacity to produce more than enough bile for the seven factories using it in fifty-six medicines made in the form of capsules, powders, ointments, oil compounds, liquor, tablets, tinctures, and suppositories. In fact, researchers were formulating new products to utilize the growing surplus of farmed bear bile. Products such as bear-bile shampoo and toothpaste.

Li showed us snapshots from the production process. In one, a bear was splayed under anesthesia, surgeons at work inside a belly incision, apparently implanting a spigot. In another, a worker in a white lab coat held a dish of food for a large brown bear standing in a small iron cage while a second worker kneeled, holding a funnel underneath the cage. Li invited us to a warm room where a worker poured fresh bile onto a shallow metal tray and slid it into an oven. Another worker opened a different oven and pulled out a tray containing a fully baked sheet of what looked like brown glass.

We left the kitchen and walked a few paces in the open air to a cement building with no windows and a metal door secured with a thick padlock.

"This is where we extract the bile," Li said. He smiled and swept his hand toward the pièce de résistance. After nearly two weeks into our first trip to China, Chris and I had arrived at our destination. We were about to see something no foreigner and few Chinese had ever seen. This was worth all the hours and days we'd spent in a fetid steam bath on wheels.

After considerable back and forth in Chinese with his staff, Li turned to us and said, "I am sorry, but the man with the keys is not here."

Not again! "When will he return?" I asked.

"We are not sure," he said.

"We'll wait," I said.

"That is not possible," he said. "He may not return today, and you must fly back to Beijing tomorrow."

"We'll change our flight," I said.

"That is not possible," our watchdog said.

"Why isn't it possible?" I asked.

"It cannot be done."

Our interminable tour of the lifeless countryside to reach a destination an hour from where we started had nothing to do with hospitality. Our hosts had been running out the clock.

3

※

FINDING THE MAN WITH THE KEYS

Seeing what was allegedly a state secret in China proved laughably easy in South Korea. I just had to lose the government escorts.

Before our trip to China, Chris and I visited Seoul for the first time. A *Christian Science Monitor* television producer there told me that one Korean bear owner was experimenting with bile milking and another rendered bears on the spot for buyers wanting gall bladders of guaranteed origin. When Chris and I asked our hosts from the national Forestry Administration about these places, they said their most recent census had found fourteen facilities nationwide holding 655 bears "for educational purposes only."

To prove their point, they drove us twenty miles south of Seoul to see a wealthy man's private collection of sixty-three Asiatic black bears. He kept them in large groups inside tidy cement grottos amid the groomed gardens surrounding his gated home. The bears' middle-aged caretaker swore they were kept for his boss's pleasure only—absolutely not for making medicine or money.

When I arrived in Seoul for a second look, alone and unannounced after being locked out of China's bile-milking rooms, I took a taxi with a Korean friend back to the rich guy's hobby bears. We hadn't called ahead, but the caretaker welcomed us. He didn't appear to remember me. He just seemed flattered that two young women were eager to see his bears.

"How many bears do you have?" I asked through my friend's Korean.

"Seventy," he said. Seven more than when Chris and I had visited five months before. There were no cubs, so the additions must have been purchased as adults.

"Where do your bears come from?" I said.

"Japan," he said. A probable violation of Japan's laws at least.

After some chitchat in Korean, he admitted to selling bears from time to time. For *ungdam*—gall bladders—only.

"Do you plan to milk your bears' bile?" I said.

"Oh, no. We want to breed them so we can sell stock to bear farms all over the country. Now we just sell the gall bladders. We let people choose the bear they like."

Our next stop had become a national phenomenon after news broke that it was the first in South Korea to milk bile from live bears. Customers came from all over the country after a man in Pusan claimed a miraculous recovery from liver cancer after drinking fresh bile from Kaya Bear Farm.

The turn for Kaya off a rural highway outside Taegu, South Korea's fourth-largest city, was easy to spot thanks to the Asiatic black bear waving from a hand-painted sign. A dirt driveway led to a modest wood house on several grassy acres dotted with fruit trees. My friend had called ahead and been told we could not visit. We dropped in anyway.

A white luxury sedan drove in behind us. As the driver parked, we braced for a command to leave. A well-dressed Korean man in perhaps his early fifties stepped out and greeted us with smiles, handshakes, and bows. He was the farm's owner, he said. He apologized for not speaking English. I apologized for not speaking Korean and said my companion would speak for me.

"We understand you sell bear bile," I said.

I thought for sure our welcome would be revoked at that point, but the man continued to smile, admitted he sold bear bile, and seemed pleased that we knew about it. "I am Mr. To Won Ho, at your service," he said, then bowed deeply.

The three middle-aged Koreans who had been his passengers—

two men and a woman—joined us. "These people have come to buy bile," Mr. To said. "Please come. Join us." He extended his arm toward a barn-like building about the size of a two-car garage.

Recent media coverage had made Mr. To famous in Korea, he said. "Perhaps I am famous outside Korea too." He tipped his head in my direction. Everyone chuckled. He led us inside and flipped a switch, illuminating five adult bears—two Asiatic black and three brown—each in an iron cage just large enough for lying down, standing, and turning around. All but one wore harnesses holding metal plates tight across their midsections.

Our host grabbed a long metal pole, prodding a female black bear to stand up and move into the narrow squeeze cage attached to her living quarters. Mrs. To walked in with a bowl of sweetened rice, which she encircled with her arms while the bear exuberantly lapped up the contents. Meanwhile, Mr. To cranked a metal panel inside the cage toward the bear's left flank until the bulk of her torso was tightly compressed. He then inserted metal rods to hold the bear's legs away from her belly. The bear began to whine like a child and claw wildly with her front legs.

The bile farmer reached through the bars and unlocked a small door in the bear's metal girdle, which released a catheter attached to a plastic pouch half full of brown liquid. The only sound was the frenzy of claws on metal and the bear's panicked mewling. Mr. To quickly extracted two syringes of bile from the bag and emptied them into three small vials. Within five minutes, he had milked the bear, secured the tap, and released her from the metal sandwich.

I had finally seen what our hosts in China had kept locked from view. But what sickened me more than the bear's torment was the fact that she would never roll in a meadow, amble through a forest, or clamber up a tree to gorge on honey. If China's model held sway, all bears might one day be like this bear, with implanted spigots forever poking their guts as they tried for a lifetime to get comfortable in cages barely bigger than themselves. And the world's forests would be forever diminished by their absence.

Mr. To packed the trio's prized purchases with ice. A $5,000 harvest in five minutes. *Ka-ching.* The bear continued to growl and snap her jaws as we left her locked away in the total darkness of the milking shed.

No one among the A-list of international wildlife conservation took issue with bear farms or bile milking. They admitted personal disgust but showed zero professional interest. Any bear not in the wild was relegated to "an animal-welfare issue."

Chris suggested I hand over all my information about bear farms to the World Society for the Protection of Animals in London, which I did. They ran with it, as did the International Fund for Animal Welfare and other groups that "science-based" A-listers World Wildlife Fund (WWF), TRAFFIC, and my scientist husband deemed "humane-iacs."

Something in my gut told me this was a major mistake. But what did I know? I was just a journalist with humane-iac leanings who happened to be lucky enough to sneak her way into the highest echelons of international wildlife conservation. And I wanted to hang with the A-listers, which, almost overnight, I was.

Encouraging news came quickly after Chris and I submitted the report on my pan-Asian shopping spree. TRAFFIC decided to take the findings to CITES (pronounced "sigh-tease"), the UN treaty on international trade in endangered wild animals and plants.[1]

At that time, 112 of the world's nearly two hundred countries had signed on to CITES. TRAFFIC, which had enormous credibility and clout with member countries and the CITES Secretariat, used my evidence to convince Denmark to propose that American black bears—the only bear species not subject to CITES regulation—be added. Such a listing would make it more difficult for criminals to pass off—or launder—the gall bladders of endangered bear species as those of plentiful, legally hunted American black bears. If Denmark's proposal were approved, no bear gall bladder could be legally traded across international borders without a CITES permit, closing a huge loophole of opportunity for illicit trade—a game changer.

The matter was to be decided at the biannual CITES conference in March 1992 in Kyoto, Japan. After Chris was invited to speak for the Bear Specialist Group, he and I agreed that I should come along since he and Denmark would be citing my work. In the hushed and formal UN setting, with its parliamentary protocols and simultaneous interpretation into multiple languages, it seemed to me as if the Croc Farm Bear had won an audience with God.

Denmark introduced the proposal on behalf of the twelve countries that made up the European Economic Community, which would later become the European Union. The CITES Secretariat said it shared Denmark's concerns about the high volume of trade in bear parts in Asia and the laundering risk posed by the look-alike appearance of parts from American black bears.

Canada, the country with the most American black bears, spoke against the proposal on grounds that most bear parts leaving Canada were hunting trophies going home with Americans licensed to hunt them. The proposed listing would "impose an unnecessary administrative burden." Canada didn't want additional paperwork!

The United States opposed the proposal because American black bears were not endangered. I wanted to raise my hand and say, "Excuse me, Country of My Birth, what about the well-being of Asia's endangered bears? What about your own law-enforcement agencies that have arrested poachers trafficking bear gall bladders on the international market? The same agencies that have likened the trade in bear parts to the narcotics trade. In fact, your own people say drug traffickers are now dealing in bear gall bladders." But I could do nothing besides flash a hairy eyeball in the general direction of the US delegation.

Mexico, home to a small American black bear population, supported the behemoth economies to its north in opposing Denmark's proposal.

My husband asked for the floor. "Thank you, Mr. Chairman. The international trade in bear parts and derivatives is pervasive and increasing. The Bear Specialist Group believes the combined populations of *all* the world's bear species cannot sustain this trade for long. Furthermore, a large number of bear scientists we polled believe a CITES listing for the American black bear is necessary to control trade in Asia's endangered bears. Thank you, Mr. Chairman."

The floor went next to TRAFFIC. A Viking of a man with a dark sweep of thick hair nearly to his shoulders and a deep, accented voice that boomed authority supported Chris's statement and Denmark's proposal.

Despite solid evidence collected across Asia over eighteen months and recommendations from the world's top bear experts, CITES voted to reject the proposal.[2] Many countries abstained, not wanting to get in the middle of a pissing match between Europe and North America. The World, as represented by CITES, cared more about avoiding paperwork and staying sweet with certain economic heavyweights than about wild bears being hunted down and eviscerated at rates entire species might not survive.

I felt gutted. I had once again failed the Croc Farm Bear.

Waitresses in geisha costumes scurried past shoji-screen doors as Chris and I strolled with TRAFFIC staff to a post-defeat dinner at a noisy teppanyaki grill in Kyoto's historic district. TRAFFIC's Viking of a spokesman sat at the head of the table. His accent was Danish, and he was Jorgen Thomsen, executive director of TRAFFIC's international network. His staff had nicknamed him the Great Dane. He sat next to his supremely articulate, multilingual American wife, Amie Brautigam, who worked for the vaunted IUCN Species Survival Commission, of which Chris's Bear Specialist Group was a part. To me, Thomsen and Brautigam were the Brad Pitt and Angelina Jolie of that time and place, and I could barely speak in their presence.

Plan B for bears emerged over teriyaki rice bowls and Asahi beer. The Great Dane decided that TRAFFIC would press Denmark to reopen the discussion. Chris and I were assigned to inform as many government officials as possible why every bear on Earth had a bull's-eye on its gall bladder.

The next day we joined TRAFFIC staff to fan out and corner

CITES delegates as they tried to grab coffee, a quick meal, a smoke, or a breath of outside air. Many a delegate's restroom break was delayed, but our efforts paid off. Just as the two-week conference was tying up business in its final day, Denmark moved to reopen the bear debate. Brazil seconded the motion. The United States objected. South Africa seconded the objection. A vote went in favor of reopening discussion.

Germany called the trade in bear gall bladders the greatest threat to the survival of Asia's bears. The United States, Canada, and Mexico repeated their opposition to Denmark's proposal and vowed to step up efforts at home to stop trade in gall bladders from American black bears. One after the other, the United Kingdom, Zimbabwe, Austria, Brazil, Kenya, Thailand, and Portugal underscored how the look-alike issue provided opportunities for laundering of Asian bear gall bladders that no amount of law enforcement in North America could contain.

The chairman closed the debate and called for a vote. I prayed.

In the final tally, forty-six voted in favor and twenty against.[3] With that, international trade in *all* bear species would be regulated under CITES. No one could legally take a bear gall bladder, bear bile, or bear paws across national borders without what amounted to a CITES-issued passport. To do so would be a crime. This victory wouldn't stop illegal bear trade, but it would make trafficking much easier for law enforcement to spot.

I mentally toasted the Croc Farm Bear.

Although the thousands of bears on farms in China did not come up in Kyoto, the handful of tigers on that fur farm near Harbin did. Many delegates missed the moment because they were preoccupied with proposals to weaken the 1990 ban on trade in elephant ivory and concerns over runaway rhino poaching. Furthermore, the matter came and went while many were literally out to lunch.

Just before the midday recess, China's delegation introduced a proposal to register its tiger farm—the Breeding Centre for Felidae Animals of Hengdaohezi, established in 1986 by the Heilongjiang

Native Animal By-Products Import/Export Company.[4] The place reportedly held sixty-two live tigers and a store of twenty-six dead ones, which medicine makers outside China were eager to buy at record-high prices. *Apparently Chris and I only saw the front of the store.*

China's delegation argued that demand for tiger products was not a threat to wild tigers because it came from a small number of Asian countries and because wild tigers had become so few in number that poachers had difficulty finding them. Therefore, China wanted permission to sell bones and skins from the farm's stockpile to keep the fledgling venture solvent.

Kenya and the United States expressed concern that trade in bones and skins from the farm would stimulate and provide cover for illegal trade in look-alike bones and skins from wild tigers. TRAFFIC argued that the extreme rarity of wild tigers barred them from trade under any circumstances.

China's spokesman said that if the request were denied, China would be forced to ask international organizations for funds to keep the farm from bankruptcy and its tigers from starving.

After countries spoke for and against, the chair deferred a vote until after lunch. But the vote never came. Immediately after the break, China withdrew its proposal.[5]

Just like that, the matter was done. Gone. I figured people had piled on China's delegation at lunch to tell them that the world would *never* stand for tigers being farmed like livestock. With scant ado, tigers seemed to have been spared the fate of bears in China.

Not long after Kyoto, tigers joined rhinos and elephants in the international spotlight. Scientists in the Russian Far East reported that at least fifty of the region's estimated three hundred to four hundred tigers had been poached.[6] Buyers were flooding in from China, Japan, and South Korea, creating what some experts termed an impending catastrophe. India's beloved Ranthambore National Park had lost more than half of its tigers to a "massacre" by poachers seeking bones to sell in China.[7] Nepal and Laos reported that their tigers also had been hard-hit.[8]

"The future of the wild tiger is at stake, and the situation is just as critical as that of the rhinos," Peter Jackson, head of the IUCN's Cat Specialist Group, declared in September 1992. "It is far more critical than the situation of the African elephant, which totals nearly 100 times the number of tigers." Despite being decimated by poachers, even rhinos outnumbered the "far fewer than 7,000" tigers left in the wild, he said.[9]

In November 1992, lawyers for WWF and the National Wildlife Federation petitioned the Clinton White House to impose trade sanctions against China, South Korea, and Taiwan for undermining CITES' bans by allowing legal domestic trade in tiger bone and rhino horn.[10] The petition also named Yemen, where men continued to buy daggers with handles made of rhino horn in defiance of a national ban and a fatwa by the Grand Mufti saying that killing rhinos was against the will of God.[11] The petition was filed under an obscure US law with an addendum nicknamed "the Pelly Amendment," which allowed the United States to punish countries whose citizens engaged in trade that weakened international agreements to protect endangered species.

During the same month, India's tiger specialists announced that demand for bones to make traditional Chinese medicine had supplanted the fur market as the driving force behind tiger poaching.[12]

In early March 1993, the standing committee that governs CITES between conferences expressed "deep concern" for wild tigers and asked all member countries to take measures to halt tiger trade.[13]

Then on May 29, 1993, China's State Council shocked the CITES world by declaring a domestic ban on all import, export, sale, purchase, transport, and medicinal use of tiger bones and rhino horns. The government broadcast news of the ban to the nation via television, radio, and newspapers. Manufacturing of all medicines containing tiger bone and rhino horn ceased, and both items were dropped from China's list of approved medicine ingredients.[14] As a result, government funding for the fledgling tiger farm outside Harbin stopped.[15]

It seemed too good to be true, and that may be why the Clinton administration issued a press release eleven days later to announce that the United States had sent official warnings to China anyway, and also to Taiwan, that trade sanctions would follow if they could not prove that their domestic trade in tiger bone and rhino horn had stopped. Actions against South Korea and Yemen were being considered as well.

"The killing of these grand creatures continues unabated today, even though they are clearly on the brink of extinction," Interior Secretary Bruce Babbitt told the press.[16] "The Pelly Amendment requires us to address this destructive trade, and we have done so."

While this unprecedented diplomatic drama was unfolding, I was obliviously working away at a master's in wildlife conservation, aiming to redesign myself so I could do more on behalf of the Croc Farm Bear.

Chris and I had separated by then, over differences I considered irreconcilable. We had agreed when we married that if I made the move to Missoula for him, he would make the next move for me. But when I brought up my dream of working for TRAFFIC in Asia, he said he would not leave Montana. The Massachusetts native had found his heart's content in the Rocky Mountain West. Having a baby was the one thing I thought might trump my promise to the Croc Farm Bear, but when I asked Chris if he wanted one, he shrugged and said, "If you do." Being the child of a father who wanted my mother to abort me and left her and me without saying good-bye when I was nine, I needed more paternal enthusiasm than that to bring an innocent into this vexing world.

I had recently returned from a third visit to South Korea, where I did field research for my graduate thesis on why an abundance of farmed bear bile might never reduce poaching of wild bears for their gall bladders. A Korean professor at Taegu's Kyungpook University had taken me under his wing and assigned his graduate students to help me survey doctors in the city's nationally renowned TCM community. The results confirmed my suspicions. Nearly half the respondents said there were grave illnesses that only bear bile could cure. And while 75 percent approved of farming bears for bile, 90 percent said bile from farmed bears was less effective than bile from wild bears.[17]

I had $110 left in my checking account and was puzzling over how to crunch my Korean data one April morning in 1993 when my phone rang. The reverberant voice needed no introduction. It was the Great Dane. He was calling from TRAFFIC headquarters in Cambridge, England, to ask if I would be willing to return to South Korea to do an undercover investigation of rhino-horn trade to determine whether US trade sanctions were warranted. Korean government officials had denounced the Pelly charges as "malicious accusations . . . based on neither fact nor verified information." My mission, should I choose to take it, was to bring home verified information. I felt as if I had won the lottery.

What came next ranks among my least honorable moments. Without a heartbeat's hesitation, I left behind my life in Montana— a faithful husband willing to work at healing a wounded marriage, a dream home perched on a mountainside, two beloved dogs, the cat-love-of-my-life, and all my worldly belongings except those that fit into a large duffle bag—to pounce on the Great Dane's offer. And I did not look back—or apologize to those I hurt—until years later. I never regretted the path I chose, but one day came when I felt sickening shame for the way I had shattered Chris's heart and abandoned my four-legged family.

South Korea was ravenous for Woo Hwang Chung Shim Won balls— small, waxy spheres containing ground-up rhino horn. They were considered so precious that they sometimes were dusted with gold. The ancient formula was credited with restoring people after paralyzing strokes and waking them from comas, though increasingly affluent Koreans had begun taking them to reduce stress, fight fatigue, and boost brainpower before all-important school exams. Korean pharmaceutical companies valued the national market for Woo Hwang Chung Shim Won in 1993 at $19 million—little compared to the amount US trade sanctions might cost the country.

"Rhinoceros could get in the way of the South Korean government's effort to revive its ailing economy," one Korean journalist declared in a story about the US threat. National decrees outlawed even the intent to sell rhino horn or tiger bone in any form. "I will leave no stone unturned in hunting down illegal traders of rhinoceros horn," the national prosecutor general proclaimed. Police swept into traditional medicine shops and clinics across the country. The one shop found with rhino horn—less than 100 grams—was closed and its owner jailed. Afterward, Korean officials declared that they had eradicated the trade.

To help get at the truth after this police siege, a sympathetic college professor in Seoul loaned me a team of his graduate students. They visited 130 traditional medicine shops and clinics in South Korea's five largest cities, asking to fill a prescription containing rhino horn for a sick relative. While they were shopping, I posed as a TCM scholar and, working with an interpreter in Seoul, interviewed twenty-three traditional doctors at length about their past and present use of rhino horn. At the same time, one of Seoul's most respected TCM colleges helped me survey its alumni by mail.

The combined results showed that South Korea's TCM practitioners retained a robust belief in the efficacy of rhino horn for treating maladies from nosebleeds and dermatitis to stroke and life-threatening fever. However, their use of rhino horn had declined because it was hard to find, exorbitantly expensive, and illegal. One shopkeeper said rhino horn was readily available in Seoul, but "only a fool" would keep it at his place of business. Another said he kept his supply of rhino-horn powder at home. More than half the shops and clinics queried claimed to use rhino horn, but only one produced evidence in the form of a horn fragment alleged to be from a rhino— a stark contrast to earlier years when investigators found widespread availability of whole rhino horns.

My TRAFFIC report, *Market Under Cover: The Rhinoceros Horn Trade in South Korea*, concluded that while allegiance to rhino horn's healing power remained high, there was "little absolute proof that trade in rhinoceros horn persists in South Korea."[18] Whether the ban had eliminated trade or simply driven it underground remained a mystery that only undercover police work could solve.

• • •

With that, South Korea dodged the economic bullet. The United States dropped threats of sanctions, citing the country's "strong intent" to eliminate trade in rhino horn and its decision to join CITES. Ditto for Yemen.

China and Taiwan were another matter. On September 7, 1993, Secretary Babbitt announced that he was taking the next step toward sanctioning both, though China—much to the dismay of the Taiwan government—continued to insist that Taiwan was simply a renegade Chinese province. "The United States cannot stand by while the world's remaining wild tigers and rhinos slip into extinction as a result of illegal commercial trade in the world marketplace," Babbitt said in a press release. "Our action today will send the message that continued unlawful trade in these rare species will not be tolerated."[19]

Despite my hard feelings about the elusive Man with the Keys to the bile-milking room, I felt sorry for China and thought my country was acting like a bully. In contrast to South Korea, China had willingly become a CITES member twelve years before and had proactively shut down its much larger market for tiger bone and rhino horn. Japan too had a continuing appetite for tiger bone and rhino horn, but that geopolitical delicacy never made it to the Pelly table. I naively failed to factor in the US military bases in Japan and South Korea and the fact that Japan was our second largest trading partner. China, meanwhile, was still scratching at the door to be let into the world marketplace regulated by the General Agreement of Tariffs and Trade (GATT).

The same week as Babbitt's announcement in Washington, the China-bashing continued at the CITES Standing Committee meeting in Brussels. Elizabeth Dowdeswell, executive director of the UN Environment Programme, said she was aware of China's efforts to stop trade in tiger bone and rhino horn, but she was "not comfortable with the degree of China's commitment," as it was put in the meeting's official record.[20]

Babbitt flew in to personally announce stepped-up US threats against China and Taiwan. Trade in tiger bone and rhino horn was of urgent concern to the American people, he said. President Clinton would inform Congress within sixty days if he intended to take the next step of imposing trade sanctions. Babbitt encouraged CITES to demonstrate similar resolve.

China's spokesman denounced Babbitt's statements as unacceptable in light of all China had done. Furthermore, the threat of US trade sanctions violated China's sovereignty. He warned that the US action would only make matters worse.

Bill Clark, Israel's amiable representative with an American accent, took the floor to congratulate the United States for its boldness. The spokeswoman for Latin America and the Caribbean stated that there was solid evidence that illegal trade in tiger and rhino products continued unabated in China and, therefore, CITES should respond with trade sanctions.

The Standing Committee ordered China, South Korea, and Taiwan to confiscate, consolidate, and lock away all of their tiger and rhino products by the end of the following month. A CITES technical mission would be dispatched to verify compliance. Meanwhile, CITES member countries were told to consider actions "up to and including immediate trade sanctions."[21]

This humiliation of China marked a moment in history that would soon become unimaginable. But in September 1993, China was a nobody economically, politically, and militarily, as it emerged from more than forty years of isolation and Mao's ruinous Great Leaps Backward.

The following month, China exploded a nuclear weapon in defiance of President Clinton's call for a global testing moratorium.[22]

The CITES "mission" that amounted to an inspection team consisted of one person from Australia's CITES Management Authority, one from the US CITES Management Authority, the head of the Endangered Species Protection Unit of the South African Police, and, thanks to the Great Dane's influence, me, representing TRAFFIC.

Our "technical delegation" spent Thanksgiving week of 1993 in China's core-chilling cold, going in and out of unheated warehouses, viewing wooden crates of confiscated horns sawed or hacked from all five of the world's rhino species and burlap bags stuffed with the moldering bones of indeterminate tiger subspecies. We eyeballed shelves chockablock with nearly two million packaged pills, medicine balls, medicated skin plasters, and tonic wines containing, according to their labels, *xi jiao* (rhino horn) or *hu gu* (tiger bone).

To comply with CITES' request, China had gathered up 11,000 pounds of rhino horns and 1,100 pounds of tiger bone from twenty-seven provinces for safekeeping inside pharmaceutical companies that were either partly or wholly government-owned. Ministry of Forestry officials reportedly travelled to six provinces to inspect stockpiles, met with forty thousand people, and inspected more than thirty thousand stores, markets, medicine manufacturers, hotels, and restaurants to round up every last morsel of tiger bone and rhino horn. Our hosts assured us that the nation's stocks had all been consolidated and securely sealed behind the long rice-paper banners with big black Chinese characters we saw draped across entries to the storerooms we visited.

Our visit to traditional-medicine giant Tongrentang was a step back into pre-ransacked China. The company's Beijing headquarters occupied a traditional one-story courtyard house, entered through red double doors under a tiled roof with upturned eaves. Red window sills framed red shutters crisscrossed with bamboo latticework.

The management team at China's oldest, largest, and most venerated TCM manufacturer explained to us that, before the 1993 ban, Tongrentang had used nearly seven thousand pounds of tiger bone— the equivalent of more than three hundred tigers—a year to supply 80 percent of the country's tiger-based medicines to treat arthritis and broken bones.[23] The company's most famous and costly product had been Angong Nui Huang Wan (Calm the Palace), whose white, waxy balls engraved with gold Chinese characters were made with rhino horn. This medicine reportedly had saved countless lives of people who otherwise would have died from brain hemorrhage, embolism, heart failure, extreme fever, encephalitis, pneumonia, and poisoning. They said China's ancient medicine practice was a precious gift to humanity but they understood people in the West might not yet appreciate its value.

Tiger bone and rhino horn were essential medicine ingredients and important to China's long cultural heritage as well as the health of China's people, Tongrentang executives told us. Changing laws won't change the people's faith in these medicines or reduce their need for them, they said. They also asked who would compensate them for financial losses caused by the ban and whether tiger farming could be expanded so they could resume using tiger bone. We were asking how they were complying with China's new trade ban, and they were telling us why the ban was naive, wrong-headed, and imposed because of foreign ignorance.

Yale sociologist William Graham Sumner observed in 1906 that "law ways can't change folkways."[24] In other words, laws don't change hearts and minds. Until hearts and minds change, laws will be ignored, skirted, and broken, righteously and in good conscience. I realized for the first time that the fate of tigers, rhinos, and bears rested in the hands of these people, and they were not on board with the program.

Even our escorts from the Ministry of Forestry, China's CITES enforcer, lamented the waste of the stockpiled bones and horns. They touted tiger farming, citing the "success" of bear farming.[25] I wanted to tell them that their own wildlife experts said that bear poaching had not decreased, even after supplies of farmed bear bile surpassed national needs. But I was a UN emissary on a fact-finding mission, so I just took notes and wondered how effective China's ban would be if neither the policed nor the police thought it was justified.

The same month I was inspecting China's stockpiles, China's president, Jiang Zemin, met with President Clinton in Seattle for the highest-level parley between the United States and China since the Tiananmen Square massacre set off a mini cold war over human rights.[26] During his stop, Jiang visited the family of a Boeing worker, while his spokesmen took every opportunity to underscore the fact that China was buying one in every seven aircraft Boeing made. Message: we pay American salaries. Clinton emerged from the tête-à-tête calling America a "commercial friend" to China.[27]

The following month, January 1994, a high-level CITES delegation came to China to follow up on our technical mission. As a show of good faith, Chinese officials burned tiger bones and rhino horns confiscated in illegal trade at two public events.[28] Afterward, CITES threats of trade sanctions against China faded away.

On March 18, 1994, thirty-nine members of the US Congress sent a letter to President Clinton pressuring him to impose trade sanctions on China because it had "been unable to account for over three tons of registered rhinoceros horn and apparently allowed the export of over one ton of tiger bone to Korea."[29]

Ten days later, a picture of a snarling tiger made the cover of *Time* magazine with a one-word cover line: "Doomed."[30]

On April 11, 1994, Clinton sent a letter to Congress stating that, as a result of China's "progress in the key areas . . . I have decided that import prohibitions are not warranted at this time."[31]

On May 26, 1997, President Clinton renewed China's Most Favored Nation trade status, even though China had achieved little of the human rights progress Clinton had made a precondition of the renewal.[32]

Not long after Clinton softened toward China, the Great Dane shipped me off to Hong Kong to open TRAFFIC's East Asia regional program, which would supervise offices in Tokyo and Taipei and monitor wildlife trade in China, Japan, Mongolia, South Korea, Taiwan, Macau, and Hong Kong. There was some racy speculation within the TRAFFIC network about why he had chosen me, but none of it was true. The Great Dane simply believed in me—more than I believed in myself. Certainly more than my TRAFFIC colleagues, who were still skeptical of me for having ridden on my ex-husband's coattails into their world.

Hong Kong was Wonderland to my Alice. It offered the best of China and England—minus the Mao baggage and English gloom— plus affordable servants, plantation shutters, ceiling fans, gentle sea breezes, outlandish affluence, and a free flow of Veuve Clicquot. I partook of dazzling balls, cocktails after work at the Foreign Correspondents' Club, and weekends motoring away on refurbished Chinese junks to feast on fresh seafood at waterfront restaurants in the outlying islands. It looked and felt like the stuff of movies. And it would be my life for six years.

Despite my infatuation with the location, my first day on the job found me at a loss. I sat at a battered hand-me-down desk in a corner of the small glass conservatory that was WWF's Hong Kong office tucked under the tram to Victoria Peak, pondering how to create a regional TRAFFIC program. I waited until the sun rose in the UK and then called the Great Dane to ask.

"You will know what to do," he told me in That Voice. *Yes, Zen master.*

While I awaited enlightenment, I decided to do what I knew how to do, which was what I had done with bears. I began piecing together a picture of the global trade in tiger bone.

I learned that TCM practitioners over millennia had used every part of the tiger as medicine. Whiskers for toothaches. Nose for epilepsy. Eyeballs for cataracts and malaria. Claws, hair, and fat were cures too at different times in history. Tiger bile as well. And blood. But by the time China announced its 1993 trade ban, only tiger bone remained in its official pharmacopeia.

I confirmed that tiger bone, unlike bear bile and rhino horn, was not credited with saving lives. It was more like aspirin—an anti-inflammatory to ease the pain of arthritis and broken bones. The fact that no human lives depended on it seemed to bode well for wild tigers.[33]

According to ancient TCM principles, tigers closest to home made the best medicine, which only partially explained the crash of China's wild tigers. Biologists estimated that around four thousand South China tigers still roamed the wild when Mao, under the Great Leap Forward of 1958, launched an anti-pest campaign that offered a bounty for dead tigers. By the time China finally banned tiger hunting in 1977, the South China tiger had been reduced to around four hundred. When China joined CITES in 1981, some experts believed that South China tigers were nearly extinct. Siberian tigers in China's northeast and Indochina tigers along its borders with Laos,

Vietnam, and Myanmar hadn't fared much better. In 1994, no one was sure China still had any wild tigers.[34]

Despite this paucity, 130 Chinese manufacturers were producing forty different medicines containing tiger bone in 1985, according to China's Bureau of National Medicine. That explained the drive to farm tigers. But the withdrawal of China's 1992 CITES proposal to sell farmed bones internationally and its subsequent trade ban in 1993 meant that the farm's tiger numbers should have decreased. After all, the place had barely enough money to feed its animals back in 1992. However, a reputable source in China told Cat Specialist Group Chairman Peter Jackson that the farm's tiger numbers had actually increased.

As I was scratching my head about this apparent contradiction, a longtime Hong Kong expat gave me a welcome gift. It was a red pocket-sized paperback—a spoof of Mao's *Little Red Book* of slogans—entitled *101 Ways to Say 'No' in China*. My eye stopped on one phrase: "The man with the keys is not here." I thought of my pathetic overtures about changing flights so Chris and I could wait for the man who could unlock the door to the bile-milking room. I had thought our hosts were lying, but they were actually saying no in a form I didn't understand. I laughed so hard that some of my new colleagues at WWF Hong Kong asked me if I was okay.

I stopped laughing when I realized how the tiger-farm numbers made sense. Tigers were next. Like bears, they were to become "like cows and pigs." And the Man with the Keys would not be there until the metamorphosis was a done deal. Yes, China had banned trade in tiger bone in 1993. But had it banned tiger *farming*?

I frantically dug out an English translation of China's ban and reread it with new eyes. Sure enough, it contained *nothing* that could be construed to apply to tiger farming. The truth had been hiding in plain sight. I had missed it. The entire conservation A-list had missed it. CITES had missed it. Tiger farming would scale up until the government had no choice but to lift the ban. With five thousand years of history, Chinese entrepreneurs had mastered the long view.

Aficionados would always prefer the bones of wild tigers, placing an enticing price on the heads of them all—most of whom lived in some of the most cash-starved places in Asia. Worse, there was a profound and potentially fatal difference between tigers and bears. Where wild bears were still one hundred thousand strong, wild tigers were down to between five thousand and seven thousand. How long could they survive if even a tiny fraction of the more than one billion people in China wanted the "best" tiger bone? And why did tiger farming in China continue to expand unless lifting the ban was in the offing?

It was a prescription for extinction—a prescription the backers of China's tiger farms intended to fill.

4

PRESCRIPTION REWRITTEN

My belief that the King of the Jungle's fate rested with the very people who wanted to grind its bones into medicines didn't endear me to anyone.

Telling China's TCM doctors they couldn't use tiger bone and rhino horn because of threats from the United States was like telling American MDs they couldn't use penicillin and insulin because of threats from China, I insisted. They might suck it up for the good of their country, but their hearts wouldn't be in it. I told anyone who would listen that we had to *enlist* rather than vilify TCM practitioners if we wanted them to do more than put tiger bone and rhino horn out of sight until we turned our backs.

The Great Dane saw the logic, but a lot of my other colleagues thought I was what people in Hong Kong called an "egg"—white on the outside but yellow on the inside. A China sympathizer. What the diplomatic community called a "panda lover" as opposed to a "dragon slayer."[1]

Because I worked for TRAFFIC, other groups viewed me with an extra serving of suspicion. TRAFFIC's archrival at the time was the Environmental Investigation Agency (EIA). We were the *New York Times* of wildlife-trade information, while EIA—in our minds—was the *National Enquirer*. They courted the media with shocking video footage taken with hidden cameras, while we primly published wordy tomes based on customs records and CITES data. We prided ourselves in working *with* governments, while EIA used gotcha exposés to call them out for being soft on wildlife crime. We were the State Department to their CIA. They thought we erred on the side of spineless diplomacy, while we thought they crossed the line into reckless espionage. They were the bad cops who drove governments into our good-cop arms. They wowed television audiences with their work, while we were invited to sit on government delegations. Jealousy, animosity, mistrust, and condescension kept both sides estranged and therefore scattershot in what was, at its core, a shared fight to save wild tigers, rhinos, elephants, and bears, as well as a growing list of other rare species of skyrocketing commercial value.

"We were like the Montagues and Capulets," Allan Thornton, one of EIA's founders, told me years later.[2] Indeed we were.

At the 1994 CITES conference in Fort Lauderdale, more than a few people besides EIA thought I was batting for China's team. I fought hard against calls to destroy the country's stockpiles of tiger bone and rhino horn. I feared that destroying medicines TCM practitioners held invaluable would close their minds to respecting the trade bans needed to save wild tigers and rhinos. I wanted to have a fighting chance to change their "folkways" so the "law ways" of CITES stood a chance of working.

In the end, I got my wish, which made me even more suspect among my peers. CITES did not call for destruction of stockpiles but did urge collaboration with the TCM industry to stop tiger bone and rhino horn consumption.[3] I felt I'd won the mandate to follow what my gut said would stop the killing—and the farming too. Had I mingled with the Capulets, though, I might have fought *with* them to make a bonfire of China's stockpiles. Had I known what they knew, I might have done many things differently—except allying with the TCM community.

Steve Galster topped the list of Capulets I should have befriended. My TRAFFIC colleagues claimed that this tall, dark, neatly trimmed American was ex-CIA. Years later, I asked him if he'd been a spy. He laughed. "I worked for the NSA but not the one you're thinking of," he said.[4] He'd worked for the National Security Archive, an investigative think tank at George Washington University, where he earned his master's in security policy. While at that NSA, he studied insurgencies in Afghanistan, Iran, and Pakistan, which led him to hang out with mujahedin and see opium exchanged for guns among people who later shot at each other. He joined the EIA while dating a woman there who was investigating how money from the ivory trade was used to arm Africa's civil conflicts.

That's how Steve came to be on a twelve-hour train ride through South China in 1993, posing as the husband of a vivacious woman from Taiwan "interested" in buying wholesale rhino horn. The "couple" was en route to see a Chinese man in Guangdong Province who an informant claimed was sitting on a fortune in illegal rhino horn. Mr. Big, as Steve called him, met their train with five black Mercedes.

"He took us to his warehouse, opened it up, and it was *full* of rhino horn," Steve said. Mr. Big told his guests he had put out a call for rhino horn and received eight tons. He claimed most of it had come from Zambia and Zimbabwe, delivered via North Korean diplomatic pouch. "He wanted to stockpile it so the price would go up," Steve said. "He wasn't going to sell it for Chinese medicine. He was banking on extinction."

Steve and his female accomplice began to worry about their safety when they realized the amount of money and corruption necessary to amass the hoard of rhino horn they were secretly filming. Mr. Big said if they needed some delivered to Hong Kong, it would be no problem. "He told us, 'I've got military and secure trucks,'" Steve said. Mr. Big also said government officials knew he had the rhino horn but wanted it kept quiet until China won its bid to host the Olympics.

EIA delivered the video footage of Mr. Big to the Chinese embassy in London so China could be prepared to save face when the evidence was presented at the September 1993 CITES Standing Committee meeting in Brussels—the same meeting where the United States would announce possible trade sanctions. "At Brussels, we were given the floor to present our findings, showed the film, handed out our report," Steve said. "Then the Chinese were given the microphone. They congratulated us on an excellent investigation." They also announced that they had found Mr. Big's rhino-horn cache and prosecution would follow.

I wasn't at that Brussels meeting in 1993, so I also missed hearing a tall British rabble-rouser say things that might have dampened my sympathies for China. Having just turned forty that year, Mike Day appeared every bit the former advertising executive he was—posh English accent, tailor-made suits, leather-soled shoes.[5] Day was brash, impatient, and attacked wildlife traffickers, governments, and the A-list conservation establishment with equal zeal. Nonetheless, in him I would have found a soul mate in my growing worry over tiger farming. In fact, at the Kyoto CITES meeting, where I was only interested in bears, Mike had been behind the scenes in near apoplexy trying to stop China's bid for permission to sell the parts of farmed tigers.

In July 1993, two months after China announced its ban on tiger-bone trade, Mike flew to Harbin to see what had become of the farm. He presented himself as the husband of a Chinese woman in Taiwan whose father sold "exotic imports." He went shopping for tiger products in downtown Harbin and by day's end had offers of three whole tiger skeletons and "any amount" of tiger skins.

At the fur farm turned tiger farm, director Liu Xinchen told Mike that resident tigers were bred to one day replace China's nearly extinct Siberian tigers in the wild. However, Professor Shi Shaoye of Northeast Forestry University, who had escorted Mike to the farm, said there was no work underway to ascertain the habits and needs of wild tigers.

The farm had received close to $1 million in government subsidies before the 1993 ban put an end to them, Liu told Mike. Liu said he planned to publicly announce that his tigers were starving, in order to restart the cash flow from government sources or, if necessary, international donors.

Mike saw gaggles of young tigers that, in the wild, would still have been with their mothers learning how to hunt. If these tigers were ever released, he thought, they would become man-eaters simply because they lacked skills to catch anything more wily. He noted an inordinate number of adult female tigers in spartan cages but only a small number of adult males. Just like the ratios in pig farms he'd seen as a boy growing up in England. No need to feed a lot of males when only a few were needed to impregnate females that, well, bred like cats.

"Everything about the place said farm," Mike wrote in his 1995 book *Fight for the Tiger*. It "was a scam to produce the maximum amount of tiger bone and return the maximum amount of profit for its owners," he said. He had a "Fort Knox Theory"—that Chinese investors were stockpiling captive tigers and their parts for the day when extinction would bring them windfall returns.

Before leaving Harbin, a man offered Mike one thousand bottles of tiger-bone wine from his factory full of fermentation vats. When Mike asked how he could be certain the wine contained real tiger bone, the man said that Mike had just visited his "most reliable source of supply"—the tiger farm.

In September 1993, while I worked long hours in the offices of TRAFFIC International down a country lane in Cambridge, England, Mike flew to Brussels. After the chairman of the CITES Standing Committee gave him the floor, he reminded his audience that more than one thousand pounds of bones—from perhaps fifty tigers—had been seized by authorities in India and Nepal during the previous two months, allegedly bound for China's "closed" market. He spoke of "sacks of tiger skin and bone . . . bartered on the Sino-Russian border for automatic weapons and four-wheel drive vehicles" that would enable Russian poachers to become more "deadly and effective" at obtaining tiger bone to sell in China. Snow was about to blanket the Russian Far East, making tigers easier for poachers to track. By the time the Standing Committee reconvened in March 1994, he said, "the effects of our actions here this week will be known." CITES "must send a message now, this week, before it is too late. A message that leaves the poachers, the middlemen, and the entire illegal network in no doubt whatsoever the market for tiger bone *is closed*."

A rangy man in pin stripes approached Mike afterward. He was from the UK's Foreign Office. He asked whether Mike intended to "pursue this matter further." Mike said he did, given that the survival of wild tigers was at stake. "Perhaps this is not quite the time to be rocking the boat with Beijing," the man said. He told Mike that certain UK leaders took "a rather dim view of your rather brusque approach to this issue."

Frustrated by the diplomatic slow dance at CITES, Mike decided to do what he could on his own to protect Russia's tigers. But he needed help. Help from someone like Steve Galster. They'd only just met, but Mike offered Steve a ride from Brussels back to EIA's headquarters. By the time Mike's blue Volvo reached London, Steve had received a job offer. The following month, the two men flew to Vladivostok.

Steve was soon on his way to Harbin from the Russian Far East in Mike's employ, accompanied by the same loquacious Taiwan-born "wife" with whom he'd met Mr. Big. She happened to run into a Chinese businessman visiting Khabarovsk who promised he could help her and her "husband" find a wholesale source for tiger-bone products. The man led the couple right back to the same factory Mike Day had found months earlier.[6]

The factory's CEO said he had recently been visited by an "English spy" and asked the woman if she was "a little spy."

No, she said, she was a *big* spy. The CEO laughed and let down his guard.

Their camera-in-a-bag filmed the factory brewing what was said to be tiger-bone wine and burlap sacks nearby full of bones said to have come from wild tigers in Russia, India, and Indonesia, as well as from the nearby tiger farm.

"If we want to order a big quantity, how much can you supply monthly?" the woman asked the CEO in a smoky room, with a government official in attendance.

"We can provide as much as you want," the official said.

Mike and Steve showed the video to the CITES Standing Committee's meeting in March 1994, nearly a year after China had announced its ban. But the committee issued no reproach to China's delegation this time. Afterward, US officials warned Steve to stay out of China. They told him that if he went in, they couldn't guarantee he'd come out.

Once threats of trade sanctions against China were off the table, I flew to Beijing to extend an olive branch to the State Administration of Traditional Chinese Medicine. I had an appointment with a senior official who kept me waiting an hour only to tell me that there was no relationship between TCM and wildlife conservation, walk back in her office, and close the door in my face.

I returned to Hong Kong at a loss. I consulted with Paul But, who was Hong Kong Chinese and understood the connection I was trying to make. Paul researched the chemical composition of TCM ingredients at the Chinese University of Hong Kong and had helped the US Fish and Wildlife Service Forensics Laboratory identify Chinese medicines containing ingredients banned from trade. Still, despite his belief in conservation and trade controls, he said he would take the last horn off the last wild rhino if his child had a life-threatening fever that nothing else could treat.

I also sought advice from the wildlife-law-enforcement team at Hong Kong's Agriculture and Fisheries Department, which had established trust within the local TCM community by using outreach and reason before arrest warrants to dissuade illegal wildlife trade.

Paul and my friends in the Hong Kong government agreed to help me convince TCM specialists from Hong Kong, Japan, Singapore, South Korea, and Taiwan to come together with leading wildlife conservationists in October 1995 for the first-ever conference on TCM and wildlife conservation.[7] Most attendees from both sides arrived thinking that there was no relationship and shouldn't be one.

I credit the calm and understanding of trilingual emcee Daniel

Kwong On Chan, a University of Hong Kong zoologist who grew up using TCM, for keeping everyone in the room. The event was basically a shouting match with simultaneous interpretation—a high-volume verbal slugfest of complaints in Cantonese, Mandarin, and English—all of which Daniel understood and found a way to gracefully placate.

"You're endangering the world's most precious wild species with your scientifically unproven medicines," the conservationists declared.

"Your ignorant, imperialist mandates are endangering a medicine system proven over thousands of years of practice and refinement," the TCM specialists countered. "Your Western medicine doesn't even know *how* to test TCM's superior efficacy."

"You've driven tigers and rhinos close to extinction," the conservationists alleged.

"We have nothing to do with the killing of tigers and rhinos," the TCM specialists asserted. "We just use their parts after they're dead."

"Once you use up the last of these species, neither TCM nor the world will have them," the conservationists insisted.

"We will never run out of wildlife because China is a vast country with boundless supplies of wild animals and plants," the TCM specialists argued.

"Entire species are disappearing to make your aphrodisiacs," the conservationists said.

"You insult us," the TCM specialists said sharply. "Tiger bone relieves debilitating pain, and rhino horn saves lives. How dare you leave us unable to help desperately ill patients."

Despite the disconnects, raised voices, and shaking of fists, no one stormed out. We reached no consensus, and neither side gave up ground. But some listening occurred, and people on both sides expressed surprise at what they heard. Like it or not, they realized that their interests *did* intersect. Conservationists could not save certain endangered wildlife without the TCM industry's compliance, and the TCM industry would only lose more and more medicines if it didn't take conservation into account.

After that, my conservation colleagues stopped looking at me like I was a paid lobbyist for the TCM industry, and Hong Kong's TCM associations started asking to meet with me.

I soon became a regular on the Hong Kong TCM-association banquet circuit. Some evenings it was just me and more than a hundred Chinese in an expanse of linen-covered tables. They usually placed me at the head table next to their leader. Standard fare included sliced sea cucumber, which reminded me in taste, texture, and appearance of rubber bands, and either shark-fin soup (like fishy chicken noodle) or bird's nest soup (nests made with bird spit). I tried to fill up on the less psychologically challenging shrimp and bok choy dishes. But it was the *guanxi*—the connecting—that mattered.

Sometimes one of my Chinese-speaking staff would come along as interpreter. Other times I would spend the entire evening among people who spoke only Cantonese, with whom I could exchange but one or two phrases. My excellent chopsticks skills were always noted. I smiled and nodded whenever I recognized a word. And we bonded.

Slowly, slowly, we embraced our common ground. They wanted TCM to grow and prosper as much as I wanted wild tigers, rhinos, and bears to thrive. We both wanted to be able to forecast which wild medicinal ingredients might become scarce and, if possible, prevent it. They wanted to grow their business globally in places like the United States and Europe, where people would shun products containing endangered species. I became convinced that they would stop consumption of tiger bone, rhino horn, and bear bile in order for TCM to go global. And they were trusted and influential enough to change centuries-old "folkways" forever.

Meanwhile, our TRAFFIC surveys of China's post-ban market continued to show a decline in availability of tiger and rhino products but still enough on offer to be worrying. Even remnant demand in the world's most populous country, with its soaring affluence, could drive a deadly amount of poaching. More ominously, our investigators noted an absence of public reminders that China's ban remained in effect. Memories of the initial media blitz in 1993 were fading. By 1996, nearly half of the TCM sellers in China visited by TRAFFIC investigators said they weren't aware of the ban.[8]

My relationship with wildlife consumers in the TCM community was far more copasetic than my rapport with the Beijing officials charged with policing them. I didn't appreciate the extent of the latter's annoyance until an incident that occurred in November 1996.

The mishap involved the man I mentally nicknamed China's Fonz. Meng Xianlin had slicked-back black hair, a toothy smile, and a faux-leather bomber jacket. Though I did not meet him at the time, he had been studying wildlife at Northeast Forestry University in 1991 when some of his professors had taken "Christ" and me on our grand tour of China's frozen North to avoid seeing bears milked. He had just joined China's CITES Management Authority when we met in 1996 at a CITES-enforcement training workshop in Hong Kong.

The class was discussing the various means by which criminals can disguise illegal wildlife trade as legal. I raised my hand to mention a possible method that had been overlooked. Bear farms could be used to launder the gall bladders and bile of wild bears because there was no way to distinguish the gall bladders and bile of wild bears from those of farmed bears.

The air in the room suddenly changed. Meng motioned over Jean-Patrick Le Duc, the CITES Secretariat's chief enforcement officer. People looked on with worried brows as a red-faced Meng whispered heated words in Jean-Patrick's ear. Jean-Patrick nodded and offered what looked like reassurance. Then class resumed.

When everyone filed out for a tea break, Jean-Patrick stopped me. "Mr. Meng said if I didn't make you retract your comment about bear farms, he was going to walk out with his delegation and return to Beijing," he said. "I assured him that you did not mean any offense. But please don't mention bear farms again."

I had hit a nerve. I had no idea that it was a central nerve.

• • •

Had I run CITES, it would have been mostly about tigers and bears, but the central drama at the 1997 CITES conference in Zimbabwe's capital involved elephants. In fact, CITES was so preoccupied with elephants so much of the time that some said the UN treaty on trade in endangered species should be renamed the treaty on trade in *elephant* species. Zimbabwe's incendiary president Robert Mugabe opened the Harare conference with polite reminders that he regarded the international ivory ban as recolonization under the guise of nature protection and a drag on his country's GDP.[9]

Botswana, Namibia, and Zimbabwe were asking for permission to sell stockpiles of elephant ivory to Japan. Proponents referred to it as "limited legal trade" while opponents feared it would trigger another bloodbath for wild elephants, which were making a robust comeback thanks to the international trade ban. "Even a partial relaxation would send a message to poachers that ivory trade is back," Dave Curry, director of the Environmental Investigation Agency (EIA), told the *New York Times*.[10]

My staff in Tokyo had similar concerns. Their investigations found Japan's trade controls inadequate to prevent illegal ivory from entering the market. However, their worries were overruled by more senior TRAFFIC staff in Africa. TRAFFIC and its benefactor, World Wildlife Fund, decided to support the so-called one-off sales, which would eventually lead to other "one-offs" that would reawaken China's sleeping giant of an appetite for ivory. Hence, in Harare, some at EIA deemed us "The Evil Ones."

I didn't do ivory. I was all about species used as medicine. Nobody was ever going to take the last tusk off the last elephant to save a child's life, I thought. Ivory name stamps and dust-collecting carvings may be linked to old Asian cultural practices, but they were still just luxury items. It never occurred to me that the same forces had their greedy sights set on all of it.

I exchanged greetings with China's delegation in the gleaming marble and brass entry to the Sheraton Harare's convention complex. Their body language said that our relations had chilled since the bear-farming kerfuffle in Hong Kong. If it was that important to them, they probably weren't thrilled about my blossoming relations with the industry meant to consume products from bear farms.

They might also have been peeved that I had convinced TRAF-FIC and WWF to convince Japan, South Korea, and the United Kingdom to propose the first-ever CITES resolution on traditional Chinese medicines. I thought formal recognition of the TCM industry as a respected stakeholder was pivotal.

TRAFFIC offered suggested wording. However, after the proponent countries created their own version in consultation with China, the proposed resolution put forward in Harare was alarming.[11] It recommended "captive-breeding to meet the needs of traditional medicine"—that is, farming tigers, bears, and fill-in-the-blank other species to produce raw materials for medicine manufacturing. We counted on the United States to undo the damage during the debate.

When the United States took the floor, it praised the collaborative effort and endorsed all of the resolution except the passage on captive breeding. Since wildlife farming could stimulate demand, the United States asked that the reference be deleted. Switzerland concurred. Japan suggested simply adding the caveat that captive breeding be considered "where appropriate and with sufficient safeguards."

"No!" I whispered to Steve Broad, the unreadable Brit with a warm smile who had become my boss after the Great Dane left us for Conservation International. "Appropriate to whom? Sufficient to whom?"

"Calm down," Steve said. "That won't get through."

I clasped my hands in front of my mouth. *Meng Xianlin must be envisioning a feedlot that looks like Noah's Ark.*

China suggested simply adding the clause "in accordance with . . . national legislation."

There was a pause while delegations conferred. Then, to my horror, the United States and Switzerland said that China's wording had allayed their concerns.[12] Farming bears to supply medicine *was* in accordance with China's legislation. My only consolation was that China's 1993 ban prohibited the sale of bones from tiger farms.

· · ·

While we parsed wonky words in Zimbabwe that might decide the fate of entire species, a British man in his early thirties named Peter Knights decided he'd had enough of the UN tug-of-war between selling and saving endangered species.[13] As far as he was concerned, we were all "chasing our tails."

Another Capulet I foolishly avoided, Peter looked like a clean-cut rocker and almost vibrated with energy. The 1988 graduate of the London School of Economics had volunteered for Greenpeace in 1989. After he finagled a way into a database of all England's ivory traders, EIA hired him to investigate the international exotic-pet trade. That introduced him in the early 1990s to what he calls the CITES "Thank You for Smoking Crowd" (named for the movie spoofing the American tobacco lobby). He entered the fray just as CITES secretary general Eugene LaPointe was stepping down amid accusations of colluding with the ivory industry—after which LaPointe built a business lobbying CITES on behalf of the ivory industry.

"I saw how the legal, regulated trade was a disaster," Peter told me years later. "It didn't replace illegal trade or illegal supply. It was enabling a massive illegal trade to be laundered through the legal trade. And it got worse and worse every year. The illegal trade was always one step ahead."

He became fed up with trade advocates distorting economic theories to argue that legal wildlife trade would supplant the illegal trade. "You basically have to view illegal wildlife as stolen goods," he said. "If you have a legal market in cars, does that stop the market for stolen cars? It doesn't. People still steal cars. Creating a legal market does not replace an illegal market. And very often it enables traders to cover illegal activity because it's confusing"—confusing to consumers and law enforcers. "There's nothing cheaper than poaching a wild animal. It's much cheaper than breeding and rearing an animal. The people stealing wildlife from the wild have no fixed costs. It's like saying you can manufacture cars cheaper than someone can steal them. You can't."

Peter decided early on that wild tigers, rhinos, bears, elephants, et al. would never be safe unless demand was "stopped at the source." The people he had met across Asia while investigating illegal trade in an array of species "were not malicious people," he said. "They didn't want to hurt animals. They just didn't understand. It became clear to me that what was needed was a massive awareness campaign to help consumers understand they were actually driving the trade in these species—to connect them to the killing. Because most of the people I met in Asia found the killing abhorrent. They just didn't connect their part in it."

Peter left EIA and took his gut feelings to the CEO of advertising giant J. Walter Thompson (JWT) in London. "Why can't we use the clever advertising used in the West to sell things to sell the idea of *not* buying things?" This was his pitch to JWT. He wanted to make wildlife conservation "aspirational—the same way you market Nikes—where it's something you want to be a part of and you think the people who aren't part of it are kind of yucky and old and insensitive." He ended his appeal to JWT with, "I want to do a campaign that we can franchise throughout Asia to *un*sell things to people—and I haven't got any money."

JWT loved the idea. A pro bono team started by creating five Hollywood-worthy television spots—one each for tigers, rhinos, bears, elephants, and marine turtles. Then Peter asked a Chinese colleague who would be the one best celebrity to win Asian hearts for wildlife. "Jackie Chan," she said.

So while I and hundreds of other CITES geeks were over-packing our bags with background documents for Harare, Peter sent a letter to Jackie Chan. "I basically told him, 'This is what's going on. These are the issues. People don't understand. Your championship of this campaign will help break down stereotypes.'" A few days later, Peter was shocked to receive a reply. Chan was in South Africa filming. He wanted to meet up. Peter weighed whether to join the warring wonks in Zimbabwe or accept Chan's invitation—for about thirty seconds.

Peter had no idea what to expect in South Africa, with Chan in the middle of making a martial-arts action movie. As it turned out, Chan filmed all day and ate dinner with Peter every night.

"How did you know I was in South Africa when you sent me this letter?" Chan asked him one evening. "Nobody was supposed to know."

"Jackie, I had no idea you were in South Africa," Peter said. "This is fate. We were supposed to meet this way."

"Good answer," Chan said. "I'm going to do this with you."

Because of our "family" feud, I had no idea that Peter and I were simultaneously flanking the same enemy—demand. While he enlisted troops in Hollywood, I continued recruiting from the TCM industry.

My efforts culminated in December 1997 with a sequel to the 1995 shouting match. At the suggestion of my new TCM collaborators, the second Hong Kong conference would highlight substitutes for tiger bone and musk.[14] We chose musk because substitutes for rhino horn were too sensitive. The horns of saiga antelope had been a recommended substitute for rhino horn until the run on saiga herds in the steppes of Central Asia caused one of the most precipitous population crashes ever seen. The tragedy was an embarrassment for conservation groups that promoted the substitute and another bitter pill for TCM practitioners who had tried to do the right thing only to have restrictions placed on yet another valued medicine. Chinese researchers were leaning toward bones of the mole rat, considered a pest on the Tibetan Plateau, as a substitute for tiger bone, and synthetic musk to replace the prized medicine found inside the scent glands of the dog-size male musk deer, distinctive for its tusk-like teeth.

The two-day gathering was cosponsored by TRAFFIC East Asia and Paul But's Chinese Medicinal Material Research Centre, with enthusiastic support from TCM leaders in Hong Kong and Singapore. We expected more than one hundred TCM and conservation luminaries from seventeen countries and territories, including China.

We chose a kitschy hotel complex with a karaoke bar and several Chinese restaurants in suburban Hong Kong as the venue. My small but unflagging staff and I prepared for months with a professional conference organizer. We were days out from picking up presenters at the airport, and running on nerves, when the call came in. No one from China would attend. No one from China was *allowed* to attend. Permission had been denied.

I called my boss Steve the moment his day started in the UK. "I think we should cancel the conference," I said. "Or maybe we can postpone it until we know mainland Chinese can attend." Tens of thousands of dollars had been spent, hundreds of details were in place, and scores of non-refundable flights had been booked.

"Someone in China doesn't want this to happen," I said. "But who? And why?"

"You can't cancel," Steve said.

He was right, of course. But I felt defeated. Again. Still, as is so often the case in life, triumph came in an unforeseen form.

We had a full house. I was the emcee and central command for guests, staff, consultants, and an unrelenting litany of urgent details. Toward the end of the harried first day, Ginette Hemley, the quietly formidable head of the species program at WWF-US, placed her hand on my elbow. "There's someone I'd like you to meet," she said. I turned and saw a Chinese woman about my age, with short hair and wearing a fitted black-and-white tweed suit. Her wire-framed glasses could not hide her high cheekbones and flawless skin. Her name sounded like "Lee-sheen Wong."

When I shook hands with Lixin Huang, the universe seemed to pause.[15] Her grip was firm and her English fluent, with a mainland Chinese accent. She smiled with her whole face and held my eyes as she talked. "Wow," she said, "I never knew this was an issue. But now I see that it is a very important one."

"I'm sorry," I said. "Where did you say you're from?"

"I am from China, but I am an American," she said. "I am the president of the American College of Traditional Chinese Medicine in San Francisco. This meeting is amazing. It has truly opened my eyes. I want to know how I can help."

There were other gratifying moments during those two days. One TCM specialist took the mic to say that he had once believed wildlife advocates were trying to "kill" TCM but now saw how the survival of TCM was inextricably linked to wildlife conservation. We also learned that there was a spy from China among us who later gave the meeting a glowing review. We produced written proceedings in Chi-

nese that were disseminated across the TCM world. But the one outcome that proved game-changing was the presence of Lixin Huang.
My gut knew it in an instant. She was the Woman with the Keys.

Lixin had been in third grade when the Cultural Revolution began.

"I didn't know what it was about," she said. "Everything became
different." Even her name. Her mother had named her Weina ("Way-
nah") because it sounded like a Russian girl's name, and China was
a close ally to Russia when she was born. "During the Cultural Revolution, that name was considered not very revolutionary, so my dad
changed it to Lixin, which means 'set up new things.'" Other popular
names of the time were Jianguo ("establishing China") and Yuanchao
("supporting Korea").

In high school PE, Lixin learned to run with a rifle and throw grenades. "We would march for hours and hours," she said. Upon graduation, she was sent to the countryside and "reeducated" by peasants
for three years. "I remember all of Mao's slogans," she said. "I can
recite them even today. It's like Mao's *Little Red Book* in my head."

Lixin was tending cows when the village loudspeaker announced
Mao's death. At that time, peasants, workers, and the People's Liberation Army chose who would go to college. She was among the one
in a thousand selected by farmers.

Known as "The Beautiful Girl with the Hair" for a silky cascade
that fell below her waist, she was far more interested in her studies
than the many young men orbiting her. She studied English at university, but her professor specialized in Russian, so Lixin turned to
the radio for instruction. After graduation, she taught English at an
architectural-engineering college and was soon promoted to associ-
ate dean. "I didn't like it," she said. "It was all meetings with old men
in smoky rooms talking about politics and how to motivate young
people with the Communist Party's philosophy."

Lixin didn't plan to become an American. However, the young
man who finally won her heart ended up going to graduate school in
the United States in 1985. A year later, she followed her husband and

entered a masters program in adult continuing education at Northern Illinois University. "If there had been no Tiananmen massacre
in 1989, we would have taken a completely different path," she said.
They stayed glued to the television as the event unfolded, seeing
what their friends and family back in China could not. "We were
angry. We were sad. We were frustrated. We were very much worried
about the future of China. And it made us question how the Chinese
government would treat returning graduate students. Once we left
China, we could never be the same. We became outspoken."

She was in Berkeley to attend a forum on the future of China
after Tiananmen when a friend working at the American College of
Traditional Medicine asked her to meet with the school's president
and dean. After an hour, they said, "We need you. The students need
someone who understands Chinese culture and American education." She started as the college's administrator in 1989 and became
its president in 1994, the same year I became director of TRAFFIC
East Asia.

Lixin was puzzled when a woman named Karen Baragona called
her from WWF in Washington, DC, and asked if they could meet. "I
thought, 'What can I do for you?'" She gave Karen a tour of the college and figured that was the end of it, until Karen called to say that
WWF wanted to fly her to Hong Kong for a symposium on TCM and
wildlife conservation. Lixin didn't see the connection, but she accepted. "I observed and listened," she said. "But I did not talk because
the subject was completely new to me. I quickly got the message and
the main problem." When she realized that no one from China had
been allowed to attend, she saw how she could add value.

Lixin decided she would attract China's TCM industry to tiger
conservation by example.[16] "I asked myself who is the key player I
can pull in for this." Her answer: Mingkang Dai, senior reporter for
the World Journal, North America's largest Chinese-language newspaper. He, in turn, enlisted Chinese American community leaders
who, like himself and Lixin, had been sent to China's countryside
during the Cultural Revolution. "If you could handle the hunger,
the thirst, the separation from family as a youth, you could handle
anything as an adult," she said.

Lixin and Mingkang quickly convinced 120 Chinese organizations and businesses in the Bay Area to form an alliance to spread what Lixin called the "saving-wild-tigers message" (which sounds better in Chinese): "If no one sells tiger products, then no one buys them, and the wild tiger will no longer be endangered."

In honor of the Chinese zodiac's 1998 Year of the Tiger, the alliance convinced the offices of the governor of California, the mayor of San Francisco, and the city's Board of Supervisors to jointly declare February 6, 1998, Wildlife Conservation Day in San Francisco. On a Friday drenched in El Niño rains, nearly one hundred Chinese Americans and all the area's Chinese news outlets gathered in San Francisco's Chinatown for the launch of a tiger campaign. In the weeks that followed, Chinese in the Bay Area celebrated wild tigers with a parade, festivals, and essay and drawing contests for children. The San Francisco Zoo set aside a day for more than one thousand Chinese American families to come for free and enjoy tiger-related games, traditional Chinese dancing, and martial-arts demonstrations.

The campaign culminated in June 1998 with a conference at what had once been a general's residence in San Francisco's Fort Mason Park. I flew in from Hong Kong to watch Lixin run with a baton I did not realize I'd passed to her seven months before in Hong Kong.

The most extraordinary part of the day was not that Chinese far outnumbered non-Chinese in the meeting room overlooking San Francisco Bay. I had grown so used to being a minority during my years in Hong Kong that I was sometimes surprised when I looked in the mirror and didn't see a Chinese face. What astounded me was the fact that Chinese were driving every aspect of an impassioned push to stop all consumption of tiger products.

They were not, like me, part of the swooning, misty-eyed Cult of the Tiger. For them, saving wild tigers was a matter of Chinese pride and responsibility. They did not want the blood of the last wild tigers to sully their beloved mother country or its treasured culture and revered traditional medicine system. The trade-off of tiger bones for the honor of the Chinese diaspora was, for them, a no-brainer.

Not long after that, Lixin's "keys" opened the door I'd been banging against for so long.

She hosted a delegation from China's State Administration of Traditional Chinese Medicine interested in the US approach to continuing education for TCM practitioners. During the course of those discussions, Lixin mentioned the Bay Area Chinese community's tiger campaign. While flying back to Beijing, one of her guests, a high-level official named Zhang Zaizeng, read some of the Chinese press coverage of the campaign. He called Lixin as soon as he returned to Beijing. "This is fascinating," he said. "This is an area we do not know how to handle. We are always criticized, but we don't know how to participate in the international dialogue. Tell me what we can do together."

As the TCM industry in the United States, Canada, Australia, United Kingdom, and, it seemed at last, China took up the call to end the use of tiger bone once and for all, poaching of Siberian tigers began to decline thanks to anti-poaching teams working with an American rumored to be an ex-spy.

When Steve Galster flew with Mike Day to the Russian Far East in 1993, they had gone directly into marathon sessions with government officials to convince them to create a special police force to stop tiger poaching. "Mike was ballsy and smart," Steve said, recounting how he got lured into spending the better part of the next seven years working there. "He was good with the Russians because he was tough, could drink with them, and he offered money."

The dissolution of the Soviet Union at the end of 1991 brought an end to strict wildlife protection in the Russian Far East. At the same time, traders from China, Japan, and South Korea gained access to the region's pristine forests. By 1993, Russian, Korean, and Chinese poachers were collecting ginseng, sea cucumbers, bear gall bladders, musk, leopard skins, tiger bones, tiger skins, and entire tiger bodies destined mainly for China but also Japan and South Korea. Organized criminal networks provided poachers with guns, vehicles, and, when needed, protection from prosecution.

Poachers were killing as many as sixty Russian tigers a year, reducing the total number to as few as two hundred. Some tiger biologists were talking "imminent extinction," according to Steve. On Mike's pledge of funding, a branch of the Ministry of Environment in the Russian Far East agreed to set up a special unit, code-named Operation Amba (after an indigenous people's word for "tiger"). The week before Christmas of 1993, Mike took off for London to find the $350,000 he had promised, leaving Steve to help select an anti-poaching brigade.

"That bank account stayed dry for a long time," Steve told me. WWF wanted in on the action too, but it and Mike took a good long time before wiring any money. Meanwhile, Steve was the only foreigner within arm's length as the Russians grew antsy about the promised funding. "I was getting nervous," he said. "This was after we'd hired fifteen guys who'd given up other jobs. They were like the Dirty Dozen. They were *ready*." Steve eventually flew to London to round up three donors willing to put up funds until Mike and WWF came through.

"There were months when these guys were buying gas and bullets with their own money," Steve said. Most of them had been in the Soviet military so they knew their way around guns and conflict. Steve trained them to use hidden cameras, arranged for local prosecutors to teach them the intricacies of relevant laws, and then brought in trainers from the US Fish and Wildlife Service experienced in wildlife sting operations.

At first, gray-bearded Commander Vladimir Shetinin and his team of tiger defenders in maroon military berets and gray fatigues were outmaneuvered, showing up at crime scenes only to find poachers had already disappeared.[17] Then they adopted what Steve termed PsyOps. They created a network of local informants, randomly checked vehicles leaving forests, and varied the routes of their three five-man patrols until they seemed to have eyes everywhere and the ability to appear anywhere at any time.

They found professional hunters selling tiger bones and whole frozen tiger carcasses directly to Chinese buyers. Middlemen transported their contraband by air to Harbin and via road or rail across remote border posts like the small, modest town of Pogranichniy, gateway to Suifenhe, a Chinese city of one hundred thousand that by 2008 would be processing more than five billion pounds of mostly Russian timber annually—half of it illegal, according to the Environmental Investigation Agency.[18]

 Amba teams uncovered corrupt local officials who employed poachers to supply Korean Russians, who then sold to Chinese and Koreans. They traced dead tigers, whole and in parts, leaving Russia aboard ships, facilitated by a corrupt customs officer in Vladivostok or carried by Russian sailors and Korean workers shipping out for Japan and South Korea. In one case, they arrested a rural poacher who turned out to be a suspect in four murders. The prevalence of Mafia ties led Operation Amba to seek backup from local police and the FSB (formerly the KGB).

In 1997, the Russian Duma approved government funding for the tiger brigades, which had become legendary for their daring and were credited with the steady drop in poaching that had allowed the country's wild tigers to rebound.

No longer needed, Steve left Russia about the same time I announced I was leaving Hong Kong.

"I feel like I'm repeating myself," I told my boss when I resigned from TRAFFIC in 1999 after accepting a job to work on wild tigers at WWF in Washington, DC.

By then, Lixin had convinced China's health ministry to cohost the next conference on endangered species used in TCM, and the International Fund for Animal Welfare had signed a deal with a Chinese organization tied to the Ministry of Forestry to close China's worst bear farms, with the aim of eventually phasing out bear farming.

I was feeling superfluous and also a bit banqueted to death by the well-meaning Hong Kong TCM community, which had recently asked me to be their Vanna White, drawing raffle winners on stage at an annual dinner. I longed for time around wild tigers rather than the bits and pieces of their poached relatives. I wanted to spread the word throughout the tiger's range that TCM demand for tiger parts was dying so poachers wouldn't waste their time and more tiger lives.

I had just three major tasks to complete before I rang in the new millennium at my last over-the-top Hong Kong soiree and flew off to a new life in my home country.

First came another UN mission. CITES had decided to send emissaries to assess controls on tiger trade in range and consumer countries. I joined the technical delegation headed by John Sellar, the tough-minded Scottish detective who was the new chief cop for CITES, to visit China, Cambodia, India, Japan, Nepal, and Russia.[19]

We spent the first week of June 1999 in China, mostly retracing the steps of my 1993 mission. The sealed stockpiles of tiger bone and rhino horn looked the same, except for advancing decay in the burlap sacks of tiger bones. The estimated value of it all had risen substantially, and Chinese officials put the costs of securing it for six years at $3.6 million. TCM manufacturers and government representatives again asked about compensation for their economic losses and still talked as if China's trade ban was temporary. I wondered if they knew that the TCM-led campaign against use of tiger bone had spread from Hong Kong to the United States, Australia, Canada, and Europe—all places China's TCM industry hoped to build market share.

We flew from Beijing to Harbin to visit the Siberian Tiger Park, opened in 1996 to raise revenues for the tiger farm that the World (as represented by CITES) assumed would disappear after China's 1993 ban. Park management threw a live chicken into a large dusty enclosure so we could watch a herd of tigers chase the squawking bird like a soccer team after a ball. As many as three hundred thousand people visited each year, we were told. None of the information displays in the park mentioned China's trade ban or the imperative to stop the use of tiger products to save wild tigers.

Once again, the numbers didn't make sense. Speed-breeding was producing two hundred tigers a year. I was shocked by the birthrate and asked why this was allowed under the ban. Both farm staff and our government hosts assured us that the baby boom was for release into the wild only—to one day set free in a corner of Northeast China that had more hunters' snares than forest cover or tiger prey. Either our hosts were delusional or lying, we concluded.

Our report back to CITES warned that the tiger farm and its

public-facing park offered opportunities for laundering wild-caught tigers and their parts and products. To put an end to the perception that China's ban was temporary, we recommended destruction of all stockpiles of tiger parts and products.

John Sellar was fearless in presenting our analysis, so I felt sure tigers would be courageously looked after at CITES.

Second on my final TRAFFIC to-do list was a symposium on the trade in bear parts, the third in a series that had grown from my initial TRAFFIC investigation. In October 1999, it was held for the first time in Asia and hosted by the country with the most tenacious consumers of bear gall bladders—South Korea.[20] Once again, Asians were taking leadership in stopping a threat posed by Asians. I sat in the audience, awed and grateful—until the first speaker on bear farming.

Fan Zhiyong, a young man with a middle-aged build from the CITES office in Beijing, revealed that close to one thousand bears had been taken from the wild to set up China's bear farms—at a time when Asian bears were already endangered. There were now nearly 250 farms housing a total of more than seven thousand bears across China. The farms were surgically constructing taps from the bears' own flesh to access their bile, creating what looked like "an anus." Bile production still far outpaced China's demand, and a request to CITES for permission to trade the surplus internationally would soon follow, Fan said.[21] Despite the signed agreement to eventually phase out bear farming, the plan was clearly to establish farmed bear bile as a global commodity. And wild bears were *still* being poached for their gall bladders.

I would have despaired if not for the delicate Chinese woman who came to the podium after Fan. Her name was Grace Ge Gabriel and she had just joined the International Fund for Animal Welfare's China team. A recent survey in Beijing and Shanghai showed less than 5 percent of families had ever used bear bile, she said. More than 42 percent of respondents didn't know about the use of bear bile in health care, and nearly 60 percent didn't know what diseases it treated. When told about the conditions in bear farms, 88 percent deemed them cruel, nearly 63 percent condemned them, and more than 70 percent said they would refuse to use bear bile. Finally, more than 86 percent said they were against relaxing international regulations to allow China to export bear-bile products. Furthermore, she said, bear farming "directly and negatively affects China's image and the reputation of traditional Chinese medicine as a cultural heritage."[22]

Thanks to this woman, I left South Korea feeling bears were in capable hands at a time of waning Chinese appetites for wildlife products.

I flew directly from Seoul to snowy Beijing to tick off the last item on my list—witnessing Lixin's miracle of a three-day conference on TCM and wildlife conservation hosted by China's health ministry.[23]

It had been scheduled to take place months earlier—until US warplanes dropped laser-guided bombs on the Chinese embassy in Belgrade during a NATO intervention in Yugoslavia that spring. Three Chinese had died and twenty others were injured. China's government called it a deliberate attack, despite apologies from President Clinton, who blamed the incident on out-of-date maps. Anti-American protests had erupted in China, and the "Healthy People, Healthy Planet" conference was postponed indefinitely.

When it finally convened at Beijing's China World Hotel at the end of October 1999, more than 120 people attended, including high-ranking representatives of China's ministries of health, science and technology, and food and drug regulation.

"If TCM is to develop, we must get past the problem of endangered species," Dequan Ren, vice general director of the State Administration and Management for Medicinal Products, told the delegates, 90 percent of whom were Chinese. "Our collective feeling is that there is no contradiction between TCM and conservation. For TCM to progress, it must take a sustainable course."

Speakers from both camps spent a lot of their time at the podium emphasizing how collaboration would determine the survival of species like tigers and the global embrace of TCM as a trusted health-care system. "The survival of critically endangered species, such as tigers and rhinos, depends, in part, on the elimination of their use in traditional Chinese medicine," WWF's Ginette Hemley said to affirming nods around the tightly packed hotel meeting room.[24]

I used my time at the podium to emphasize the "symbiotic match" of TCM and wildlife conservation but cautioned that some species would forever remain off-limits. "The tiger's condition might be called a triage situation in medical terms," I said. "While tigers do breed well in captivity, farming them for their bones is not a viable option. Unscrupulous traders could easily sell the bones of wild tigers as bones from farmed tigers. All efforts for tigers now should be focused on conserving them in the wild." I noticed nervous shuffling and many eyes examining the floor after I mentioned tiger farming.[25]

When the time came to agree on the meeting's consensus declaration, representatives from what had been the Ministry of Forestry before it was renamed the State Forestry Administration—home of Meng Xianlin—pushed for endorsement of wildlife farming to supply TCM. Because it was my last chance to do so, I pushed back hard. There were no harsh tones or sharp words, but the pushing was intense and stubborn on both sides. In the end, there was no declaration.

I left Beijing, for what I thought was the last time, unsettled, worried about who would push back in my absence. I told myself that Meng Xianlin and his cohorts were simply stuck in the 1980s, in denial that the prescription for extinction had been rewritten—by the TCM industry itself. I convinced myself that withering Chinese demand for medicines containing parts of tigers and bears would soon eliminate any market the backers of farms hoped to supply.

5

※

INTERMISSION I

The Wild Ones

The tiger attacked the fifty-five-year-old Nepali woman when she went to the loo in the forest. It was just like in my sleepless nightmare during my first overnight in Glacier National Park years before, only what was an imaginary bear for me was an all-too-real tiger for her. People from her village saw her leave and called for help when she didn't return by nightfall. Trackers on elephants from Royal Bardia National Park found her torn clothes first, then what was left of her body.

I visited her village just after the incident in March 2001. My World Wildlife Fund Nepal colleagues and I were leading a National Public Radio crew across what we had named the Terai Arc—the place we hoped would one day form a ribbon of broadleaf forests, towering grasslands, and rivers fed by the world's highest glaciers, connecting eleven protected areas on either side of the India-Nepal border. Tigers shared this subtropical expanse with rhinos, elephants, leopards, sloth bears, striped hyenas, sambar deer, wild pigs, river dolphins, and more than five hundred bird species. Our envisioned swath of Eden, about the size of an elongated state of Maryland, was also home to two million people and at least that many scrawny cows granted run of the place by their sacred status among Nepal's Hindu majority.[1]

"If there used to be tiger, there can be tiger again," Anil Manandhar of WWF Nepal told me. I never saw Anil without a smile under his thin mustache, and he, like me, was all-in on this dream of restoring an international greenbelt in which the region's several hundred tigers could expand and thrive in perpetuity.

"Is there some way to get rid of these cattle that are everywhere overgrazing the forests?" I asked him during my first on-the-ground look, in 2000.

"You cannot talk about these things," he said.

The threat posed to wild tigers by TCM was centuries old and potentially more than one billion people strong. But it seemed simple to me compared to the poverty, religion, cattle run amok, and burgeoning Maoist insurgency that came together where India meets Nepal at the base of the Himalayan foothills.

I wanted NPR listeners to hear the complications but also sense the adrenaline rush of possibility. So we took reporter John Nielsen and crew first to Nepal's Royal Chitwan National Park, at the Terai Arc's eastern extreme, for what John dubbed a "rhino roundup." His story aired just after Nepal's royal family was assassinated by one of their own in June 2001, ushering in a period of political instability that brought even greater jeopardy for the Terai's tigers, rhinos, and bears.

John's narrative began with what sounded like a sledgehammer hitting wood and men shouting in Nepali.[2] "When the 1,500-pound rhinoceros wakes up inside the wooden crate, it gets angry," he said. "On top of the crate, men with hammers bounce around like ping-pong balls. A crowd of anxious men waits to push the crate up a ramp into the truck. The driver has orders to travel all night on the only highway in lowland Nepal, past rice paddies, crowded towns, and shredded forests. The truck won't stop until it reaches Royal Bardia, a park in western Nepal that has lost its rhinos to poachers. But how, exactly, do you get a rhino into a wooden crate? Is it sane to even try? To answer those questions, we need to go back several hours, to the start of this rhino roundup."

With jungle creatures trilling and hooting in the background, John said in a hushed voice, "It's before dawn now, and a line of

Asian elephants is carrying at least forty people towards a shallow river and a forest shrouded in fog. Three of us ride an elephant called 'The Queen.' The driver, or mahout, sits in front of me, steering by pushing his bare feet into the pink spots behind the elephant's ears. Behind me, Anil Manandhar stands, like some kind of surfer, on the elephant's back."

My elephant trailed behind John's. I snapped photos of him while trying not to fall off the padded cloth saddle as the elephant stepped down to ford the river and climbed up into high grass on the other side, breaking into a trot to keep up with the others.

"We're moving into the forest now," John said. "The idea is for the fifteen elephants in this group to surround the rhino, gradually collapse the circle, then shooters hit the rhino with a dart containing M-99—it's a little bit like morphine. The elephants move through the forest in a horizontal line—hunting formation."

Someone spotted rhinos, and the elephants closed in. There was a lot of frantic chatter over walkie-talkies. A Nepali raised a gun; NPR listeners heard the *pop*. The dart reached its target, who ran in a panic between the elephants before the drug could take effect. Men shouted and elephants bellowed as we gave chase, praying that the rhino wouldn't go down in brush too thick to find it and administer the antidote needed to restore consciousness. The rest went perfectly.

"Veterinarians check his pulse," John said. "Somebody puts a blindfold over his eyes. Over the years, dozens of rhinos have been safely captured in this way. . . . But a ride in a [crate] in the back of a truck is no way to migrate. That's why Anil Manandhar hopes to rebuild the grasslands and forests that used to connect these parks. . . . But if the Royal Bengal tigers are to return, these corridors will need fresh water and lots of smaller animals."

"When you conserve and protect a tiger," Anil told him, "you have to protect and conserve its habitat, its prey species, everything."

Our car caravan was following the rhino's forced migration via highway when word came of the tiger attack near the border. We rushed to the site, arriving at the dead woman's village just outside the park the day after trackers had found her remains. They were there again when we arrived, trying to determine whether her killer was sick or aged and prone to kill again or an able-bodied tiger that had mistaken her for a deer. The latter would get a second chance. No one from the village demanded that the tiger be removed or shot, testimony to the tolerance in Nepal and India that allowed wild tigers to survive in human-dominated landscapes.

John asked the weathered village headman what his people needed to prevent another tragedy of this kind.

Toilets, he said.

John and soundman Bill McQuay reached into their pockets and together came up with the $100 needed for WWF's local team to build the village a batch of outhouses.

Once I left TRAFFIC, I didn't look back. I couldn't. I missed everything about my work there—the family my gifted staff had become, the high-octane Hong Kong lifestyle, the geopolitical soap opera of a UN treaty built around charismatic megafauna. Looking back brought too much longing. And I figured all was well because of the work of certain people. People who would become my heroes. Capulets, for the most part.

Belinda Wright was one. She had scared me when we first met in 1994. She had a proper English accent and fair, rounded cheeks that spoke of her British ancestry, but she wore the long tunic and loose trousers favored by women in India. My desktop study with cat specialist Peter Jackson, *Killed for a Cure: A Review of the Worldwide Trade in Tiger Bone*, had just been published, and WWF's global communications machine had spun it and me into a cause célèbre. Upon our introduction, Belinda hissed something about how little I knew about tiger trade. My good friend Ashok Kumar, then director of TRAFFIC India, had known Belinda since her youth and promised me she was good-hearted. Still, stung by her initial rebuff, I sneered behind her back about her Mata Hari exploits, which included wearing a blonde wig and cherry-red satin trousers to woo information from tiger traffickers.

She was born in Kolkata to a father who was head of the British

Citizens' Association and a mother who had advised Prime Minister Indira Gandhi on setting up India's first tiger reserves. At one time or another, Belinda's childhood home hosted a tiger, a lion, and a leopard rescued from animal markets.

At fourteen, she announced she was going to be a wildlife photographer. *National Geographic* hired her when she was just twenty. She eventually became an author and wildlife filmmaker. But she set all that aside in 1989 when tiger poachers put an end to what she called the "golden years" for India's national animal.

Her first bust happened after she stopped to make a call from a phone kiosk in the Indian state of Madhya Pradesh and the kiosk owner offered to sell her four tiger skins. She smiled warmly and said, "I don't want any skins, but I know who does." Then she drove an hour to the next phone to notify police.

It didn't take Belinda long to trace this new threat back to the fact that China had run out of tigers to supply bones to medicine factories. However, she didn't appreciate the magnitude of the menace until she took a nine-week trip across central India in 1994 and received offers of forty-nine dead tigers. That's when she founded the Wildlife Protection Society of India (WPSI) to help law enforcement officials catch the perpetrators.

"I was able, in those days, to do stings, mostly with the police, sometimes with the forest department," Belinda told a TED audience in Goa, India, in 2012. "I was shot at. I was stabbed. But that's not really what matters. What matters is how this crime had become so big."[3]

Between 1994 and 2011, WPSI investigated 966 cases of tiger poaching. Poachers were killing tigers using electrocution, steel traps, poison, and guns. They came mainly from nomadic hunting communities and sold to "masterminds" living in big cities like New Delhi and Kathmandu. To transport tiger skins and bones from India and Nepal to China, their conduits used Himalayan mountain paths plied for centuries by yak caravans carrying wares such as spices and fine wools.

In sum, Belinda had more than earned the right to hiss at me for gliding into her world by virtue of crunching some numbers on tiger-bone trade to create what was received by many as a definitive report because it had come from TRAFFIC. Knowing that Belinda, Ashok, larger-than-life raconteur Valmik Thapar, and others were unrelenting in their influential advocacy of India's tigers made me think they were safe from trade.

Steve Galster's evolving work also reassured me. Not because actress Angelina Jolie had bought a helicopter for an anti-poaching team he trained in Cambodia, but because he was spreading what he had learned in Russia across Southeast Asia. Interpol and CITES were acknowledging what he, Mike Day, and the Environmental Investigation Agency had been saying all along: only trafficking in drugs and guns was bigger business than the illegal wildlife trade, and organized crime had its fingers in all three. In fact, some drug traffickers had switched to wildlife because it was just as lucrative but with less risk of getting caught or penalized. However, while the smuggling of drugs and guns was on the radar of customs and security forces in Asia, wildlife trade was not. Steve had dedicated himself to showing them that wildlife crime was serious crime and equipping them to combat it.

In 2003, Thailand's environment minister signed an agreement for Galster's new organization WildAid—started with Peter Knights— to help Thai law enforcement crack down on wildlife crime. By 2004, Thai police were arresting wildlife traffickers nearly every day. "After a tip to our hotline, I went with fifty investigators to a slaughterhouse . . . where we found live and dead animals, tame bears, tigers in cages ready to be slaughtered and sent as meat to exotic restaurants, and tiger cubs that looked wild," Steve told Outside.[4] The police ended up seizing one hundred pounds of tiger bones, forty-six pounds of tiger meat, three tiger skins, and twenty black bear paws that day. He was determined to stop "the Chinese vacuum cleaner sucking up Southeast Asia's wildlife left and right." By 2005, his efforts had catalyzed the ten-nation ASEAN Wildlife Enforcement Network (WEN) and would later spawn WENs in South Asia and Africa.[5]

While Steve worked to contain the supply side, WildAid cofounder Peter Knights continued to tackle demand through the program that had grown from his evenings with Jackie Chan in

South Africa. He worked the Hollywood end while fellow Brit Steve Trent worked to enlist buy-in from powerful government and business leaders in China. Together, they grew a slick franchise of television spots, billboards, and magazine ads that reached millions of people across Asia.

Eventually, China's state-run CCTV would broadcast celebrities carrying WildAid's message—"When the buying stops, the killing can, too"—to perhaps a billion people or more via its multiple channels. After Jackie Chan, more and more newsmakers signed up to echo the slogan with their fame: Olympians Yao Ming and Maurice Greene, actors Michelle Yeoh and Harrison Ford, movie director Ang Lee, billionaire Richard Branson, and many more household names.[6]

On the ground in China, more Chinese, such as Grace Ge Gabriel and her staff at the International Fund for Animal Welfare in Beijing, were keeping an eye on trade while working with TCM specialists to mainstream the use of herbal substitutes for tiger bone, rhino horn, and bear bile. At the same time, an endearing blond Brit named Jill Robinson, who could have been just another ladies-who-lunch wife of a Cathay Pacific pilot in Hong Kong, worked tirelessly through her new Animals Asia Foundation to rescue as many farm bears as possible while mentoring a Chinese-led campaign to end bear farming.[7]

Everything seemed on course to put an end to the demand that had made tigers, rhinos, and bears worth a fortune more dead—or farmed—than alive in the wild.

The success of rhino relocations and seeing firsthand what $100 could buy for wild tigers on Nepal's side of the Terai Arc made restoration of the wild tiger's realm seem within easy reach during my honeymoon at WWF. Then I began to see that Big Brother India was not so keen to coordinate efforts for tigers with Little Brother Nepal. I learned that while India's central government continued to make wild tigers a national priority, some state governments did little to carry out the mandate. Helping wild tigers seemed endlessly complicated by politics, unequal distribution of wealth, entrenched cultural practices, and insidious business interests.

I thought if only tiger conservation had the amount of money needed to buy just one fighter jet, the King of the Jungle would be home free. But even in places where adequate money was earmarked to protect them, forest rangers often patrolled on foot, without sturdy shoes, weapons, life insurance, or, in some cases, regular paychecks. When tiger traffickers were arrested, ignorance—and sometimes corruption—among police and judges often let them go unpunished or with no more than a hand slap. Meanwhile, powerful economic forces wanted to take timber and minerals out of the tiger's realm and bring in dams, roads, and palm-oil plantations.

When I resigned from WWF eighteen months after starting, I told Anil and his devoted Terai Arc team that I was leaving to find them more money. I knew money wasn't a panacea, but it could shift the balance in favor of tigers in the Terai Arc. A week before Al Qaeda operatives flew planes into the World Trade Center and Pentagon, I became Asia grant director for the $125 million fund that the Great Dane was running inside Conservation International. The fund's goal was to get money directly into the hands of local people who wanted to protect intact forests. The job wasn't about tigers, but I was hell-bent on making it about tigers whenever I could.

I was too busy trying to give away money wisely, adjusting to a post-9/11 world, and falling in love with the investment banker I would eventually marry to notice when a theme park called Sanya Love World opened in China's Hainan Province in 2002 with the stated goal of becoming the world's largest tiger farm. Thailand's Sriracha Tiger Zoo shipped one hundred live tigers to the farm on Christmas Eve that year—for which a Thai deputy prime minister would eventually be charged with "abuse of power, failing to carry out his duty, and/or corruption" and then released on a $4,000 bond.[8] I didn't see the 2004 *China Daily* story that mentioned the joint Sino-Thai venture's "ambitious plans to breed 200,000 animals in the next five years"—at least thirty times the number of wild tigers on the planet.[9]

I also missed the announcement of a "massive expansion" at Harbin's Siberian Tiger Park[10] and the explosive growth of another tiger farm down south in Guilin owned by a man who told the *People's Daily*, "My ambition is to become the tiger-rearing king of the world."

I did hear about the rich and glamorous Chinese woman who said she intended to bring back the extinct South China tiger. In 2003, she flew two South China tigers from the Shanghai Zoo to South Africa, where they were to be taught how to be wild so they could one day return to the ruined habitat of their forebearers.[11] I learned of her through a *Wall Street Journal* reporter who called me to ask what I thought of her plan.

"I can't think of anybody in the world of conservation who would tell you this is a good idea," I told him. "This is not science. It's not conservation. It could be a major biological disaster for Africa."

I then undiplomatically deemed it "a circus sideshow dressed up as eco-tourism" and said the woman's money would be better spent on efforts to keep wild tigers in the wild.[12] In 2004, she flew three more South China tigers from zoos to South Africa just as poachers were snatching the last wild tigers from one of India's most famous reserves.[13]

6

CROUCHING DRAGON
SELLING TIGERS

"It's me. John."

It was the deep, deadpan voice of John Seidensticker, the man I referred to as the Obi-Wan Kenobi of Tigers. Famed for being on the first team to track Nepal's secretive tigers by radio collar, he was chairman of Save the Tiger Fund and one of my heroes.

"To what do I owe this pleasure?" I said.

We hadn't spoken much in the four years since I had left World Wildlife Fund (WWF) to make grants at Conservation International (CI). I'd put close to $10 million into projects that benefited tigers, but it wasn't nearly enough. I was restless from funding others on the front lines rather than being there myself.

"China's going to reopen tiger trade," John said. "From the farms."

"*What?* How do you know?"

"Lu Xiaoping told me."

Lu Xiaoping was from China's State Forestry Administration, the ministry I had come to think of as the Dragon because of its apparent determination to devour tigers, bears, and too many other wild species via commodification. Lu was tall, well spoken in English, and, according to John, tasked with assessing how lifting China's twelve-year ban on tiger trade would impact wild tigers.

I cursed. "Even the hint of reopening trade will send poachers into the forest to kill tigers. What are we going to do?"

What we did was call together people who knew about tiger trafficking, China, traditional Chinese medicine, and CITES to brainstorm a way to stop the Dragon from unleashing more than a billion potential consumers on the last wild tigers, whose numbers had dropped to as few as five thousand. China's demand for bone had nearly doomed wild tigers in the early 1990s, when there were 178 million fewer Chinese with far less buying power and many fewer economic tentacles in countries where tigers ranged. If just a fraction of China's newly rich wanted the Dom Pérignon of tiger bone, the run on Asia's forests could be catastrophic.

Despite the dire tidings, I felt intoxicated to be at the center of breaking tiger news again. But my exhilaration soon turned to desolation. I learned that tiger farming had fallen off the radar of conservation's A-list. The consensus that March afternoon in 2005 when we put our heads together was that we had dropped the ball. We all, in various misguided ways, thought China's 1993 ban would dry up both tiger trade and tiger farming. We had checked China's tiger consumption off the list of top threats to wild tigers, given each other high fives, and moved on to shiny new conquests like saving multinational swaths of tiger habitat—places that could become little more than hunting reserves for poachers if China ever reopened trade. We had prematurely declared the death of demand for tiger products in China, while demand was being enticed back by the growth of tiger farms.

Why had no global alarms sounded when the number of tigers on farms rose to 1,000, then to 2,000, then 2,500? Now there were a mind-boggling 3,000.[1] *How could that be?* Meanwhile, hedging their bets, Cambodia, Indonesia, Laos, Thailand, and Vietnam all had nascent tiger farms.

We had to intervene with something that hadn't been tried before. Something big. ASAP. Whatever we did, we would have to take into account Sun Tzu's famous treatise *The Art of War*, because the Dragon certainly had.[2] "All warfare is based on deception," Sun Tzu said. We'd allowed the deception by leaving the battlefield, smug with perceived victory. We'd won at checkers, but the Dragon was playing chess.

John called again a few days later. He asked if I wanted the job of mounting this new campaign, which I could define. The offer awakened the best parts of me. I hadn't realized how diminished I'd become so removed from tigers and the fight for their wildness. The Great Dane, as worried as I was, arranged for CI to lend me to Save the Tiger Fund for three years.

Before I could wind down my grant-making and move offices, John called with more troubling news.

"I had to apologize to Lu Xiaoping," he said.

"For what?" A Chinese news report had confirmed the Dragon authorized a farm to sell tiger skeletons to hospitals, so John hadn't leaked a secret.[3]

John said he had to make amends for waking up those of us who'd fallen asleep on the job. Lu had somehow found out we were agitating and he was livid. He complained to David Wildt, chief panda-breeding expert and China liaison at the Smithsonian, John's employer. Lu felt John had betrayed a confidence, and Lu was coordinating China's panda loans to US zoos at that time. The breeding pair at Smithsonian's National Zoo had just produced a cub that finally lived beyond a few days, and America had fallen in love with the bald pink creature the size of a stick of butter, who would eventually be named Tai Shan ("Butterstick"). Millions of Americans would watch him grow 24/7 via live "pandacam." Zoo visits would shoot up 50 percent. "So many cameras click you'd think you were on the red carpet on Oscar night," Lynne Warren would write in *National Geographic* of Tai Shan's public debut.[4]

"They made me apologize," John said. That was a lot for a man I didn't think anyone could force to do anything.

While I waited for a China visa in August 2005, a Scottish woman in her mid-thirties with thick waves of blond hair and unflinching blue eyes drove into a grimy village on the grassy expanse of the Tibetan Plateau. The dirt streets were overrun with tourists.

"With so many foreigners, we were sure everything we came to see would be hidden away," Debbie Banks recounted to me.[5] Debbie loves to laugh with the lads over pints at the pub but has the heart of a hardened cop when it comes to tiger traffickers. She leads the Environmental Investigation Agency (EIA) on tigers, and in that late summer of 2005 she was on the Roof of the World in China's Tibet with India's fearless Belinda Wright, a veteran Chinese investigator, and an EIA filmmaker.

The foursome had come to check out the summer horse festivals, where natives of the high plains—called Khampas—congregate for what is part rodeo, part country fair, and part place to see and be seen, where ponies are dressed nearly as colorfully as the riders who race them. They wanted to check out the Khampas' *chupas*— traditional long tunics with wide shoulder sashes worn at festivals, weddings, and Tibetan New Year. Since the start of the new millennium, increasing numbers of *chupas* were being trimmed with tiger and leopard fur. The team wanted to learn where the fur had come from and who was selling it. What they saw as they entered the Litang fairgrounds nearly stopped their hearts.

"We spilled out of the vehicle, cameras rolling," Debbie recalled. "People were wearing *chupas* made of *entire* tigers and leopards. Not just strips of trim. We saw the whole head of a tiger on one costume. We're talking *hundreds* of leopards and tigers."

Men were marching, dancing, and playing tug of war, skirted and sashed in what had been tigers and leopards. The iconic photo from the trip captured a chiseled young man proudly posed in Ray-Bans, a wreath of gold discs set with coral around his head, and heavy gold and coral necklaces layered over a tiger-skin shoulder sash trimmed in brocade. These men and their families had become rich from tourism and from trading an indigenous caterpillar fungus coveted for TCM, which had soared to as much as $13,000 a pound. While nouveau riche in other parts of the world coveted Rolexes and Armani, these men desired tiger and leopard.

"It was so brazen and there were so many," Debbie said. "I felt the pit of my stomach drop, and I had to fight hard to keep back tears. We thought we might see one or two people wearing skins and a couple skins for sale. What we saw was more dead tigers and leopards than I'll ever see alive. The fact that Tibetans were wearing these skins was all the more heartbreaking because of my empathy for the Tibetan people and my support for their freedom."

Debbie and her colleagues began asking questions. "Most people had no concept of an animal dying so they could wear its skin. They had no idea that a tiger had been snared, speared, shot, or beaten to death with a club for them. They weren't exposed to natural history programs on television. Everything was censored. And they were being encouraged by the government to wear their best at horse festivals to show they were prospering under Chinese rule."

It was unlike any undercover investigation they had conducted before because nothing was undercover. "It was like going to buy vegetables at a farmers market," Debbie said. "Everything was out and on display. We were offered whole tiger skins." People felt at ease saying their skins came from India, usually via the high Himalayan passes of Nepal. An Indian poacher could get $1,500 for one tiger skin when most Indians made less than a dollar a day. That skin could sell for $20,000 in China—enough to leave worthwhile profits at every change of hands from forest to consumer.

What the team saw at Litang repeated itself at other horse festivals and towns, even in the shops lining the narrow streets of the Barkhor in the holy city of Lhasa. One Chinese policewoman eagerly posed for their cameras next to a man swathed in tiger skin.[6]

Like me, Debbie had been transformed by her first encounter with a wild tiger. It happened when she was surrounded by grass as tall as the elephant she was riding through the wide river valley that cuts through India's Corbett Tiger Reserve. She struggled to see what the mahout was pointing to with the stick he used to goad his elephant. Finally she saw a young tiger hissing and baring its teeth. "Then we heard a deep, sinister growl," she said. "We had walked between a tigress and her cub." The mahout jabbed his heels into the elephant's neck to prompt a hasty getaway. A tigress fearing for her cub could leap onto an elephant's back in a heartbeat to neutralize a perceived threat.[7]

"So my first experience seeing a tiger was fleeting," Debbie said.

"It was more what I heard than what I could see. It was that growl that rumbles through your chest. I held my breath for a long time."

I asked her what the tiger meant to her. "The tiger *is* wilderness. It's freedom, the future. If you see one in the wild, whether you're filled with fear or awe, you have reverence for the intense feeling it instills. Even if you don't see a tiger, there's electricity in the jungle when one is nearby. You hear the alarm calls from monkeys or deer. Everyone—I mean every living creature—is anticipating the tiger's appearance. It's a supreme being. You are nothing in its presence. It *is* the King of the Jungle."

What Debbie saw on the Tibetan Plateau in August 2005 impaled her spirit. She had wanted to go to the region in 2002 and 2003, but every application for funding was rejected. Donors told her that the skin trade was no longer an issue despite repeated seizures in India of tiger skins with bones bound for China. By 2004, India's Sariska Tiger Reserve had lost all of its tigers to poachers.[8]

"If we'd had money to put people on the ground in China in 2002 or 2003, they might have picked up intel that poachers were taking the last tigers out of Sariska," Debbie said, pausing to fight back tears. "When it all came together, and we finally had the money to go in 2005, it was too late. I felt that the tigers we saw people wearing at the horse festivals had come from Sariska because so many said they'd bought the skins from India one or two years before. I couldn't help feeling that we could have stopped this, that all those tigers died needlessly, that we could have stopped it if we had had the funds to get out there sooner."

Debbie dragged herself from the horse festivals in rural Tibet to Urumqi, the city of two million in far western China best known in recent years for its restive Uigher population. Emotionally drained, she boarded a plane in Chengdu and landed in Urumqi scared because she sat across the aisle from Steve Galster, who was also en route to the "Silk Road" CITES-enforcement seminar organized by the Dragon. This was Steve's first return to China since he and his "wife" from Taiwan had used a hidden camera in 1994 to capture a government official selling tiger bone in violation of China's ban.

"Steve freaked me out with stories of US officials telling him not to come back to China after that because he might be arrested," Debbie said. And there she was about to expose widespread illegal tiger trade in China's politically explosive Tibetan region at an international workshop proudly hosted by the people charged with stopping illegal tiger trade.

I landed in Urumqi with fears of my own. The workshop marked my reentry into the CITES fray after a five-year absence. I would debut what was then a one-woman show called the Campaign Against Tiger Trafficking, or CATT, which I was pitching as "an organized response to an organized crime." When I left TRAFFIC, some factions within the conservation community loathed one another almost as much as the wildlife traffickers who were their common enemy. My task was to herd these fiercely territorial cats. My only leverage came from the fact that they all knew me—though didn't necessarily like me—and my employer, Save the Tiger Fund (STF), had funded, was funding, or might one day fund their work. The urgency to herd them had intensified a few weeks before when a trusted Chinese informant with close ties to the Dragon sent me an e-mail that said, "China will approve the sale of tiger bodies in farms for traditional Chinese medicine use. It has been confirmed by a friend of mine who is a senior officer in the CITES division."

Debbie and I had met during my TRAFFIC days, but the Montague-Capulet divide kept our interactions brief. Given the grisly scene she had just left in Tibet and my recent confirmation of the Dragon's aim to unfetter tiger-bone trade in China, we were drawn together by our shared view that the sky was falling. So began my friendship with this heroic woman. The other cats I hoped to herd were friendly but wary.

The three-star hotel's stuffy conference room was full of familiar faces from tiger countries, the CITES Secretariat, the conservation community, and, of course, the Dragon. Meng Xianlin was there, hair still slicked back but wearing a real leather bomber jacket in place of his faux one from the 1990s. His wiry protégé, Wan Ziming, distinct for his nasal voice, was with him. Also Fan Zhiyong, who, the last time I saw him, was proudly announcing the Dragon's plans to sell farmed bear bile as an international commodity.

As everyone mingled before the meeting's late-morning start, I approached Fan. After warm mutual greetings, I told him I had heard China was going to let tiger farms sell bone. "We are getting a lot of pressure from the farms," he said. "They have more than three thousand tigers now. They want to know why they cannot trade. It is a big problem." No confirmation; no denial. *The Art of War.*

"What I don't understand is why they were allowed to continue breeding *any* tigers after the 1993 ban," I said.

Fan Zhiyong's eyes looked past me as I spoke. When it came time for his answer, he abruptly excused himself on urgent business.

During three single-spaced pages of opening remarks, Liu Hongcun of the State Forestry Administration's Department of International Cooperation did not mention China's intention to reopen tiger trade or the illegal trade in tiger skins that was running amok on the Tibetan Plateau. He did, however, touch on the farming and utilization of endangered species as mainstays of China's wildlife protection efforts.

John Sellar, the CITES Secretariat's head cop, livened things up with his droll Scottish delivery. He emphasized the need to fight wildlife crime like organized crime because increasingly it was just that.

Most of the rest of the first day was taken up by whitewashed summaries of the mostly disappointing wildlife-law-enforcement efforts of the ten Eurasian countries represented. Little had changed during my five years away—except that tiger farms had more than tripled in size and wild tiger numbers continued to plummet.

Debbie dropped her bombshell on the second day, startling everyone awake with slide after PowerPoint slide of men wearing and selling the skins of hundreds of tigers and leopards. Representatives from India, Nepal, and Russia probably wondered how many had been stolen from their forests. Others may have wondered how so many yaks, trucks, and suitcases loaded with tiger and leopard skins had breezed across China's borders. The Dragon must have thought, "How can we stop this woman from destroying our claim that we keep an iron grip on tiger trade so we can justify reopening it?"

At the coffee break, the Dragon's men surrounded Debbie. "They were shouting at me, and I was worried because I had given my passport to the local police to get an extension on my visa," she said. They demanded proof of her accusations—where she went, with whom, what she saw. Some didn't believe her. Her charges were "very sensitive" because they concerned Tibetans and their sacred traditions.

"It wasn't about arresting Tibetans who were wearing the stuff," she said of her frustration. "It was about where the hell this stuff was coming into China. How was it coming through? When? Who was bringing it in? The problem was, they weren't out on the front lines looking for this information. If any one of them or their people had been at the festivals, there's *no* way they could not have known what was going on."

I was the only presenter to bring up tiger farming and I was blunt. "Any use of tiger parts will be fatal to wild tigers," I said. "Selling products from farmed tigers will pave the road to the wild tiger's extinction." Even limited trade—if it could be limited—would reignite demand for the more desirable bones of wild tigers and provide a place for criminals to launder and sell poachers' wares. A confused public wouldn't know legal from illegal tiger goods, nor would the police. And all of this risk to wild tigers would be for a medicine ingredient that leaders of the global TCM community no longer wanted or needed.

Had Debbie not just torn off the Dragon's face with her exposé, my remarks might have brought aggressive pushback and claims of insult. But the one-two punch seemed to give everyone pause. The Dragon demurred. And, to my surprise, representatives of Conservation International, the Environmental Investigation Agency, the International Fund for Animal Welfare, TRAFFIC, WildAid, the Wildlife Conservation Society, and WWF all agreed to let me list their organizations on the slide in my presentation underscoring why tiger trade of any kind, from any source, was dangerous to wild tigers. None of us knew then that this marked the beginning of an alliance that would move the world.

China's president Hu Jintao was the next VIP to receive an introduction to my new cat-herding program. It came in the form of a letter, dated September 19, 2005, signed by my boss Mahendra Shrestha, the Nepali tiger biologist who was Save the Tiger Fund's director. The core message, embedded in praise for China and a polite outline of the issues, was to "strongly discourage" any lifting of the 1993 ban.

Two weeks later, official Chinese media quoted the Dragon as saying reports of China reopening tiger trade were "completely groundless."[9] Within days of that, the Dragon's chief tiger-farm promoter showed up on our doorstep.

Wang Weisheng, a slip of an officious man who appeared to be in his thirties, worked for the State Forestry Administration's Department of Wildlife Conservation, which was responsible for wildlife in the wild and on farms. In fact, he was supervising the Chinese dilettante's attempts to make wild South China tigers out of the zoo cats she had flown to South Africa—the effort I had trashed in the *Wall Street Journal*.

Hunkered over a cup of tea, Wang Weisheng told John Seiden-sticker, Mahendra, and me that the use of tiger bone had become necessary because of SARS (severe acute respiratory syndrome). Arthritic conditions, which could only be treated with tiger bone, were among the residual effects of the virus, he said. Given that SARS sickened fewer than nine thousand people worldwide and hadn't been seen since 2004, this didn't seem to justify the enormous threat to wild tigers that would be unleashed if China lifted its ban, I said.[10]

When Wang switched his argument to the need to generate revenues for China's efforts to stop tiger trade, I stared at him with incredulity. Did he really expect us to believe a country with an economy growing by more than 10 percent annually and foreign exchange reserves greater than $800 billion needed to sell tiger bones to pay for law enforcement?[11]

Finally, he said China simply could not eliminate demand for tiger bone. I didn't say that TCM's global campaign against tiger trade made a liar of him or remind him that one of the top ten medical developments in China, according to the Ministry of Science and Technology, was the formulation of artificial tiger bone, which had been proven effective and was licensed for retail sale.[12]

I gained two insights that day. First, Wang Weisheng was not a friend to wild tigers. Second, the push to legalize tiger trade in China was not about sick people, underfunded law enforcement, or popular allegiance to ancient medicine formulas. So then what was it about? Stubborn will to make tigers into "cows and pigs"? China's sovereignty? Payback for threats of trade sanctions in 1993? Or something more insidious?

The Dalai Lama entered the fray two weeks after Wang Weisheng's visit. Ashok Kumar, UK wildlife crusader Barbara Maas, and other wildlife advocates had gone to His Holiness with evidence of the slaughter brought by the growing material desires of wealthy Tibetans in China. As a result, on October 23, 2005, the Dalai Lama told an estimated ten thousand Buddhists gathered in Dharamsala, India, that he was disturbed by Tibetans buying, selling, and wearing the pelts of endangered animals. He asked his followers to stop.[13] Afterward, demand began to take a noticeable downturn.

As the Dalai Lama's words began to do what the Dragon said the government of China could not, I flew to China to find out whether the traditional Chinese medicine industry there had reneged on its earlier pledges to quit tiger bone.

"Reopening tiger-bone trade is driven by the farms, *not* by TCM," Lixin insisted when we met up in frigid, smog-choked Beijing in early December 2005. I hadn't seen her in years, but she was just as dogged as when she'd launched the Chinese-led campaign for tigers in the late 1990s. Still president of the American College of Traditional Chinese Medicine, she also was leading the US Council of Colleges of Acupuncture and Oriental Medicine. She was pretty much TCM royalty. She remained firmly against any use of tiger bone and believed China's TCM leaders remained with her.

Sources at the Chinese Academy of Sciences and TRAFFIC's China office confirmed that reopening tiger trade was a done deal though it had not yet been announced to the general public. However, the Dragon rather than the TCM industry was the main driver, they said. There were even rumors that the Dragon also wanted to permit canned hunting of farmed tigers.

The true test would be what Lixin and I learned at the World Federation of Chinese Medicine Societies, a quasi NGO tied to China's State Administration of Traditional Chinese Medicine and run by its retired leaders. The federation had member organizations around the world and represented the global TCM mainstream. I had not seen its leaders since their landmark 1999 conference on TCM and wildlife conservation in Beijing.

Upon our arrival at the federation's modest headquarters, a deferential young woman seated Lixin and me in the boardroom with lidded cups of steaming jasmine tea. Moments later Vice Secretary General Jiang Zaizeng, the man with the kind eyes who had been so taken with Lixin's San Francisco tiger campaign, walked in smiling with outstretched hands.

"How have you been?" he said, shaking our hands with both of his to let us know he meant it. "*Where* have you been? We have been waiting for you for five years."

What? Had no one from the conservation community come round since 1999? Jiang said no. Not one. I was stunned.

"I'm sorry." It was all I could say while thinking, *How could that golden moment have been squandered?* I was especially sorry because there were only about six hundred tigers on farms back then, and shutting them down would have been far less complicated. It was a betrayal of wild tigers. One that could prove fatal.

Jiang said he'd heard that tiger farms were not profitable as tourist attractions, so farm owners were pushing hard to lift the ban. Also, pharmaceutical companies wanted to sell the tiger-bone medicines they had kept locked under government seal since 1993. But he and his colleagues had had no direct communication about the matter with the Dragon. The push was about launching a tiger-bone wine industry—about making a lot of money. Nothing had changed from his side. The TCM industry still viewed use of tiger bone as a hindrance to its global ambitions. Using tigers was bad for PR.

"Why not let us take the lead in a campaign to stop the use of tiger bone?" Jiang asked. Such an effort would fit perfectly into Premier Wen Jiabao's five-year plan to achieve harmony between humans and nature, he said.

Not only was this major player in the global TCM industry still with tigers, its leaders wanted to take the lead against China lifting its ban. It seemed too good to be true. As we rode down in the elevator, I hugged Lixin and told her she was the tiger's most powerful secret weapon.

Three days later, Jiang presented a three-pronged plan that we agreed to in a signed memorandum of understanding.[14] In 2006, the World Federation of Chinese Medicine Societies would hold a conference of "high-level" government officials, TCM leaders, and conservationists to discuss TCM's role in saving wild tigers. In 2007, the federation would organize a cross-China journey for a group of TCM doctors to "educate the public at large about why it is important not to use tiger bone in medicine and wine or tiger skins for clothing and décor." Finally, on the eve of the 2008 Summer Olympics in Beijing, the federation would hold a ceremony at the Great Wall to present, as a gift to the green-themed Games, a petition signed by TCM specialists around the world calling for an end to all uses of all tiger products from all sources for all time.

The latter was huge. China had been campaigning to host the Olympics since the early 1990s. Fulfilling this goal was a key milestone in China's ascendancy to world leadership.[15] Anything associated with it would be unassailable.

The slogan for the Beijing Olympics was "One world, one dream," chosen for China's hope of global harmony between humans and nature.[16] That's what the federation's campaign would mean for tigers: one world committed to tigers in one form—alive, in nature, and wild. All I needed was to find the money to pay for it.

• • •

The Dalai Lama upped the ante in January 2006. He told more than one hundred thousand Buddhists from around the world, who had converged in southern India to pray for peace at the Kalachakra festival, that wearing animals skins was un-Buddhist. "I am ashamed and don't feel like living when I see all those pictures of people decorating themselves with skins and furs," he said. He asked celebrants to return home remembering his words and to never use, sell, or buy wild animals or products made from them.[17]

By early in the next month, Tibetans in China had begun mass public burnings of their fur holdings.[18] In Amdo, birthplace of the Dalai Lama, crowds of men, women, and children gathered to chant, ring bells, and blow conch-shell horns in celebration of carrying out the wishes of His Holiness. Encouraged by applause and whooping from the audience, *chupa* owners formed a circle and ripped the fur of tigers, leopards, and other wild animals from their treasured garments. The owners then gathered their contraband and walked forward to toss it on a towering stack of burning branches. Circling the pyre, a man squirted gasoline to make the flames leap higher and burn hotter.[19]

Media coverage went global, telling the planet that the Dalai Lama still led the people of Tibet despite China's iron rule and his exile to India since 1959. The skin trade so dramatically exposed by Debbie and Belinda's team was no longer just a stick in the Dragon's eye. It had shamed the entire government of the People's Republic of China.

The government struck back in the spring. On April 28, 2006, Radio Free Asia reported that Chinese authorities had ordered Tibetan television broadcasters to sew fur onto their *chupas*. When broadcasters complained that they couldn't afford to buy fur, the government promised $1,250 per person for its purchase. Asked about the order to buy and wear fur, a Chinese source was quoted as saying that government officials "came to the conclusion that it is not right for people to follow and obey the instructions of His Holiness."[20]

The burnings continued, although less publicly. As a result, the team Debbie and Belinda sent to Tibet in the summer of 2006 saw significantly fewer tiger- and leopard-trimmed *chupas*. Many of those they did see were worn by local government officials, likely on orders from their superiors. Most Tibetans who could exercise free will were done with wearing tigers and leopards.

The team found a chilling scene in Lhasa's Barkhor, however. Urban Chinese were filling the void left by Tibetans. Displays of fur-trimmed *chupas* had been replaced with whole tiger and leopard skins sold as rugs and wall hangings. One trader said that 80 percent of his buyers were Chinese from big cities like Beijing and Hong Kong looking for prestigious home décor. Others reported brisk business from Chinese government officials and army officers.[21] A year after Debbie's exposé in Urumqi, the Dragon still had not cracked down. It was as if the Dragon wanted illegal trade to flourish.

The starvation ploy used by Harbin's tiger farm to restart government financial aid in the 1990s resurfaced in August 2006, when the manager of the Siberian Tiger Park told the media that he was having difficulty feeding his seven hundred tigers. "We're happy to see new cubs being born, but we're worried about how to feed them properly with our limited funds," manager Wang Ligang was quoted as saying. He said each tiger needed $10 worth of meat every day, which totaled more than $2.5 million a year just for food. Ticket sales to visitors were bringing in only $1.5 million.[22] Media reports did not question why the farm continued speed-breeding tigers that it couldn't afford to feed.

The next day the *New York Times* published an opinion piece headlined "Sell the Tiger to Save It."[23] The author was libertarian Barun Mitra, director of India's Liberty Institute, who had once been a hired gun in ExxonMobil's campaign to deny climate change. "Which country is thinking about applying free-market principles to wildlife preservation and, in the process, improving the survival chances of a long-endangered species while giving its economy a boost?" he wrote. "Communist China, of course."

To Mitra's credit, he did disclose that he'd accepted an all-expenses-paid trip to China earlier in the year to learn about tiger farming from the Dragon. "Market economics greatly favor the tiger," he concluded. "If China decides to unleash the tiger's commercial potential, the king of the forest might be more secure in his kingdom."

Ten days later, *China Youth Daily*—renowned for its openness—released an incendiary scoop about illegal tiger trade at Xiongsen Bear and Tiger Mountain Village in Guilin Province, owned by the man who had once told the *People's Daily* he would become "the tiger-rearing king of the world."[24]

Xiongsen employees told reporter Zhang Kejia that the farm did not generate enough income from tourism to feed its 1,500 tigers, while also touting a revenue source bringing in more than enough to do so. They took her to a dank, dimly lit wine cellar where, they said, hundreds of tiger skeletons were steeping in vats of pungent rice liquor.

"This is a whole tiger carcass," said a manager as he pulled on a rope tied to a muck-covered leg bone attached to a tiger-sized skeleton that emerged from the depths of one vat. Zhang noted the stripes on the fur still attached. "We have four hundred vats, each containing a tiger carcass, in this cellar," the manager said. Another cellar was being completed to increase production capacity, he said, but sales had already reached two hundred thousand bottles annually.

Xiongsen sold this wine in tiger-shaped porcelain bottles, each packaged in a wooden box with a label from the State Forestry Administration and the State Industry and Commerce Administration granting "permission for its sale." Zhang found the wine on offer at the farm's Science Education Museum and at stores in three nearby cities and two of the region's airports.

The oldest vintage was claimed to have steeped six years, which would mean Xiongsen had been producing illegal goods since at least 2000. Costs ranged between $41 and $135 for a half-liter bottle (just under seventeen ounces), priced according to the number of years the contents had commingled with tiger bones. Even at the lowest price, revenues from the two hundred thousand bottles allegedly produced each year would exceed $8 million—several million more than what Xiongsen said it needed to feed resident tigers.

Xiongsen sales personnel repeatedly assured Zhang that what was called Bone Nurturing Wine was made with tiger bone by permission from the Dragon. "Who would dare sell tiger-bone products without permission from relevant authorities?" one staffer said. An official from the local forestry bureau told Zhang that Xiongsen's owner Zhou Weisen had the only permit in the province for selling tiger-bone wine. He also said the State Forestry Administration had given Zhou nearly $1 million to speed his tiger breeding and to build a winery.

After her visit to Xiongsen, Zhang discussed what she'd seen with Professor Zhou Fang of Guangxi University's College of Animal Science and Technology. "The Chinese term to describe the Forestry Administration is 'forestry industry,'" he said. "It is the word 'industry' where it goes wrong." He said keeping China's ban in place was essential to wild tigers but a hindrance to the tiger-farm industry.

Zhang also interviewed me. I told her, "Lifting China's trade ban will satisfy the greed of a few tiger farmers yet destroy years of effort by the world to save tigers in the wild."

Cat herding was slow going. My invitations to ally forces against tiger farming were answered with complaints about other groups, rants over lame anti-poaching efforts in India, and trepidation about the Dragon's sensitivity to discussing tiger farms. I was reminded of that little red book listing 101 ways to say no without saying it. A breakthrough yes finally came in the summer of 2006. And it came from within China, where people and organizations had the most to lose from broaching any subject deemed sensitive by government officials.

International organizations had to register in China to open a bank account and receive funds from abroad. Registered or not, every foreign group had to find a government agency to vouch for them— what was called a "mother-in-law," according to Grace Ge Gabriel. Mother-in-law agencies allegedly could kick any one of their charges out of China at any time, for sins real or imagined. World Wildlife Fund (WWF) was registered under the State Forestry Administration, while the other cats I was trying to herd were in various stages of pursuing registration. All trod carefully and, as it happened in the summer of 2006, courageously.

At a meeting with Lixin and me in July 2006, China staff from Conservation International, the International Fund for Animals, TRAFFIC, the Wildlife Conservation Society, and WWF announced that they wanted to herd for the sake of wild tigers. As long as they were all in and had backing from their powerful mother ships outside China, they would join Save the Tiger Fund on September 1 to issue an open statement to Premier Wen Jiabao asking that the 1993 ban stay firmly in place. The threat to wild tigers was that dire, and they were that brave. Most had only Chinese passports.

I worried throughout August that they would reconsider and opt for the safety of silence. But on September 1, 2006, we issued an international press release, in Chinese and English, announcing our joint statement to China's premier.[25] "The recent proposal by China's tiger farms to legalize trade in tiger parts and derivatives will jeopardize the great efforts that the Chinese government and the world have invested to save wild tigers," the statement said. In closing, we played the Olympics card. We said we hoped China, in the spirit of the upcoming "green" Olympic Games, would reiterate its 1993 ban, prohibit all tiger trade from all sources, and continue to play a "leadership role in protecting the world's few remaining wild tigers." This may not have seemed like much outside China, but inside it was audacious.

Lixin also sent a letter to the premier on behalf of more than fifty TCM colleges in the United States. She said they wished to "offer a gift to the Green Olympics by stating, strongly and without condition, that we support China in enforcing wildlife trade-control laws, in particular the existing ban on trade in tiger derivatives from any and all sources."[26]

Once those letters went public, my phone started ringing. Other cats wanted to know if they could join the herd.

The Dragon was on the defensive by the time the CITES Standing Committee convened in Geneva, Switzerland, during the first week of October 2006. The first sign of stress was the spectacle of normally dignified Lu Xiaoping losing his cool in public. In an otherwise subdued corridor outside a UN auditorium, Lu's face became contorted and his index finger stabbed the air as he berated petite Linda Kruger of the Wildlife Conservation Society (WCS). The Dragon was not happy with preliminary results from a survey of China's market for saiga antelope horns.[27] WCS had sent twenty-three investigators across the country and found widespread illegal trade. The tallies made China look like it was out of control and eating the world, one species at a time.[28]

Debbie also received a verbal drubbing from Lu, assisted by Wan Ziming, over the twenty-five-page report she had brought along to document tiger-skin trade in Tibet. The tiger-draped stud in Ray-Bans on the cover of *Skinning the Cat: Crime and Politics in the Big Cat Skin Trade* was drawing in a lot of delegates. Lu and Wan told Debbie that the photos had to be fake because people in Tibet can't afford to buy Ray-Bans. "I thought, 'Have you *been* there?'" she said. "People are parading around in brand new SUVs and tiger skins that cost $10,000, $15,000, $20,000."

The CITES Secretariat's John Sellar referenced *Skinning the Cat* when he told the Standing Committee that neither tiger-range countries nor tiger-consuming countries were doing enough to stop tiger trafficking. He beat up on India for lax efforts to stop tiger poaching but acknowledged that it was plagued by "demand beyond its borders," which everyone assumed meant China. It was time the matter be addressed "at the highest levels of government," John said, calling for a ministerial summit.[29]

The United States also alluded to *Skinning the Cat* and suggested that the Standing Committee recommend trade sanctions against CITES member countries that didn't demonstrate "substantial progress" in stopping tiger trade before the committee met again in June 2007.

The Dragon rejected both ideas, which spurred another minor miracle of cat herding. I never thought I would see the day when fourteen organizations—Montagues and Capulets, great and small, science-headed and "humane-iac," at odds over so much for so many years—delivered a joint statement for tigers. Under the auspices of our new alliance, they supported a ministerial tiger summit, a mission to China to verify crackdowns on tiger trade, and, if necessary, sanctions to punish noncompliance.

One of the last speakers on tigers was a guy who had always reminded me of Crocodile Dundee. Hank Jenkins had been with Australia's CITES authority and had chaired the CITES Animals Committee during my TRAFFIC days. Although he farmed crocs, I always assumed we were on the same side because he and the Great Dane were on friendly terms. Since I'd last seen him, Hank had retired, grown a belly, and hired himself out as a CITES lobbyist. He told the Standing Committee that perhaps it was time to "explore a legal trade regime" for tigers.

I craned my neck to make sure this was the same Hank Jenkins I had once looked up to. As I took in his defensively crossed arms and wicked grin, I realized I was gaping at the Dragon's chief foreign advisor on how to sell tiger farming to the World (as represented by CITES).

The Standing Committee decided to kick the crisis down the road eight months to the full CITES conference in June 2007. Jaws dropped. All of the evidence from Tibet, combined with China's evasiveness over whether it had reopened or would soon reopen tiger trade, hadn't moved them.

By the grace of John Sellar's moxie, tigers came up again under "enforcement matters." He said he had written to the Dragon repeatedly concerning the blatant skin trade in China and a rumored reopening of trade in tiger bones from farms.

The United States said it too was concerned about these issues and suggested, in diplomat-speak, that a mission be sent to China to verify what the hell was going on.

With no intervention from the Dragon, the Standing Committee agreed. China was asked to report to the CITES Secretariat by January 2007 on its efforts to stop tiger-skin trade and clarify whether tiger-bone trade had reopened or would reopen. It also ordered the CITES Secretariat to go to China to verify the situation and report back to the June conference.

The Dragon suddenly awoke, asked for the floor, and protested the decision because it had been made while the head of China's delegation was out of the room. The CITES Secretariat pointed out that the agenda item had been taken in order, allowing plenty of notice for the right people to be present. End of discussion.

The Dragon was on the UN hot seat once again.

Three Chinese men caught the eye of Justin Gosling, a former British police detective, as they exited the 2006 Standing Committee meeting.[30] Justin, who worked for Debbie, was sitting at the coffee bar checking e-mail when the trio appeared. After hovering a while around the table stacked with documents for CITES delegates, one of them scooped up the hefty pile of *Skinning the Cat* reports and walked across the foyer toward the exit. Justin decided to follow him.

"I thought he was putting them in his car so he could distribute them at work," Justin said. The man walked quite a distance. "I thought maybe his car was parked a ways away. Then he found a big dumpster, opened the lid, and threw in all the reports. After that, he walked back to the conference center. He never noticed me."

Justin went to the dumpster, took some photos, and left the reports there. He found Debbie and took her to the dumpster. She asked if he could identify the thief. Justin pointed him out to Debbie and me. Combed back hair, black leather bomber jacket. The Dragon's Meng Xianlin, by then deputy director of China's CITES authority.

Debbie reported the incident to the CITES secretary general and basked in the satisfaction of knowing that her exposé had prompted such a desperate and undignified move. "It proved the report was right," she said.

On the last day of the Standing Committee meeting in 2006, the Dragon dropped a bombshell of its own. In a written statement, it said that the newspaper exposé about the Xiongsen tiger farm selling tiger bone wine had been investigated and found baseless.[31] However, it said, continuing illegal tiger trade called into question the effectiveness of bans, especially when China's farms had more than four thousand tigers with which to feed consumer demand.

Never mind that no one seemed to be policing illegal tiger trade on the Tibetan Plateau and Chinese government officials were lobbying for commodification of tigers—in writing, at a CITES meeting. More importantly, where had another one thousand farmed tigers come from?

7

TIGER LILY AND
THE ART OF WAR

Someone had tipped off the ITV News crew. Their target was in the open. Three young men carrying a video camera, a long microphone, and a fistful of documents spilled out of a van and hurried along the hotel's driveway.

The sun was warm at 4,600 feet in the Kathmandu Valley that mid-April afternoon in 2007 as I mingled during a coffee break at the International Tiger Symposium. Most participants gravitated toward the balcony above the pool and manicured gardens. Conversations in Nepali, Hindi, Chinese, and English mixed with birdsong.

The uninvited trio swept across the lobby toward our gathering. They were locked onto a Chinese man in his mid-forties who looked as if he'd just come off a golf course—Zhou Weisen, CEO of Xiongsen Bear and Tiger Mountain Village, by then China's largest tiger farm. He had come with the Dragon to lobby for reopening the tiger trade.

John Ray, Beijing correspondent for the British television network, had been rebuffed in his efforts to interview Zhou in China. Ray wanted to ask the businessman about a dish served at a restaurant on his premises. So the cherub-faced English newsman with a riot of blond hair had followed him to Nepal. Ray, his cameraman, and a Chinese interpreter approached Zhou with audio and video rolling. The tiger farmer took a bite from a shortbread cookie and sipped lukewarm tea, ignoring his sudden entourage.

"Mr. Zhou? John Ray from ITV News. We want to talk to you about your tiger farm."

Zhou refused to look at him, flicking his free hand as if waving off a fly.

"This is a DNA test that proves the meat you sell in the restaurant is tiger meat," Ray said, trying to show Zhou some papers.

Zhou's brow was pinched as he finally turned toward his questioner. "You tampered with it!" he shouted in Chinese, stabbing the air with his index finger. "You made it up! Wherever you got the tiger meat, it has nothing to do with us!"

As Zhou stormed away, Ray asked him if he knew that selling tiger meat was against Chinese and international law. Zhou stopped, reared back, and tossed his tea into the ITV camera lens. Then he smashed his teacup on the stone floor and delivered a powerful swipe at Ray's interpreter with the hand still holding a saucer.

"Hey, hey, hey," Ray said with a calm he surely didn't feel. A couple of Nepalese reached for Zhou, urging him to back down. Just as it seemed he would, he pivoted to throw a punch toward Ray's cameraman.[1]

"Bred for the Freezer: How Zoo Rears Tigers Like Battery Hens," read the headline that ran in the UK's *Guardian* newspaper just before the Kathmandu meeting. Writer Jonathan Watts described the sights and sounds at Xiongsen Bear and Tiger Mountain Village:

> The park is part farm, part zoo, and part circus. Its nursery is the start of a production line that churns out hundreds of tigers each year and ends in the freezer packed with carcasses. In between, most animals spend their lives in tiny cages that are lined up in rows around the perimeter wall, each jammed with as many as four animals, which lie around listlessly or pace back and forth between wire and concrete. . . . Others are trained to perform in the Dream Theatre—a circus where they jump through flaming hoops—or in an outdoor show that

also has monkeys riding camels and a bear cycling across a high wire without a safety net.

For most of the hundreds of tourists who come each day, the most memorable part of their visits is feeding time, when a tiger is released into a pen with live cattle. Earlier this week, tourists gasped but watched in fascination as the predator chased down a cow, sinking its teeth and claws into its victim, which cried and defecated in pain and fear. The bloody spectacle lasted 15 minutes before the tiger—too domesticated to kill its prey in such a short time—meekly returned to its cage, and the wounded cow was taken away for slaughter by zookeepers.[2]

This is what the Dragon would have all tigers become—diminished prisoners stripped of their role as dignified monarchs and mighty protectors of deep, rich jungles and grasslands—so that a handful of rich guys like Zhou Weisen could become vastly richer. Zhou's reaction at teatime in Kathmandu was unsettling, but the

Tigers are bred like livestock on farms throughout China, including this one in Guilin, the country's largest. (Courtesy of Belinda Wright)

owner of China's largest tiger farm revealed himself on camera as privileged, imperious, and guilty. All of the symposium participants saw it and the world would too once John Ray's story aired.

By Kathmandu, our international alliance had grown to thirty groups from the conservation, animal welfare, zoo, and TCM communities, representing more than one hundred organizations, with more than a million members around the world, speaking for the first time with one voice. And we had arrived with a name: the International Tiger Coalition (ITC). We tagged our campaign End Tiger Trade. Our slogan, placed beneath a tiger's hypnotic gaze: "The eyes of the world are watching."

The Dragon was still playing coy about whether China would reopen tiger trade. In January 2007, the official Xinhua News Agency said China had "no intention of easing" its ban.[3] However, a source on beers-with-the-boys terms with the Dragon told me that China's State Council had approved a request to reopen tiger trade after the Beijing Olympics. "You must kill it before it is impossible to stop," he told me.

China's obsession with an untainted Olympic debut bought us time, but the June 2007 CITES conference in The Hague would be the pivotal event. If the World (as represented by CITES) did not say no to all tiger trade then, it could be too late by the time of the next conference in 2010.

I marveled at the ITC's enthusiasm for allying efforts. With a limited budget, the donation of WWF's Pulitzer Prize–nominated Jan Vertefeuille to coordinate communications, and so many varied organizations amplifying our shared message, we had global reach. ITC members vowed to counter the Dragon en masse at every turn on tiger farming, starting in earnest in Kathmandu and sustaining a steady drumbeat of press coverage through the CITES conference in The Hague.

On the drive from Kathmandu's airport, symposium delegates were greeted at a major downtown roundabout with a huge "The eyes of the world are watching" banner and a smaller version as they reached the conference location. Our presentations praised China's ban as we politely pressed tiger-range countries for an official statement asking China to make it permanent.

The Dragon came prepared to counter our efforts. Its delegation of thirteen included Tiger-Farm-Promoter-in-Chief Wang Weisheng, his like-minded boss Wang Wei, the CEOs of China's two largest tiger farms, and a consultant who called himself a TCM researcher. Hank Jenkins was there too, along with Kirsten Conrad, another of Wang Weisheng's small gaggle of hired foreign "experts." Kirsten was a spunky, marathon-running, blonde mom with a freckled face and Harvard education who kept exotic cats at home and functioned as a one-woman cheerleading squad for tiger farming. She and I had met when we both lived in Hong Kong, and I liked her in spite of her belief that selling tigers could save them.

The Dragon's entourage declared that China's tiger farms had borne "tremendous economic burdens" because the 1993 ban prevented them from selling bones to medicine manufacturers. The farm CEOs stated, "We have never engaged in illegal use of tiger bones and meat."[4] Meanwhile, Wang Weisheng refused to answer whether China planned to lift its ban but promised that any change in policy would benefit wild tigers. He said he had been convening meetings of "experts from the scientific community" to weigh the pros and cons of lifting China's ban. Experts like Aussie croc farmer Hank Jenkins, libertarian opinionator Barun Mitra, tiger-farm evangelist Kirsten Conrad, and a handful of contrarian resource economists. Bona fide experts promoting tiger trade could be counted on one hand.

To make the case for the TCM industry, Wang Weisheng brought along Jia Qian, a retiree from the Ministry of Science and Technology who was working as a consultant on "the development of TCM"—apparently through commodification of endangered species. He told the symposium that China needed 22,000 pounds of tiger bone—at least one thousand tigers—to meet yearly medical needs. He showed slides of Chinese men and women with limbs contorted at painful angles by arthritic conditions from SARS. I wondered why these poor people hadn't been given any of the growing number of effective TCM and Western arthritis treatments made without tiger bone.

"Why not spend less on farming and more on saving wild tigers in China?" suggested Rina Khatau, the Singapore-Chinese woman who cofounded the Corbett Foundation with her Indian husband.

"Legalized trade could easily wipe out all of China's wild tigers by making it much easier for local poachers and traders," said Sarah Christie of the London Zoological Society.

"We need better facts before acting," said Urs Breitenmoser, co-chair of the Cat Specialist Group. "Does the world really want to use tiger parts? There are huge risk implications."

"Let's not reopen tiger trade," said renowned Indian tiger biologist A. J. T. Johnsingh. "Let's ask people to stop using tiger bone."

"Crocodile farming has not prevented Asia's crocodiles from becoming endangered," said Bivash Pandav of WWF India.

"We need to understand what exactly is being considered," said TRAFFIC's Steve Broad.

Representatives of Bangladesh and Russia thanked China for its ban and asked that it stay firmly in place.

"Wildlife is not a resource if it is not used!" said an Indian protégé of Barun Mitra, horrifying all his countrymen in the room.

Wang Weisheng reiterated that the ban was "under review" and that China welcomed input to the review process.

India would respond to the invitation because reopening tiger trade in China would seriously impact the wild tigers of other countries, said R. B. Lal, a senior official from India's Ministry of Environment and Forests. "The wild tiger is not just the heart and soul of India," he said. "It is the symbol and the essence of our country."

ITV News aired the tea-throwing scene on April 20, 2007. An enraged Zhou responded with a lawsuit against Ray and his employer, charging defamation.

The US Fish and Wildlife Service Forensics Laboratory reviewed the DNA analysis of Ray's meat sample by Chinese scientists and agreed that the results showed the genetic sequence for tiger.[5] The CITES Secretariat asked China to investigate the Xiongsen farm for illegal tiger trade.[6] The Dragon—the farm's champion and financial supporter—sent investigators, who reported finding no evidence of wrongdoing.

In contrast, a team of Chinese investigators for the International Fund for Animal Welfare (IFAW) found an abundance of evidence that Xiongsen and other tiger farms were selling not just tiger meat but also tiger-bone wine and tiger bones, teeth, claws, and whiskers. "Tiger farms in China are purely commercial operations," concluded *Made in China: Farming Tigers to Extinction*, which IFAW published after giving the Dragon its findings in advance.[7]

What IFAW investigators found was more disturbing than previous allegations. Four of the five registered farms investigated had been established by permission of the Dragon *after* China's 1993 ban. For every tiger in the wild in China (perhaps fifty), there were one hundred tigers on farms (five thousand). Xiongsen's winery was established in 2004. The winery affiliated with China's first tiger farm near Harbin opened in 2005. Xiongsen had had a tiger skeleton steeping in a special brew for eight or nine years, exclusively for a local government official's use. The "science education centres" at the Harbin farm and its affiliated Siberian Tiger Park each had a large glass tank full of wine containing a tiger skeleton. Empty bottles with "King of the Forest" labels sat nearby for visitors to fill and buy.

Worse yet, Xiongsen was "actively expanding its sales network, recruiting wholesale outlets to distribute its products nationwide," according to IFAW. The Harbin winery already took phone and mail orders for tiger-bone wine. One of Xiongsen's employees told investigators that pharmaceutical companies, including China's famed Tongrentang, were seeking tiger bones to restart medicine manufacturing. Managers at both tiger farms said they expected large-scale trade in tiger products would be allowed in China after the 2008 Olympics.

Despite the 1993 ban, "several wealthy businessmen still made the decision to invest in tiger farms, to speed-breed tigers, and to stockpile tiger carcasses," the report said. Furthermore, "they have started producing and selling tiger parts openly in an effort to pressure the Chinese government and the international community to accept the 'reality' of trade in tiger parts." Theirs is "a product looking for a market rather than a response to market demands." Finally, it concluded, "China's image is being tarnished by the illegal tiger trade from which only a few individual businessmen in China profit."

And there the report stopped, one step shy of implicating the Dragon. A brilliant strategy to allow the Dragon to save face, nail a couple of scapegoat entrepreneurs, and avoid staining China with the blood of the last wild tiger.

This *Art of War* delivery could only have been the work of one person. Among the Chinese I so admired for all they risked to challenge the Dragon, one stood out for her daring. I think of her as Tiger Lily, for the quiet poise of her physical presence and the inner ferocity she attributes to being born in the Year of the Tiger. She was the woman I had first met in 1999, when she told the bear symposium in South Korea that a majority of people in China found bear farming appalling—Grace Ge Gabriel.[8]

Grace's college-professor parents gave her the name Ge Rui ("guh-ray") when she was born in Zhengzhou, China, during their persecution for being "intellectuals" at the time of the Cultural Revolution. Her love of animals became apparent in the hungry years she spent as a child in the countryside, where her mother was sent for reeducation while her father was assigned to operate a lathe in a distant factory.

That love didn't turn into a career until she was working in television and video production out of Salt Lake City, where she had gone to college and met her American husband. The transformation took place in the Chinese village of Yuexi one sunny December day in 1996. She had been contracted by the International Fund for Animal Welfare to make a video of eight rescued farm bears as they were released into a sanctuary newly built just for them.

She stood on a footbridge looking down, through the lens of a video camera, at a grassy enclosure strewn with apples, bananas, and grapefruit when someone yelled, "Doors open!" An Asiatic black bear named Chu Chu emerged. He was easy to spot because his back was scarred from his incessant rubbing on the bars of the small cage that had been his lifelong home. Chu Chu gingerly placed one front paw from the concrete to the grass and immediately jerked it back. "As if he had received an electric shock," Grace wrote later.[9]

The conflicted bear paced back and forth, nose fixed on the smell of fruit. He again touched the grass and again recoiled. Anything other than a cage or concrete was alien. However, once he finally dared the grass with all fours, he quickly went about exploring every corner of the sanctuary, standing on hind legs to taste honey for the first time from where it was placed up a tree to stretch his atrophied limbs. "The moment Chu Chu took his first step to freedom, I stopped being an observer and became an advocate," Grace said.

Grace was first bewitched by wild tigers, as I had been, with Ashok Kumar in the fairy-tale setting of Ranthambore. "It was dusk," she said. "We heard the monkeys calling and saw the deer running away, but we couldn't tell where the tiger was. The setting sun through the leaves was amazing camouflage. I could feel the tiger getting closer, though I didn't see it. Then a tigress sauntered out of the forest and walked right past our jeep. She was doing what she normally does, but she carried this power. I was surprised I felt the magic before I saw her."

They later saw the same tigress tirelessly dragging a large sambar deer under her belly down one hill and up another. "It was then I realized that all of that power and magic was so vulnerable—to us," she said. "*We* are the ones who will determine if it continues to exist."

At the Kathmandu symposium, Grace presented what she and her China team had uncovered about tiger farms and their wineries. She used photos from Xiongsen Bear and Tiger Mountain Village as illustration. Xiongsen's owner Zhou Weisen was puzzled about why he wasn't allowed to sell tiger products after breeding so many tigers, Grace said. "Because the State Forestry Administration gave him money to breed tigers and build a winery, he thought he would be able to sell tiger-bone wine. Then the same agency turns around and uses the argument, 'The tiger farmers are pressuring us to open trade.' In fact, they had already promised him he could trade."

The Dragon didn't dispute Grace's presentation or the report that spelled out the details. "They weren't pleased," she said, "but there was nothing they could pull out as not true."

Some of this mind-bending truth was openly presented to John Sellar when he went to China in the spring of 2007 to verify for CITES what seemed to be outright disregard for the international ban on tiger trade as well as China's own ban.[10]

When John visited Xiongsen Bear and Tiger Mountain Village, he asked Zhou Weisen why he bred so many tigers when China prohibited tiger trade. Zhou said he continued with hope that the ban was temporary. He said national and provincial forestry authorities approved and monitored his operation and knew exactly how many live and dead tigers he was amassing and how fast. While Zhou denied making tiger-bone wine, John found tiger-shaped bottles of Xiongsen's wine in his hotel, where the salesperson insisted it was made with tiger bone. However, he noticed the product was gone from the shop's shelves the next day.

Zhou presented John with a written rationale for reopening commercial trade in tiger products.[11] The document said that $47 million had been invested in developing Xiongsen's tiger breeding and wine making *after* China's 1993 ban. The State Forestry Administration, Northeast Forestry University—alma mater of the Dragon's Wang Weisheng and Meng Xianlin—and the agriculture and animal husbandry university of the People's Liberation Army all provided assistance. "Patients of rheumatism" often come pleading for tiger bones, "but we could give them nothing, even when they get down on their knees pleading," the document said.

If there was no hope of legalizing tiger trade, Zhou said, he would need $150 million to close down the farm.

•   •   •

"The art of war teaches us to rely . . . on the fact that we have made our position unassailable," Sun Tzu said. And that's what the thirty-five organizations that made up the International Tiger Coalition by June 2007 did at the CITES conference in The Hague. We dissected the fallacies the Dragon used to promote commodification of tigers and countered each with well-referenced facts.

Recognized authorities on conservation breeding, wildlife trade, and tiger conservation published a letter in the prestigious *Conservation Biology* exposing the Dragon for not consulting "recognized experts" to determine whether China's tiger trade should be reopened.[12] "Opening a market of tiger parts from any source would offer a clear avenue to 'launder' illegal parts and products from wild tigers and sell them as legal," the authors said. They cited surveys documenting China's success in nearly eliminating tiger bone from its market—an achievement being undone by stepped-up tiger farming. "Tiger farmers have no vested economic interest in securing a future for wild tigers," they wrote. In fact, extinction would give these investors "exclusive control on supply of the global tiger-parts market"—a world monopoly. Conclusion: tiger farms could be speculating on, hoping for, and perhaps even encouraging the extinction of wild tigers.

Some of our strongest arguments against lifting China's ban came from the People's Republic of China itself. A public-opinion survey we commissioned from Beijing's respected Horizon Research Consultancy Group showed that a large majority of urban Chinese who had consumed tiger products in the past preferred those from wild tigers. Among all the people polled across six major cities, 88 percent said they knew that buying and selling tiger products was illegal, and 93 percent agreed that China's ban was necessary to save wild tigers.[13]

We launched an Internet petition asking people to send in a photo if they wanted China to keep its ban in place. Each photo became a pixel in a tiger "mosaic" that we unveiled at The Hague. The result was a two-story banner of a tiger's head, erected outside the front doors of the convention center, made up of thousands of pictures from people across the world asking CITES, in Chinese and English, to "end tiger trade."[14]

At our booth outside the main meeting rooms, delegates gathered to watch our continuously looping video of a tiger walking elegantly through a lush forest. "What does the tiger mean to you: King of the Jungle? Deity? Symbol of the wild?" asked a melodious British male voice. "Or this?" Frames of a tiger in a foot snare shot to death by a poacher's bullet, merchants selling tiger skins, a slimy tiger skeleton pulled from a murky wine vat, and tiger-shaped bottles of wine in a tiger farm's gift shop. "The magnificent tiger reduced to nothing but luxury products for our vanity and consumption? That may be all that's left unless the Chinese government keeps its tiger-trade ban in place. . . . Ask China to make its tiger-trade ban permanent."[15]

We flew in India's mesmerizing tiger wallah Valmik Thapar from India to captivate delegates with a side event featuring drinks and tales from the Cult of the Tiger, as seen in art and lore across Asia for millennia. "Over thousands of years the impact of the tiger has been deep and powerful on the people of Asia," he told his entranced audience. "In many ways, the tiger is the soul of Asia." He also said, "If there wasn't a ban on the tiger trade, I assure you there wouldn't be one single tiger left in India today." As for tiger farming, he said, "It's not civil to have tiger farms. It's not part of anyone's dreams."[16]

We offered choice freebies—scarves, ties, stuffed toys, luggage tags, pens, buttons, stickers, and lanyards to hold required CITES ID badges—all tastefully tiger striped. By the end of the first day, orange and black stripes were everywhere, silently disseminating our message that the eyes of the world were watching.

At the welcome soirée of drinks, nibbles, and speeches, Grace walked over to Meng Xianlin, who looked as Fonz-like as ever, and slipped a tiger-striped lanyard over his head. I watched with Bruce Weisgold of the US delegation. He gasped. "I can't believe Grace just did that."

Grace walked back to us smiling.

"What did he say?" I asked.

"He warned me to be careful," she said.

•   •   •

Grace rode down a hotel elevator the next morning with members of Japan's delegation, who were busy lobbying to open trade in elephant ivory and whale meat. They normally looked past her as if she didn't exist. But this morning they were staring at her and grinning. She understood why when she picked up the day's new CITES documents.

According to a glossy ten-page report outlining the Dragon's position on tigers, Xiongsen tiger farm and its winery were suing the International Fund for Animal Welfare (IFAW) for "dissemination of false information and/or distortion of facts." This was the first Grace had heard of it. The document implied government support for speed-breeding tigers and lifting China's ban. It portrayed tiger-farm investors as hapless victims who had not been compensated for huge financial losses incurred because they could not sell products from the thousands of tigers and growing stockpiles of tiger products they had amassed *after* China's 1993 ban. It said trade bans were ineffective, ignoring all evidence to the contrary, including the dramatic rebound of wild tigers in the Russian Far East.[17]

Grace looked drained when I found her. "How am I going to find the tens of thousands of dollars it will take to fight this?" she said. Nowhere did the government's document dispute IFAW's findings. In fact, it verified some of them. The lawsuit was a warning to Grace and anyone else trying to thwart the Dragon's plan. (The case was later dropped for lack of evidence, but only after IFAW had spent $50,000 on its defense.)

With the Dragon's position made clear in black and white, our more than fifty representatives of the International Tiger Coalition (ITC) fanned out among delegates from the 171 CITES member countries represented in The Hague. Our collective request was support for (1) keeping China's ban in place, (2) phasing out tiger farming, and (3) destroying all stockpiles of tiger parts and products.

We put our Asian members out front to show we weren't just a bunch of imperialist white folks trying to have our Western way. India bravely took the lead among like-minded tiger-range countries, with muscular backup from the United States. The Dragon berated and threatened the Indians and argued heatedly with US delegates.

Meanwhile, we encouraged countries in Africa, the Americas, Europe, and the Middle East to voice their support for ending all tiger trade from all sources. We slept little and refueled frequently at the convention center's espresso bar.

Tigers first came before CITES in The Hague on June 12, after ten days of intense geopolitical maneuvering.[18] Black walls and lights mounted on metal scaffolding made the conference hall look like a sound stage. As usual, all of the drama was muted by stylized UN protocol, delivered via headphones in the language of choice.

John Sellar opened the CITES Secretariat's report by noting the "precarious state of tigers" and the sorry state of law enforcement within their range and the countries that consumed their parts and products. He said trade in skins was down "substantially" due to awareness-raising—a reference to the mass change of heart by Tibetan consumers, which surely goaded the Dragon. Sellar said he believed that legalizing domestic trade in tiger parts and products from farms would put China in "noncompliance" with the treaty's resolution on Asian big cats. He said he was concerned that tiger farms were already selling tiger-bone products and tiger meat, which China had yet to clarify.

India took the floor to introduce a proposed decision on tiger farming. In a move that would have pleased Sun Tzu, the Dragon agreed to cosponsor the proposal with India, Nepal, and Russia. The draft text read: "Parties with operations breeding tigers on a commercial scale should implement measures to restrict the captive population to a level supportive only to conserving wild tigers." Read one way, it could mean tiger farms should be scaled down to the very few tigers actually needed to keep a captive store of the wild tiger's gene pool. However, it could just as easily be interpreted as an endorsement of the Dragon's dangerous premise that selling farmed tigers on a massive scale could somehow save wild tigers.

We had hoped that the Dragon, after learning of widespread op-position to tiger farming at home and abroad, would work with India, Nepal, and Russia to propose a face-saving phaseout of tiger farming. But in the tempest of negotiations, it was clear the Dragon intended no such thing.

The proposed decision could not be considered until it was available in all languages of the treaty—English, French, and Spanish. Translation bought us twenty-four hours to pull off a miracle. We hoped to convince the United States or United Kingdom to make an end run that India, Nepal, and Russia could support. Unfortunately, the United Kingdom was sidelined because it acted as a bloc with the European Union, and the German head of delegation feared a decision against tiger farming might hurt Germany's zoos. That left the United States, which opposed tiger farming and relaxing China's ban but had not intended to be out front on tigers. A lot had changed geopolitically since it had strong-armed China on tiger trade in the 1990s. In 2007, China was the second-largest foreign holder of US government debt and a primary manufacturer of the consumer goods that kept the US economy humming.

Many ITC members pleaded with US delegates during that twenty-four-hour window, including me. Grace went to Marshall Jones, chief advisor to the head of the US delegation, to underscore that the Dragon was *not* China. "This is only one agency of China's government, and this agency has a conflict of interest," she said. She told him other Chinese agencies see tiger farming as a liability that damages China's international image. All of the Dragon's threats were nothing more than "a bluff charge."

The wild tiger's fate rested on an hour-long discussion that took place on June 13, 2007.[19] Those sixty minutes felt like waiting for a jury to decide between a firing squad or freedom for someone innocent of any crime.

The deliberation began with India. Rajesh Gopal, director of India's Project Tiger, said his country was "strongly" opposed to "any scenario where tigers are farmed." He asked countries to "desist" from the notion that farming would somehow reduce rather than stimulate demand for parts and products of wild tigers. He encouraged strengthening the TCM industry's efforts to discourage use of tiger bones. He thanked China for its ban, which he said helped the world retain its beloved wild tigers. Then he appealed to China to phase out tiger farms and destroy its stockpiles of tiger parts and products.

The Dragon responded by reassuring everyone that China's ban was still in place while "different approaches" (code for legalization of trade) were explored.

Bhutan reminded the room that "the eyes of the world are watching" and asked China to keep its ban in place.

Cambodia, Indonesia, and Russia supported the ambiguous decision on the table. Nepal followed suit. I was disappointed with Nepal, but what else could a tiny, impoverished country do with goliath China breathing down its northern flank?

The chair recognized the United States. This was the last, best chess move for tigers—if the US delegation chose to make it. The spokesman said the United States believed that *any* legal trade would increase poaching, so maintaining China's ban was in the best interest of wild tigers.

Good.

Therefore, the United States proposed adding the following sentence: "Tigers should not be bred for trade in their parts and derivatives." With this caveat, the proposed decision would amount to a call to phase out farming tigers for commodities trade.

Yes! The country that had threatened trade sanctions against China in 1993 for the sake of wild tigers had not lost its mojo.

Thailand, which had tiger farming interests of its own, supported the original wording.

Swaziland said it believed tiger farming would complicate law enforcement since distinguishing farmed and wild tiger products was impractical if not impossible. Given that Africa's wild rhinos faced similar pressures, it supported the US addition.

India accepted the US suggestion.

China took the floor to ask that the word "international" be inserted into the US wording.

Disaster! The revision would then read, "Tigers should not be bred for international trade in their parts and derivatives." In other words, farming them for *domestic* trade in the most populous country in the world would be fine, à la China's bear-farm industry.

Kenya supported the US proposal without the extra word, as did the Global Tiger Forum, the International Union for the Conservation of Nature, and WWF, speaking for the International Tiger Coalition's thirty-five member organizations.

The China Association of Traditional Chinese Medicine, part of the Dragon's contingent, made a statement that was blessedly incomprehensible.

Lixin Huang followed on behalf of TCM colleagues across the United States working in collaboration with China's TCM leaders. "The request to reopen tiger trade does *not* come from the TCM community" but rather from "business interests," she said. "TCM does not wish to be responsible for the extinction of the wild tiger."

Sensing the building consensus against tiger farming, an angry Dragon lashed out, saying China needed a "scientific reason" to keep its ban in place rather than "political discrimination."

In the end, it all came down to one vote on one word. The word was "international." A single word to decide whether the most majestic wild animal still walking the earth would remain a creature of the forest or be lost forever to the feedlot.

Grace was so nervous that the nails of her clenched fingers drew blood from her palms. The clock ticked, ticked, ticked as the voting commenced. I had to remind myself to breathe and could tell Debbie was doing the same.

There was whispering at the dais among the chair and CITES staff. Finally the chair spoke. The proposed insertion of "international" was rejected 45 to 19, with 11 abstentions. A lot of countries were out of the room, some surely for fear of displeasing a superpower.

The chair asked if the countries present agreed on the decision. No one said a thing. This meant the World (as represented by

CITES) had made a decision that tiger farming should be phased out and tiger parts and products should not become luxury commodities. Full stop. No tiger trade from any source.

The Dragon asked to speak. The room tensed. I was not alone in thinking the Dragon was going to call for an up or down vote on the decision. But all the spokesman said was that China wanted the record to note that it regretted CITES had stepped beyond its remit of regulating international trade and into "sovereign" domestic issues.

We suffered through the final day's wrap-up session worrying that the Dragon would try to reopen debate on tigers, just as Denmark had done to turn around the vote on bears in Kyoto. The Dragon did ask for the floor on tigers, but only to underscore its dissatisfaction with the new decision and to put in a plug for farming tigers.[20]

8

OFF TO SEE THE WIZARD

Five days. That's how long we were able to relax believing the deadly threat posed to wild tigers by tiger farming had been vanquished.

Then the state-run *China Daily* harpooned our balloon. "China will inevitably lift its ban on the trade of tiger bones and body parts," Wang Wei, boss of Tiger-Farm-Promoter-in-Chief Wang Weisheng, was quoted as saying. "The ban is in place. But it is open for review. . . . The ban won't be there forever, given the strong voices from tiger farmers, experts, and society. It will be a waste if the resources of dead tigers are not used in traditional medicine."[1] *Never mind the voices of the World (as represented by CITES) that said tiger farming should end.*

At the same time, we learned that the Dragon was going ahead with an international workshop in early July 2007 to discuss the reopening of trade in tiger parts and products from farms, essentially flipping off a UN treaty signed by nearly every country on earth.

An eruption of communication crisscrossed the planet as the International Tiger Coalition (ITC) debated whether to boycott or attend the workshop. Attending would give tiger farming legitimacy after CITES had just agreed it had none. With only two weeks notice, getting visas might be impossible and airfare would be pricey after we all had just spent down our budgets on nearly three weeks in The Hague. Furthermore, the Dragon was barring attendance to anyone who didn't first take an official tour of China's two largest tiger farms, which some coalition members refused to do on principle. In the end, the ITC boycotted, but a few members went as individuals to be our eyes and ears.

Tiger-farm CEO Zhou Weisen sent his minibus and driver to the airport to pick up Belinda Wright, arriving from India. She was later joined at the hotel by Justin Gosling, eyewitness to Meng Xianlin's dumpster escapade. Belinda and Justin learned that they were among only a handful of workshop participants whose travel expenses weren't being picked up by the Dragon. The VIPs with a free ride included croc-farming Aussie consultant Hank Jenkins, the irrepressible Kirsten Conrad, Indian libertarian-for-hire Barun Mitra, plus the gaggle of foreign economists courted by Wang Weisheng.

"Throughout the visit, Wang Weisheng behaved like a proud and enthusiastic salesman, promoting every aspect of the facility as if he owned the place," Belinda wrote of the tour of Xiongsen Bear and Tiger Mountain Village in a diary about the workshop.[2]

"We saw endless enclosures with herds of tigers," Belinda wrote. Such a strange sight for a woman who once made a living capturing wild tigers' solitary ways on film. She saw tigers of dubious lineage, "tigers without tails ('lost in fights')," an industrial fridge containing a bloody mound of dead tigers, and "extremely fat, lazy bears that could barely walk." Zhou said the farm had more than 1,300 tigers and 400 bears.

"People were asking what happens to the tigers when they die, so they opened up this cold-storage room," Justin recounted later. "There were tiger carcasses just thrown in a pile. But for the size of the farm, there weren't that many bodies. Maybe twenty. So where were all the tigers that had died since the farm opened fourteen years before?"

They were not shown Xiongsen's winery.

Belinda asked Wang Weisheng why he so blatantly promoted the farm. He said because Zhou Weisen had been "wronged," which was "a shame to China." In the United States, this would be the equivalent of an official from the US Department of Agriculture, which regulates circus animals, acting as pitchman for a circus accused of selling tiger-meat hotdogs and beer fermented with tiger bones in a brewery paid for with taxpayer dollars.

Workshop participants flew to Harbin the next morning and then were bused by police escort to the Siberian Tiger Park, the public face of China's first tiger farm. While the eight hundred or so tigers there had more space than their counterparts at Xiongsen, Belinda noted, there were only males herding about in the open enclosures. The females were busy in "breeding cages" pumping out litters like battery hens.

"Barun Mitra talked endless rubbish," Belinda wrote. As they drove past tigers in the park's "safari" section, Mitra "commented on how curious and happy they were to see us." Belinda replied, "No, they are following the food van behind us." He then admitted that he knew "absolutely nothing about the subject, which makes it so much easier to write about." This from the man who received prime placement to promote tiger farming in the *New York Times*.

"Mr. Barun Mitra, an Indian, unfortunately, was the key spokesman for revoking the ban," said distressed Indian tiger wallah A. J. T. Johnsingh after he had attended a similar "workshop" six months earlier. "We told him several times that, as an Indian, he should never be a supporter of the idea of reducing India's national animal to the level of a chicken," Johnsingh reported. He shared Belinda's alarm at the lack of ecological knowledge among Wang Weisheng's cadre of so-called experts and was incredulous that they would not accept how much cheaper it is to poach a wild Indian tiger than spend years raising farmed tigers to adulthood. Poaching a wild tiger could cost a hunter in India as little as $10 compared to the $10 worth of meat per day needed to keep a tiger in captivity.[3]

Belinda asked her workshop cohorts for a show of hands to see how many had seen a tiger in the wild. Other than those from India—minus Mitra—few arms went up. "There was much discussion during the workshop on what is 'best for tigers,'" Belinda wrote, "but there was seldom any distinction made between wild tigers and the herd of tigers in the farms." Most of Wang Weisheng's hand-picked experts knew dangerously little of the habits and needs of wild tigers or their intricately woven kingdom.

In his opening remarks, Wang's boss said that 24,000 businesses in China were involved in farming fifty-four different wild species. He brushed aside the CITES decision in The Hague against tiger farming, predicting it would never be enforced. He bragged that China's farms could accommodate as many as seventy thousand tigers, though the Dragon had quietly touted one hundred thousand in The Hague.[4] He invited workshop participants to share their opinions "freely and candidly," although he made it clear his mind was already made up.

"*All* the Chinese speakers promoted tiger farming and the reopening of trade," Belinda said.

Urs Breitenmoser, the earnest Swiss scientist cochairing the Cat Specialist Group, told the workshop that he had asked the world's top tiger specialists whether they thought a legal supply of farmed tiger products would end or bolster the black market for wild-tiger parts. They overwhelmingly believed lifting China's ban would increase poaching and illegal trade, he said.[5]

The Dragon repeatedly assured workshop participants that no one would dare smuggle the parts of wild tigers into China, given the penalties in place for doing so. When Justin privately reminded Wang Weisheng of the free-for-all skin trade on the Tibetan Plateau, his host sputtered something about nongovernmental organizations not providing "real facts."

"The meeting was 95 percent Chinese and 99 percent pro-trade, with only a handful of real conservationists," Justin told me. "This was pitched as a meeting looking at conservation options when, in actual fact, it was almost all about how real conservation of tigers in the wild was *not* an option. The participants were *chosen* to come up with this conclusion. It wasn't democratic. It wasn't representative. It was *crazy!*"

After debriefs from attendees Belinda, Justin, Urs, and Craig Hoover of the US Fish and Wildlife Service, I felt dispirited. The World's decision in The Hague was more than I had dreamed possible, yet it meant nothing to these Chinese bureaucrats who were clearly best-friends-forever with tiger-farm investors. Maybe they were themselves tiger-farm investors. If the global body charged with regulating wildlife trade could not deter them, could anyone or anything?

After the workshop, Wang Weisheng's boss told China's Xinhua News Agency, "Tiger bones have been a key item in Chinese traditional medicine for several thousand years, and not using them is a waste." China's tiger farms had been set up "according to Chinese law," he said, and "there should be no problem" using the tiger bones they produce.

Urs, speaking for the Cat Specialist Group, was quoted as saying, "No country, including China, can make decisions affecting the existence of a species and take risks on behalf of humanity. . . . China cannot simply go its own way regardless of others."[6]

Meanwhile, an American of Korean ancestry assigned to the US consulate in Guangzhou visited Zhou Weisen's tiger farm around the same time. He found sales staff eager to sell him tiger-bone wine. They offered to ship it to South Korea, assuring him that their illegal offerings were legal—even though exporting them would have violated the laws of China and South Korea. What had been unfolding before The Hague continued to unfold.[7]

The Dragon put an end to our Olympic dreams in January 2008.

The conference to kick off the three-part tiger campaign devised by the World Federation of Chinese Medicine Societies had been delayed several times. Finally, the date was set for early 2008 in Beijing. The agenda had been decided, and the invitations sent. And I had wired $70,000 to pay for it.

At our final planning meeting, the federation's polished Secretary General Li Zhenji announced that "the time for preparation is insufficient." He apologized for the abrupt change. He started talking, in what sounded like Dragon-speak, about ensuring a "scientific outcome" that would not "cause confusion for the public." He said he wanted to visit tiger and bear farms at the invitation of his "friends" in the State Forestry Administration.[8]

"The Dragon got to him," I wrote in my notes.

Sure enough, Wang Weisheng had come calling the previous month. The Dragon wanted our conference to be a "debate" about the merits of farming tigers and allowing legal trade in tiger products. The Dragon wanted to turn it into a platform for reversing the Chinese medicine industry's opposition to the use of tiger bone. The fact that Li put off the meeting meant that he was still on our side but was unable to openly defy a government ministry's request.

I asked for a $70,000 refund.

The Dragon had disregarded the World (as represented by CITES) and silenced China's TCM leadership on tiger farming. John Sellar had once told me that wild tigers could only be saved by the intervention of world leaders and a supertanker full of money. I was acquainted with only one place that had that kind of convening power and that much cash: the World Bank.

Everyone said I was crazy. My investment-banker husband said tigers were so far outside the World Bank's remit that they may as well live on a different planet. People I knew at the World Bank agreed. What did tigers have to do with the bank's mission to reduce poverty in developing nations? Still, I had it in my head that if what I thought of as "the World's Bank" said tiger farming must stop, then China's leaders would tell the Dragon to desist. After that, I thought, the World Bank could easily come up with the hundreds of millions of dollars needed to phase out China's tiger farms.

When I heard that WWF's US CEO Carter Roberts had a scheduled meeting with the World Bank's president, Robert Zoellick, I asked my former colleagues if they would ask Roberts to bring up tigers. They told me that Roberts would not waste his precious time with Zoellick on an issue so far afield from the bank's interests. Meanwhile, some Indian members of the International Tiger Coalition declared that the World Bank was evil incarnate, blaming it for pillaging the tiger's realm with dam, road, and mining projects—succeeding at nothing more than making India's rich richer and poor poorer.

I listened to none of them. I figured that enlisting the World Bank was like enlisting the TCM industry—powerful by virtue of its unlikelihood and its potentially enormous sway. So I went knocking.

I went first to the door of resource economist Richard Damania, an animal-loving Indian who looked and sounded like an Oxbridge Brit. I had approached him the year before, after reading a journal article he'd coauthored on the economics of farming wildlife. He and his fellow author had examined the idea of rhino farming and concluded that the criminal control of wildlife trafficking meant that the normal laws of supply and demand did not apply. They said legalization could "result in greater poaching pressure and perhaps accelerate the likelihood of extinction." I asked Richard if the same applied to tigers. He said it probably did.

This time I asked Richard if he, under the auspices of the World Bank, would produce a definitive economic analysis of what the Dragon's plan would likely mean for wild tigers. He was keen, and his boss gave the green light.

Not long afterward, Richard called to say, "China kicked back harder than you can believe." By "China," he meant World Bank staff working in China. They feared that an analysis of tiger farming would "enflame" China's government.

Did that mean the commitment to farm tigers went far higher than the Dragon, or was this anticipatory self-censorship on the part of the bank's China team? Richard said he didn't know. His colleagues suggested that he focus instead on poaching and illegal trade rather than legal trade of farmed tigers. I felt uneasy about the change but trusted Richard. He said it was the only way forward. "There is extremely high-level support for this," he said. "It's far more than I'd hoped."

Then came news that Zoellick, who had a strong relationship with powerful Chinese ministries from his days as US trade representative and deputy secretary of state under President George W. Bush, felt a personal passion for tigers. *At last, a means to make an end run around the Dragon to get to China's leaders!*

Around this time, Richard introduced me to the bank's Keshav Varma, an impish, balding Indian man close to retirement age. Keshav specialized in urban planning and disaster relief, but he took eagerly to riding the tiger. And it soon became clear he was hell-bent on not dismounting. He was shameless and relentless in selling the World Bank on becoming the wild tiger's savior, but always with a broad smile and loquacious joviality.

When Keshav wanted to meet a tiger expert, I introduced him to John Seidensticker. Gradually, others were added to what became a weekly talkfest, with Keshav doing most of the talking. As word of the World Bank's interest spread among the ITC and beyond, more tiger advocates of every stripe—including tiger-farming advocates—sought private appointments with Keshav.

Against all odds and to the consternation of some of his staff, Robert Zoellick said in early 2008 that he would launch a World Bank initiative to save wild tigers. Zoellick had one major caveat, Keshav said. He would go forward only if he had a major celebrity by his side to draw in media interest.

"I can get Harrison Ford," I said, not knowing if I really could.

"Harrison Ford would be perfect," Keshav said. Zoellick was a fan.

So I went to see the Great Dane. He was a senior vice president at Conservation International (CI), and Harrison Ford was CI's most celebrated advocate. The nature-loving megastar—for whom Nobel Prize–winning scientist E. O. Wilson once named a Central American ant (*Pheidole harrisonfordi*)[9]—had been an active CI board member for a decade. His latest video promo for CI featured him taking off his shirt and sitting in what looked like a dentist's chair. "When a rainforest gets slashed and burned, it releases tons of carbon into the air we breathe," Ford said. "It changes our climate. It hurts." Then a young woman in white painted a patch of his chest hair with hot wax and smoothed a strip of cloth over it. "Every bit of rainforest that gets ripped out over there," he said, grimacing as the woman ripped clean a swath of chest, "really hurts over here."[10]

Ford was also a close friend of CI's founder and CEO Peter Seligmann, who barely knew of me and showed little affinity for tigers. The Great Dane arranged for us to meet Peter and did most of the talking. By virtue of his charisma and creativity, Peter had convinced former World Bank president Jim Wolfensohn to give CI $25 million to start the $125 million fund for which I had been Asia grant director before returning to tigers.[11] I told Peter that I hoped Zoellick would create a similar pool of funds for wild tigers. Lending Harrison Ford to the effort was a bit of a hard sell, but the Great Dane said all the right things. Peter promised Ford would be there if he was amenable and not shooting or promoting a film.

That's how the World Bank's highly unlikely tiger initiative came to be launched in June 2008, with Harrison Ford as its star attraction.

News of a World Bank tiger effort was received with both applause and rotten tomatoes by the forty-two organizations that made up the International Tiger Coalition (ITC) by 2008. Most thought the bank's involvement would elevate awareness of the wild tiger's predicament to the highest levels of world governance—far higher than the Dragon could manipulate. Others saw in it—and began surreptitiously pursuing—World Bank funding exclusively for their own tiger work. A small faction from India became enraged, accused me of courting the devil, and threatened to resign.

In essence, the effort I hoped would bring world leaders and hundreds of millions of dollars to rescue the King of the Jungle from the Dragon's mouth threatened to blow apart the ITC—the most powerful alliance for tigers in history. I thought if I listened, reasoned, and reassured, the coalition would hold. How I wished later that I'd remembered the dogs I passed every day on my walk to school during my graduate research in South Korea.

Each day there were six or seven different dogs in the small cage under a tree on the sidewalk outside this dog-soup restaurant near Kyungpook University. One day, thinking I was giving them a savory last meal, I threw each one a hot dog. Instead of delight, a melee ensued. The dogs viciously attacked one another. Only the two victors ate.

Sun Tzu counted "six ways of courting defeat" in his *Art of War*: "flight, insubordination, collapse, ruin, disorganization, and rout." In courting the World Bank for tigers, I had unknowingly invited all six.

The unraveling became evident on June 1, 2008—eight days before the World Bank was to unveil its tiger initiative. "The bank will merely use the ITC's credibility, give out consultancies, and make you feel good in meetings, and then go out and do exactly what they want," said the e-mail that came that day from ITC members Belinda Wright of the Wildlife Society of India and P. K. Sen of the Ranthambore Foundation. What the bank wanted, they said, was to replace forests with tree plantations, build highways through the tiger's realm, and create "scores of new open-pit coal mines in prime tiger and elephant habitat." They lamented that some ITC members "have clearly decided they would rather align themselves with the bank than preserve the unity and integrity of the coalition." In closing, Belinda and P. K. said: "We are committed to saving wild tigers in India and believe that any affiliation with the World Bank will be detrimental to this cause. Consequently, we have decided we have no option but to leave the ITC."

I felt slapped in the face, kicked in the gut, and guilty as charged. But I believed we had to stop the Dragon or none of the rest of it would matter. The World Bank seemed our only hope of doing that.

Meanwhile, the Wildlife Conservation Society (WCS) and World Wildlife Fund (WWF) were secretly proposing, with TRAFFIC, to take over the relationship with the World Bank on tigers. Without telling fellow ITC members, WCS had quietly applied for a $1 million grant from the Global Environment Facility (GEF) to establish the three organizations as the bank's main NGO partners on tigers.[12]

That alone could shatter the ITC. If there was going to be World Bank or GEF money for tigers, I'd hoped a substantial sum would be shared with smaller ITC members—like the Capulets who had moved the bar so significantly for tigers with small sums of money. I had hoped that grants would be given contingent on working in alliance because together forty-two organizations were too powerful for the Dragon and CITES to ignore. I wanted funds to flow to people like Debbie and Belinda, who would be able to pick up the "intel" that would prevent another Sariska. If the big three got all the money, as they usually did, I feared we wild-tiger advocates would once again scatter our forces to resume fighting each other for donor favor while those banking on extinction marched on, resolute and in lockstep.

I tried to explain this to my old friend Josh Ginsberg at WCS after expressing my fears to the World Bank about the $1 million grant. This man, who had once complained to me for hours about WWF's greed and deception around fund-raising, warned me that if I tried to interfere, regardless of my good intentions, I would be professional dead meat.

Any mention of tiger farming had vanished from the World Bank's Global Tiger Initiative by the time Robert Zoellick, with Harrison Ford, announced it on June 9, 2008, at the National Zoo in Washington, DC.[13]

From early morning, the day felt equatorial—unusually stifling for late spring. A stage facing rows of folding chairs filled the wide walkway that circled the back of the zoo's tiger grotto. With a thicket of bamboo along one side and a couple of Sumatran tigers lounging atop a shaded hillside on the other, the place resembled a jungle-themed wedding venue. In fact, the World Bank was about to pledge its troth to wild tigers.

Peter Seligmann arrived with Ford at the same time as Zoellick and other VIPs began to appear, including WWF CEO Carter Roberts, Bo Derek, and Robert Duvall. During the show, Ford said little but listened with his signature half smile, while others said a lot of what was expected.

To his credit, Zoellick said trade was the threat to tigers that trumped all others. "Conservation efforts are continually being undermined by poaching and illegal trade," he said. "Wild tigers are slipping away." Part of the World Bank's five-point tiger strategy would "address the illegal tiger trade" and "counter the demand for tiger products worldwide." The latter was especially good.

The ITC was given two minutes at the podium, which I insisted go to Grace because I believed an Asian face should represent us. She was the only speaker who was not a white, forty-plus male, and she was the only one to mention the CITES decision that tigers should not be farmed for their parts and products.

As Zoellick had anticipated, the press coverage went global thanks to Ford's presence. News outlets from Beijing to Sydney to Hollywood picked up a tiger story that they—and their audiences—most likely would have ignored otherwise. *Washington Post* coverage came under the tantalizing headline, "Indiana Jones and the Temple of Celebrity."[14]

A select group was invited to a lunch hosted by Zoellick in the World Bank's elegant top-floor gallery. As I walked under the soaring atrium ceiling into the crowd of round linen-covered tables, someone from Conservation International approached me in a panic. Peter Seligmann had not been assigned a seat with Harrison Ford at Zoellick's table, she said. I immediately went to Keshav for remedy, but he shrugged off my request to correct the seating arrangement.

"Keshav, you *cannot* do this to Peter," I said. "Peter is why Harrison Ford is here. He alone made it happen."

"I'm sorry," Keshav said, "there's nothing I can do." He then walked off to receive more accolades for the morning's event and mentally prepare for his victory speech at the lunchtime podium.

As I tried to appeal to a higher authority, Zoellick took the microphone and asked everyone to be seated. Every chair at the president's table was quickly filled. Ford sat on one side of Zoellick and WWF's Carter Roberts sat on the other—possibly the hardest slap in the face for the CEO of competitor Conservation International. To my mortification, Peter sat across from me at a table of mid-level World Bank staff. I didn't hear a word of the speeches. All I could think of was Peter's humiliation. I also knew that I was now officially dead to him. Worse yet, any hope of adding CI's might to the fight to save wild tigers had died.

Keshav called a meeting of World Bank staff and "partners" the following afternoon to discuss how to implement Zoellick's plan. John Robinson, the Wildlife Conservation Society's chief conservation officer, and WWF's chief scientist Eric Dinerstein announced to all present that while they appreciated the International Tiger Coalition's role in bringing about the bank's Global Tiger Initiative, WCS, WWF, and TRAFFIC had the right stuff to take over as the initiative's lead partners from that point forward. These biologists, who knew little of the ways of the Dragon, wanted to sideline the ITC—of which their organizations were members.

My mind reeled with disbelief. *If you do this, you will silence the one voice big enough to stop the Dragon from unleashing a force that will leave your beloved tiger landscapes emptied of tigers.* I argued for ITC's diversity of skills, reach, ethnicity, and boots on the ground in tiger-range and tiger-consuming countries. But I could see it was a done deal. Just as Josh Ginsberg had warned.

Not long after that, the ITC received another blow. One of the major donors funding my cat-herding role decided not to re-up. The trustees "continue to have considerable reservations about the involvement, perceived or otherwise, of the World Bank," said the e-mail announcing the decision. The Great Dane helped me appeal, but to no avail. Certain people in India had gotten to them. Without this donor's support, matching funds from another major donor had to be denied. The ITC no longer had a budget, and I was back at CI, sneaking in tiger work where I could, thanks only to the Great Dane's love of them.

The Dragon quickly sensed advantage, which became apparent soon after the Olympic flame left Beijing in late August 2008.

As the Dragon continued to snub the CITES decision against tiger farming, the International Tiger Coalition wrote of its concerns to the World Bank's president on December 16, 2008. "Unfortunately, China's tiger trade ban is being undermined by a handful of investors in tiger farms and a few of their advocates within one government department," the letter said. "The time could not be better than now to ask China to take another bold step toward saving wild tigers by turning its current trade ban into law, broadening it to include all tiger parts (not just bones), and phasing out tiger farms—to highlight the commitment of China and its treasured traditional medicine system to a healthy planet. . . . Your interventions in these matters stand to make the Global Tiger Initiative a success by stopping the catastrophic threat posed by the potential lifting of China's tiger trade ban."

Robert Zoellick replied a month later. "As you may know, I recently visited China and had the opportunity to raise possibilities for cooperation on tiger conservation with several senior Chinese officials," he wrote. "In particular, I explained the importance of maintaining China's ban on domestic trade in tiger parts, which the officials positively affirmed. . . . I alerted them to the sad stories of tiger farms, explaining I hoped we could follow up with more information in hope we could cooperate on finding a solution."

We wrote to Zoellick again the following month to say we were "encouraged by your discussions with Chinese authorities," to explain that China had two more weeks to report to CITES on its progress in phasing out tiger farms, and to ask for his "assistance to bring this deadline to the attention of those authorities."

Zoellick replied on February 23, saying, "I fully appreciate your concern. I recently raised these matters with a number of senior officials, and our team in Beijing is following up with the State Forestry Administration." *Home of the Dragon.* Unless the World Bank took the matter higher than that, nothing would change.

On February 27, 2009, the Dragon sent a one-line response to an official request from CITES for details about the phaseout of China's

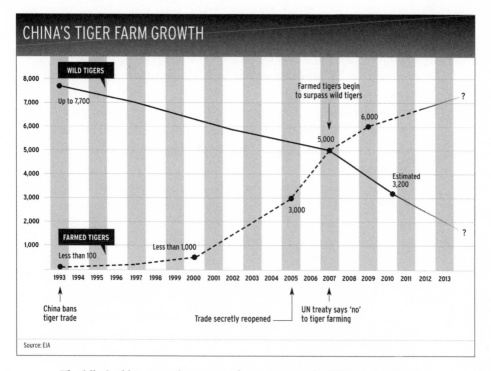

CHINA'S TIGER FARM GROWTH

WILD TIGERS

8,000

7,000   Up to 7,700   Farmed tigers begin
                                                        to surpass wild tigers   ?

6,000   6,000

5,000   5,000

4,000   Estimated
                                                                                   3,200
3,000
                                                    3,000
2,000
                                                                                                      ?
1,000   FARMED TIGERS   Less than 1,000

         Less than 100

         1993 1994 1995 1996 1997 1998 1999 2000 2001 2002 2003 2004 2005 2006 2007 2008 2009 2010 2011 2012 2013

         China bans   UN treaty says 'no'
         tiger trade   Trade secretly reopened ——— to tiger farming

Source: EIA

The fall of wild tiger numbers against the soaring growth of China's tiger farms.

tiger farms. It simply said that China prohibited commercial import
and export of tigers and their parts and products.[15] Nothing about the
status of tiger trade inside China. Nothing about tiger farms.

In an even greater rebuff of the World (as represented by CITES),
China's tiger farm population had risen by one thousand, to six thousand tigers.[16] For the first time, there were many more tigers in farms
than in the wild.

By May 2009, Wang Weisheng's cadre of foreign tiger-farm pro-
moters was on the international media circuit again.[17] I continued to
hound the World Bank for a strong stance against tiger farming and
received only vague reassurances from Keshav Varma.

In June 2009, the International Tiger Coalition sent an open letter to the CITES Standing Committee underscoring the fact that
the treaty had "endorsed the view that tiger farming for commercial

purposes is a threat to the survival of wild tigers and needs to be stopped." We urged the committee to ensure full compliance.

At the July 2009 meeting of the Standing Committee in Geneva, Switzerland, India insisted that tiger farming "should be stopped on a priority basis" and urged sanctions against countries that did not report on the matter. The European Union supported India's suggestion if there was no reporting within ninety days. The United States, Iran, and Australia, as well as the Global Tiger Forum, supported the EU suggestion.[18]

Hank Jenkins, in support of the Dragon, took the floor to say that there was "no empirical evidence" that tiger farming stimulated poaching of wild tigers.

Then Keshav Varma delivered a statement I had hoped to hear from the World Bank for more than two years. Reading a message carefully crafted with Richard Damania's help, he said:

> Tiger farming has proven to be a divisive issue and one that has distracted many in the conservation community from the common goal of saving wild tigers. . . . There are clever theories that tell us that tiger farming . . . is the panacea for conservation. But there are an equal number of experts . . . who inform us otherwise. . . . There are several unknowns and even more unknowables that no amount of research can cast light upon. Will legalized farming facilitate laundering? Would it create new markets and an even higher demand for wild tiger products for those who want a luxury good—the "real thing," the organic tigers? And why, if farming is so effective, are wild bears still poached when there is a surplus of farmed bear bile in the world? The truth is that we cannot provide answers to these counterfactuals that can only be known after the fact. And this is why we need to exercise caution. Extinction is irreversible, so prudence and precaution suggest that the risks of legalized farming of tigers for their parts and derivatives are too great a gamble for the world to take. Having carefully weighed the economic arguments, we urge the CITES community to uphold the ban on wild tiger products and for all

countries to continue to ban the domestic trade of wild tigers or any commercial exploitation. This is the only safe way to ensure that wild tigers may have a future tomorrow.

The Dragon, speaking for China, opposed the request for reporting on tiger farms because the only official mandate of CITES was to regulate *international* wildlife trade.

John Sellar, speaking for the CITES Secretariat, said that China was "technically correct" but member countries had agreed by consensus that tigers should not be farmed because farming stimulated demand for tiger parts and products from all sources, including critically endangered wild tigers.

In the end, the Standing Committee agreed to require reporting within ninety days, and I sent Keshav's statement in an e-mail to the ITC with the subject line "Victory for Tigers!" "The Bank's decision to announce its opposition to tiger farming in a UN forum, in the presence of a large delegation from China, may well be a game-changer," I said.

Three months later, tiger specialist Dale Miquelle reported that the Russian Far East had lost up to 40 percent of its wild tigers to poachers.[19]

The Year of the Tiger dawned on Valentine's Day 2010. Four days later, the editorial board of the *New York Times* gave wild tigers a gift:

> One particularly horrifying practice is Chinese tiger farms.
> . . . These farms are thinly masked as efforts at tiger conservation. In reality, their purpose is to raise tigers to be butchered and consumed.
>
> The tiger farms also do nothing to take pressure off the dwindling population of wild tigers. Chinese consumers believe parts from wild tigers have greater medicinal potency. In China, there are only some twenty wild tigers left. And Chinese demand—heightened by the farms and the beginning of

the Year of the Tiger—has caused sharply increased poaching in India, which has only about 1,400 wild tigers left.

The Chinese government seems to be doing little or nothing to shut down tiger farms or punish those who buy or sell tiger parts. And it has made no attempt to persuade Chinese consumers that tiger parts have no real medicinal value.

Unless China does both—shuts down the tiger trade and finds a way to alter consumers' tastes—the wild tiger is almost surely doomed.[20]

Exactly. Except for the part about no real medicinal value, which was a bit of an insult to the tiger's friends in the TCM industry, the editors were spot-on.

Then more good news came from the World Bank. Robert Zoellick wanted to convene world leaders for a tiger summit.

9

THE VLADIMIR PUTIN SHOW

Never before had world leaders come together solely to discuss an animal. The November 2010 tiger summit hosted by Russia's prime minister Vladimir Putin would make history and perhaps decide the fate of wild tigers.

In my mind's eye, the summit took place atop a pyramid of bodies—those of the many tiger advocates who had been thrown under a bus since the World Bank had launched its tiger initiative on that sticky June morning in 2008. But what disturbed me more than the intrigue and betrayal was the loss along the way of that one overshadowing, deal-breaking menace that had sent me on the yellow-brick road to the World Bank in the first place. It had vanished not just from the summit agenda and summit documents but from mere mention. The term "tiger farming," both written and spoken, was verboten.

The surrealism of this fact sent my mind back to the door of the bile-milking room nearly twenty years before when the Man with the Keys wasn't there and was never going to be there because the Dragon didn't want the door opened to expose the scheme to transform some of the world's most magnificent wild animals into livestock. But that was then—in barely-past-Mao China, witnessed by only me, my husband, and a bunch of low-level, Communist Party tools saying no without saying no to a stubborn American woman with a bear-gall-bladder obsession. This was *now*. On the world stage, set by the World Bank, showcasing a gaggle of world leaders.

In the years since I'd seen that handwritten ledger of orders for tiger bones at China's first tiger farm, what had really changed? Wild tiger numbers were down by more than half, to perhaps three thousand. The number of tigers on farms in China had grown a hundredfold, from sixty to six thousand.[1] All the while, the Dragon's commitment to farm tigers, bears, and fifty-two other wild species "like cows and pigs" had remained steadfast.

After China banned tiger-bone trade in 1993, tiger farms had stepped up their speed-breeding. Furthermore, the very government agency charged with *saving* wildlife and enforcing China's tiger-trade ban had actually invested substantial sums of money in wineries where skeletons of farmed tigers had been steeping in alcohol for years in anticipation of launching a multibillion-dollar-a-year venture to sell tiger-bone wine to the world. And now China's stature as an emerging world leader gave the Dragon a good many more than one hundred ways to say no to the CITES order to shut down tiger farms, including the sway of China's 2010 global trade surplus of $2.68 trillion.[2] (Sun Tzu: "The clever combatant imposes his will on the enemy, but does not allow the enemy's will to be imposed on him.")

I truly had thought when I approached the World Bank in 2007 that I was engaging a monolithic global body that could rule against tiger farming and make it stop. How naïve I was! And how outmaneuvered. I could almost hear the Man with the Keys laughing.

By the time I boarded a plane bound for St. Petersburg in November of that 2010 Year of the Tiger, I had been out of the game for months. My mother had died the first week of January, and my father passed three weeks later. In between, my husband had taken a leave of absence from our life together.

I had been pretty much emotionally comatose as I carried out my volunteer cat-herding duties for the International Tiger Coalition at the CITES conference in Doha, Qatar, in March. Inside a convention center under the relentlessly sunny skies of the Persian Gulf, ITC members lobbied mightily to hold on to the decision against tiger farming hard-won in The Hague. The Dragon came armed and ready to make it go away.

Rather than argue the facts of tiger farming, the Dragon sent a heat-seeking missile straight for the deep values of every developing country that had ever felt pushed around by the West. The Dragon's delegates called on developing nations to band together and stand up for their sovereign rights to natural resources. Never mind that China was the world's third-largest economy and sucking up many of their resources, the messaging about defying the dictates of "outsiders" resonated.

The marketing was so successful that even India set aside its usual friction with the Dragon to root for Asia's home team, agreeing that countries with no tigers should butt out of the matter. The West was on the defensive for the first time since CITES was founded in 1973. In the words of my Doha roommate Amie Brautigam—still married to the Great Dane and now a policy advisor at the Wildlife Conservation Society—Western governments and conservation groups were "outgunned, outmaneuvered, and severely under-resourced."

The saving grace for tigers was that unless a CITES member country asked for the decision against tiger farming to be deleted, the decision would automatically stay in force. A lot of people froze when the Dragon stated on the floor that the decision was "outside interference," beyond the mandate of CITES. But most tiger-range countries did not want to go there, despite their "Kumbaya" moment of anti-colonial unity.[3]

India, as ever the leader on tigers, said demand for tiger parts outside its borders was "dampening" protection efforts and survival of its tigers depended on quashing that demand. Spokesman Rajesh Gopal said India supported China's ban and the decision against tiger farming. Tiger-range countries Bhutan, Indonesia, Nepal, and Vietnam supported India's remarks. Malaysia, Myanmar, and Thailand sided with China.

In the end, the 2007 decision against tiger farming remained intact. But everyone felt the tectonic shift in Qatar, and it looked as if Vladimir Putin's tiger summit eight months later might well determine whether that decision would ever be implemented.

After Qatar, I took time off to adjust to life as a daughter with no parents and a wife with no husband. Through summer and early fall, I grieved and hid in sleep. Without my incessant prodding, the cats did not herd. The International Tiger Coalition fell silent, but I was too bereft to care.

In mid-October, a smelling-salts moment revived me. A reliable someone told me that the Dragon had summoned Beijing representatives of ITC stalwarts WWF, the Wildlife Conservation Society, and TRAFFIC for a pre-summit chat. By then all ITC members but these three had pretty much been elbowed out of the inner circle of summit planning. If they went soft on tiger farming, any hope of it making the agenda would be lost—a fact not missed by the Dragon, which let them know that raising the subject at the summit could jeopardize their future work in China.

I e-mailed a trusted source close to the Dragon seeking confirmation of this threat. The source confirmed that Wang Weisheng had indeed warned the triumvirate to keep mum on tiger farms or else. (Sun Tzu: "One need not destroy one's enemy. One need only destroy his willingness to engage.")

On November 3, 2010, with less than three weeks till the summit and feeling deep remorse over conceding the fight against tiger farming, I e-mailed the ITC to announce a conference call the next day—our first in five months. On that teleconference, WWF confirmed that tiger farming was not on the summit agenda. And while tiger-range countries were supposed to make bold summit pledges toward saving tigers, none was yet in evidence.

Before I had been squeezed out of the World Bank's "tiger core group," I had advocated asking China to pledge an end to tiger farming. WWF had wanted huge new protected tracts and a multi-donor trust fund to dispense millions, perhaps billions, of dollars for projects to "stop the bleeding." However, on the eve of the summit, the only assured outcomes were two paper tigers—a lengthy Global Tiger Recovery Program plan prescribing how tiger-range countries *could* save wild tigers *if* they had the money, and a short, feel-good declaration about pulling wild tigers back from the abyss.[4] Neither so much as hinted at tiger farming. The ITC had asked that the words "end all tiger trade" be included in both documents. But the more we pushed for these four words, the more we were excluded from the drafting process. "Illegal" tiger trade was the only trade that made the cut, which implied that *legal* tiger trade would get a pass.

After the ITC meeting, WWF's Ginette Hemley and I met to catch up on personal news over coffee. Just as we were about to ask for the check, she shared a recent incident she'd experienced at the World Bank with its president. Robert Zoellick had called together top officials of major conservation groups to rally support for the Russia summit and to ask if anyone could rustle up some celebrities to make an appearance. At the end of the meeting, he asked Ginette to come to his office. She happily obliged, proud that he'd singled out WWF for a one-on-one. "I thought he was going to thank me for all of WWF's support in making the summit happen," she said. (In fact, WWF Russia was pretty much running the show.)

Instead, Zoellick closed his door and began a tirade. Ginette said he was livid about a letter WWF International and the Wildlife Conservation Society (WCS) had sent to the head of the bank's sister organization, the Global Environment Facility (GEF). The letter implied that the GEF was better suited than the World Bank to run the Global Tiger Initiative (GTI), according to Ginette. It was true that the GEF had billons of dollars in grant monies that it could award to governments and conservation groups like WWF and WCS while the World Bank mostly just made *loans* to developing countries. Nonetheless, the GTI was Zoellick's creation, and he felt thrown under a bus by the very groups that had put themselves forward as his go-to partners.

I then attended a US State Department meeting about the summit, at which one participant said officials from China's Ministry of Foreign Affairs were puzzled over why tigers would be discussed by heads of state. She asked State Department officials to "work your magic" to help Chinese diplomats grasp the urgent necessity of high-level intervention.

Rumor had it that Zoellick had been removed from the summit's list of speakers, so I asked who *would* be speaking. That was now a matter of "yelling and screaming," according to John Seidensticker, who had become a consultant to the World Bank on tigers.

As I left the State Department, I noticed several calls had come in to my cell phone from Keshav Varma, now head of the GTI. When I called him back, he sounded as dejected as a little boy scorned by his best mates.

"What's wrong?" I asked.

"He who plays with tigers gets mauled," he said. More catfights between the World Bank and WWF Russia, I assumed.

"How can I help?" I asked.

"You can attend a luncheon I'm having for partners this Friday," he said. *Things must really be bad if I'm being asked back to the partners' table.*

Dejection seemed epidemic. The usually stoic and ever-positive Kristin Nowell invited me to "whine over wine" at her mother's DC condo. Kristin was one of TRAFFIC's best investigators, a respected member of the Cat Specialist Group, and founder of ITC member Cat Action Treasury. The last time we'd spoken, she'd just started working for Keshav. He had summoned her from her rural homestead in Maine to help appease the many players frustrated with the all-show, no-dough GTI, she said. So she agreed to move to DC to become the World Bank's cat herder. Ten days later, she was out of a job. She didn't know what had gone wrong, but she had decided to save her anger until after the summit. "I just said to myself, 'Screw my feelings. Screw everybody else's feelings. This is the event of the century for tigers!'"

Kristin told me we needed to do everything possible to bring tiger farming to the attention of China's top leaders. By "we" she meant the sidelined ITC. It was up to us, she said, because tiger farming had become the summit's "bête noire."

The report I was not supposed to see came to me by US mail with no return address.

The draft of TRAFFIC's "Getting Off the Tiger: How China Can Eliminate Illicit Demand for Tiger Parts and Products and Deliver on Its Trade-Related National Tiger Recover Priorities" detailed how China could stop international tiger trade if it stopped the "leakage" of products from its tiger farms.[5] The report asserted that tiger farms had kept alive demand for tiger-bone wine in spite of China's 1993 ban.

Overall, demand was low, thanks to the ban, according to the report. However, low in the context of a population of 1.4 billion citizens translated into "a potential consumer base of millions of people." Young Chinese men coveted tiger products because they "demonstrate prestige in social settings." This nontraditional use was growing because China's farms were selling them without penalty. Since wild-tiger products were considered superior, poaching of wild tigers was up and the numbers of wild-tiger parts and products seized on the black market had doubled in recent years.

The report underscored all that the International Tiger Coalition had been saying, with new evidence to back it up. "A well-publicized crackdown on the tiger farms could have a profound freezing effect" on all tiger trade, it said. The authors concluded that saving wild tigers depended on China "firmly closing the door on use of captive-bred tiger products." *Bravo, TRAFFIC!*

The report was a godsend. It was fact-based, persuasive, and timed perfectly to draw the attention of China's leadership during the summit. Only TRAFFIC was not going to publish it, according to my Deep Throat.

I e-mailed my former boss, Steve Broad, TRAFFIC International's executive director, and his right-hand man, Sabri Zain, praising the report and asking if they planned to release it before or during the summit. Several days of silence followed. Finally, Sabri replied saying, "We actually have no plans for publishing and distributing it at the tiger forum."[6]

The report said everything that needed to be said, and it had been spiked. *Mission accomplished for the Dragon.*

By the time the woman who was St. Petersburg's governor officially opened the pre-summit symposium on November 21, 2010, the Global Tiger Initiative had already spent more than a million dollars to host preparatory confabs in Kathmandu, Bali, a Thai resort town, and New Delhi. Not one wild tiger had been saved. In fact, many had been lost. But Keshav Varma told me that his strategy was to first get tiger-range countries to agree to a unified plan to double wild tiger numbers by 2022—aka "Tx2"—then the money would come. *Then the saving of wild tigers?*

I sat on the gold-velvet cushion at my designated chair in the third rounded row of UN-style seating between the EU representative and the Wildlife Conservation Society duo, who probably winced at the thought of the Dragon seeing them sitting next to the woman who refused to shut up about tiger farming.

Crystal chandeliers reflected the gilding that outlined the white columns, porticos, and balconies surrounding the Great Hall inside Mariinsky Palace. Built in the 1840s by Czar Nicholas I as a wedding gift to his eldest daughter, the palace was now city hall. In this splendorous place that had witnessed historic triumph, deceit, revolution, and revival, I was ready to be wrong, to be humbled, to apologize for my skepticism, cynicism, criticism, and anger over all the ways I thought the Global Tiger Initiative had sold out wild tigers and played into the hands of the Dragon.

Environment ministers from every tiger-range country had RSVPed—except India, for which a pouting Keshav labeled his motherland "negligent." Five heads of tiger-range countries were to attend the summit, including China's premier, Wen Jiabao. Leonardo DiCaprio was tweeting about it, and Ilya Lagutenko—the rocker called "Russia's Mick Jagger"—had planned an elaborate concert to honor it.

Despite all the hype, the opening sessions were a slow-moving slog of scripted speeches and PowerPoints delivered from a white podium so large it dwarfed all but the tallest presenters. The term "unprecedented" was used by nearly every speaker to describe the summit, although nothing without precedent was said.

Bangladesh declared, "Our children must not learn about tigers only in books"—but announced no bold actions to prevent that from happening. Bhutan implored the audience to ensure that tigers are "not only seen in cartoons and toy stores"—but prescribed no means of doing so. Cambodia, Indonesia, Malaysia, and Myanmar outlined what they would do to protect wild tigers *if* they received funding from the international community. Action-upon-receipt-of-funds was the overriding theme of the day. China, which in August 2010 supplanted Japan as the world's second-largest economy, called on the international community to ante financial support for tigers but did not offer up any itself. Even host Russia made no monetary pledge.

India, which had sent a civil servant as its representative, announced the most significant strides for tigers. It would spend more than $1 billion to move people out of core tiger areas, expand its Wildlife Crime Bureau, put tigers back in reserves that had lost them all to poachers, employ satellite technology to stop tiger poaching, and use metal detectors to find and remove tiger snares, plus add eight new tiger reserves to its existing thirty-nine. Never had a snub of the World Bank been so fruitful for tigers!

Outside the Great Hall, amid more gilded columns and a good deal of cigarette smoke, tiger countries, conservation groups, and the World Bank had set up booths to showcase their tiger efforts. The only one to so much as allude to China's tiger farms was the Dragon. A handout entitled *To Save Wild Tigers: China in Action* noted that the farms were "strictly supervised and inspected." Full stop. Mere months before, at the CITES conference in Doha, the Dragon had distributed an uncharacteristically slick color brochure that confirmed China had six thousand tigers on farms and stated that the government had "no right" to restrict them unless the in-

ternational community bought out farm investors and helped close
down their operations.[7]

Tiger-farming enthusiast Kirsten Conrad came up to ask me what
I knew about the summit's ban on discussing tiger farms. She said
she was not there on the Dragon's dime—thus claiming to have no
insider knowledge—but confided that the Dragon had been livid at
Keshav for his statement against tiger farming to the CITES Standing Committee. She claimed measures had been taken to make his
superiors shut him up. Something about panda loans to US zoos,
she said.

When I reentered the Great Hall, WWF's senior scientist Eric
Dinerstein called me over and hissed, "Why are you talking to *her?*"

"Know your enemy," I said. "Don't you want to know what's going
on with efforts to legalize tiger trade in China? Besides, Kirsten's a
nice person."

"China will *never* reopen tiger trade," he said. "Once wild tigers
start coming back in China, they will *not* want tigers to be farmed."

His naïveté astonished me. This man was a world-renowned tiger
biologist yet clueless in the ways of the Dragon.

When all was said and done, tiger farming was not spoken of once
during the pre-summit sessions. The closest anyone came was when
Charles North of the US Agency for International Development
mentioned in passing the role of the United States in securing the
2007 CITES decision against the practice. (Although he refrained
from using the f-word, the Dragon reportedly was furious.) TRAF-
FIC's Steve Broad dared a hint when he slipped in mention of the
necessity to "stop trade from any source."

(Sun Tzu: "The best victory is when the opponent surrenders of
its own accord before there are any actual hostilities.")

Dinner that evening at the Palace of Catherine the Great convinced
me that game-changing pronouncements for tigers were still in store.
Snow was falling as we walked through the iron gate and across the
brick courtyard toward the uniformed brass band that welcomed us
with oompah revelry. Inside, a chamber quartet greeted us at the top

of a wide marble staircase. We entered a gilded ballroom of mirrored walls and mural-covered ceilings, where a string orchestra was in full flight. We were handed champagne flutes that never emptied and served course after course of fresh Russian cuisine.

Vladimir Putin did not join us, but he made us feel as if we were guests of Catherine herself.

Tensions arose the next day when a committee charged with recommending urgent actions on the ground for wild tigers convened around a vast oblong table under still more chandeliers and gilding. Tiger-range countries were increasingly antsy about where the $350 million would come from to pay for their newly minted Global Tiger Recovery Program (GTRP).[8]

I had watched Keshav time and again draw in rapt audiences— from Wall Street financiers to conservation CEOs to government officials far above his pay grade—by implying that the World Bank would secure the necessary money. He never said the money would come from the World Bank, but many assumed it. That lure had engendered a lot of bad behavior en route to St. Petersburg by those who thought that a pot of gold with their names on it sat at the end of the GTRP rainbow. In reality, there was little if any World Bank money for tigers, unless a tiger country wanted to take out a loan—to be paid back with interest.

Bhutan said it was "confused" about where the money would come from. Malaysia underscored the necessity of "resource mobilization." Nepal asked for "more clarity" on the tiger trust fund long dangled as catnip by Keshav and his team. One after another, tiger-range countries more or less said, "Show us the money!"

Finally, Keshav intervened. "We have to put pressure on international institutions, including the World Bank, to create a multi-donor trust fund. Without serious money, we will not be able to implement the GTRP." But it was all good, he said, because tiger-range countries now had the heart, the unity, and a joint plan to save tigers. They now had what they needed to *raise* the money, he said.

After that, some delegates said they were "not authorized" to commit to anything beyond the written plan. The Dragon questioned whether conditions were "mature enough" to commit to actually implementing the plan. India's S. P. Yadav was bold enough to say he had expected to see cash on the summit table, "but my expectations were not met."

Ignoring the obvious frustrations, a smiling Keshav said the World Bank was "fully satisfied" with summit outcomes as they were.

I figured that Robert Zoellick would announce the pot of gold when—and if—he took the stage with Vladimir Putin and other world leaders the next day. Surely all this business about no money was a ploy to make the heads of state look like heroes.

The day of the summit unfolded inauspiciously with news that North Korea had bombed a South Korean island in the Yellow Sea, killing four people and sparking talk of impending war.[9] In St. Petersburg, a Chinese medical student had decapitated a fifty-nine-year-old Russian secretary at First Medical University and taken her head with him in a taxi.[10] These were some of the topics of chatter that morning among delegation heads in buses escorted by police motorcade out of St. Petersburg under falling snow toward the summit location.

The sky had cleared by the time our convoy arrived at the yellow and white Konstantinovsky Palace, which sits on 444 meticulously manicured acres overlooking the Gulf of Finland and was the site of the 2006 G8 summit. After lunch, elaborate security checks, and another short bus ride across the estate, we ascended marble stairs to an ornate, sky-blue room heavy with requisite gilding and crystal chandeliers. Videos of live tigers were projected on the wide crown molding above the stage, giving the impression that they were looking down on history being made on their behalf.

The stage was set with a line of white armchairs, with white end tables in between. The summit logo—appropriately a white human hand superimposed on a larger black tiger paw print—repeated itself on the podium and across the backdrop.

Prime Minister Putin and China's premier Wen Jiabao entered first and took the center seats. The prime ministers of Bangladesh,

Laos, and Nepal, the president of the World Bank, and the CEO of the Global Environment Facility took up their flanks.[11] Everyone wore some variation of a dark suit, except Nepal's leader, in traditional white pajamas with a black blazer and colorful wedge hat, and Bangladesh's prime minister, who chose a sari swirled with blues and greens.

After being struck from the speakers' list, Robert Zoellick ended up with the largest speaking role of all—summit moderator. Before introducing Putin, he talked of a "new business model" for bringing back wild tigers that expressed the "collective will" of tiger countries. He did not announce the multi-donor tiger trust fund long ballyhooed by Keshav and company, though he did say that he "would be pleased" to help establish one. *Am I the only one who thought that's what he'd been doing the past two years?*

Putin talked lyrically about the wild tiger's majesty and intrinsic value, calling its decline from one hundred thousand in the nineteenth century to three thousand in 2010 a "calamity in the history of our planet." He said that it was "our direct duty" to stop "mercilessly killing" tigers for "cruel amusement" and profit in a "selfish economy." He recounted with pride Russia's success in securing a dramatic comeback for its Siberian tiger in the late 1990s but made no mention of the recent resurgence in poaching.

Putin had recently banned harvest of Korean pine in the Russian Far East for the sake of the pine nuts that feed the wild boar that feed tigers, he said. "Everything is interrelated." He borrowed from Mahatma Gandhi ("The greatness of a nation and its moral progress can be judged by the way its animals are treated"), saying that "where tigers live well, everyone lives well," and confirming Russia's commitment to double the number of wild tigers by 2022. I was still poised for his announcement of vast new sums to make Tx2 a reality when he closed his remarks.

China's premier was up next. Wen Jiabao's delivery was less passionate than Putin's, but the fact that he was talking about tigers at all had China watchers like me parsing every dispassionate word. He said loss of wild tigers would be "disastrous" for tigers and people. *This sounds promising.* He said economic development should be "in harmony" with nature's diversity. *Harmony is a key Chinese concept, and heaven knows tiger farming isn't in harmony with anything natural except human greed.*

"We need to protect wild tigers and at the same time help local communities improve living standards," Wen continued. *Hmmm. That could be construed as a plug for tiger farming.* Finally, he said, "Every country should implement stronger laws and regulations and vigorously combat poaching, trade, and smuggling of tiger products." *He said trade. Not illegal trade. Trade without qualification.* It wasn't a promise to specifically close down tiger farms or a pledge of $350 million to save wild tigers, but it was significant.

During her turn at the podium, Bangladesh's prime minister, Sheikh Hasina, sent a jab in China's direction for "superstitious cures" that had "systematically killed" her country's tigers, but she made no sweeping promises to stop the killing. Remarks by the prime ministers of Nepal and Laos, GEF's CEO, and, in closing, Robert Zoellick, were aspirational but contained the same number of game-changing pledges: zero.

As the world leaders who had met for the first—and likely only—time in human history to discuss the needs of wild tigers exited the stage, I looked up at the ceiling tigers. They looked around, flicking their ears and blinking their eyes as if they too were wondering what it all meant.

I turned to the woman seated to my left and said, "That's it?"

Lixin Huang flashed a warm but sly smile and said, "There is a Chinese saying. 'We have an East wind; now we can make the boat move faster.'"

"What does *that* mean?" I said.

"When you don't have wind, you struggle," she said. "Now you have it. How do you take this opportunity?"

Translation: she also thought Wen Jiabao's use of "trade" without "illegal" was significant.

New money finally found its way to the summit that night at the ornate and heavily gilded Mikhailovsky Theatre, known for fine ballet and opera since it opened in 1833. Rock star Ilya Lagutenko cohosted his gala spectacle with supermodel Naomi Campbell, fiancée of a Russian oligarch, on a stage done up as the Broadway version of a forest temple. The tiger-lover had flown in Malaysia's "queen of rock" and the "godfather of Chinese rock" to perform. He had even learned enough Chinese to emcee and sing in Chinese, Russian, and English. Wen Jiabao did not attend, but Vladimir Putin was there.[12]

Once seated, we waited. Thirty minutes. Then an hour. Another thirty minutes. Even Putin waited. The audience grew restless. More than a few of us needed to use the loo, but we were afraid the KGB-looking theater staff wouldn't allow us back in.

At long last, there was a flurry of humanity at the main entry and in walked Leonardo DiCaprio in a dark suit and tie, with his signature combed-back hair. He slipped into a seat several rows from the front, across the aisle from Russia's prime minister.

When Putin leaped to the stage to open the show, he seemed starstruck. He called DiCaprio a "real man" because he had arrived despite his Delta Airlines flight having been interrupted by an emergency landing, after which he'd hired a private jet that had to make an unplanned stop in Finland when it ran low on fuel. "If tigers are in the hands of people with such character, we are doomed to success!" Putin declared to enthusiastic applause.

WWF International's CEO Jim Leape took the stage after Putin to announce that the actor had pledged $1 million for anti-poaching efforts.[13] DiCaprio reportedly had a net worth of $100 million, making his gift worth 1 percent of his wealth. Had the wealthiest tiger-range countries, Russia and China, given even .01 percent of their 2011 annual budgets, wild tigers would have been flush with protection through 2022 and beyond. But that did not happen.

I left the concert's after-party exhilarated by all the champagne, shots of vodka, caviar, and proximity to Putin and DiCaprio. But when I awoke the next morning, I thought of lone tigers padding through Asia's shrinking forests rigged with hidden wires set to ensnare a misplaced paw, while ragtag rangers patrolled for poachers without proper clothes and equipment, and their paltry paychecks sometimes arriving weeks late. How many tiger protectors could have been trained, outfitted, and paid adequately and on time *for years* with the dollars spent on just our dinner with the ghost of Catherine the Great?

If TRAFFIC's calculations were correct, more than 250 wild tigers may have died in the two years and five months that had passed since Harrison Ford stood beside Robert Zoellick to launch the Global Tiger Initiative (GTI).[14] Jockeying for GTI spoils had taken an incalculable toll on the unity of the tiger conservation community. And now this culminating moment may have missed its intended mark. The *Guardian*'s Jonathan Watts summarized the summit's outcomes best:

> Change remains possible. Tiger products have been removed from [China's] pharmacopeia of traditional medicine ingredients. Chinese officials are also discussing whether to impose a breeding ban on tiger farms as a step towards changing the way they are managed. This—along with the burning of existing stockpiles of carcasses and more undercover investigations by police—would send a clear signal that the tiger market is closed for business in China. But Premier Wen has not made that happen yet. Until he does, the political power of Putin and the conservation money from the World Bank will *not* just come to nothing. It will be helping to extend the longevity of the tiger traders.[15]

And, he might have added, ensuring that the King of the Jungle may have no future outside a feedlot.

10

INTERMISSION II

In the Valley of the Shadow

The knock at the penthouse door was insistent.

Go away.

I stayed under the bed covers cuddling my Jack Russell terrier-mix with two mongrel tabbies curled on either side of my feet.

More knocking. Louder. "Police. Please open the door."

Police?

I dragged myself up and opened the door. Two uniformed DC police officers searched my face to assess my state of mind. They said a friend of mine had called them "all the way from London" because she was worried I might harm myself.

"I'm fine," I said.

They wouldn't leave.

"Do you know who called us?"

"Yes," I said. "I'm sure it was Debbie Banks. I told her I wanted to die. But I promise you I'm *not* going to kill myself."

They still wouldn't leave.

It occurred to me that they might haul me off to a psych ward, so I straightened my posture, tried to smooth my bed head, and calmly reassured them. Yes, I'd had a really tough year. I'd lost both my parents, my marriage had broken down, and then I'd lost funding for the best job I'd ever had, leaving the world's favorite animal in the lurch. But I was too cowardly for suicide and, no, I had not considered methods for ending it all.

They left when I promised to call Debbie and tell her I was okay, which I did once I was back under the covers, safe from reality once again.

After the tiger summit, Debbie and I had stayed on an extra day to see more of snow-covered St. Petersburg. On what was Thanksgiving Day 2010 in the United States, she and I ate a quiet dinner with a bottle of wine in a sleek bistro down a slushy side street whose exteriors probably hadn't changed since Tolstoy had passed by. It was clear the International Tiger Coalition had lost its momentum and I had been sidelined, though Debbie tried to assure me we would bring it—and me—back, along with world attention to the Dragon's pernicious intentions.

The lowest point in my life came just before the planet swooned over Kate Middleton marrying Prince William, the Duke of Cambridge, on April 29, 2011. It was the first and only time offing myself felt like a soothing option. I was suffering from what mental health professionals call "complicated grief"—stuck in bereavement, unable to find a way back to life's meaning.[1] I call this heavy, hopeless time my Long March Through the Valley of the Shadow of Death.

Debbie and Grace tried to cheer me and updated me from time to time on tigers. The news, when I could bear to hear it, was grim.

In June 2011, *Time* reported that a TCM company named Longhui, a subsidiary of a Chinese arms manufacturer, had begun farming rhinos with 121 animals imported from South Africa. "Longhui aims to produce various rhino-horn products . . . and projects annual sales revenue of $60 million." It quoted Jia Qian, whom I hadn't heard of since he stood up at that 2007 tiger symposium in Kathmandu and proclaimed the utter nonsense that China needed to farm tigers to help arthritic SARS victims. In the article, he said that the Chinese government had banned the use of rhino horn "because some people were Western trained and tainted by Western thought. Other people were weak and gave in to foreign pressure."[2]

Meanwhile, it was as if the 2007 CITES decision against tiger farming had never happened. Tiger farms in Vietnam were laundering wild tigers smuggled in frozen from Laos, according to Doug Hendrie of Education for Nature–Vietnam.[3] Steve Galster reported that tiger farms in Thailand also were serving as Laundromats for wild tigers smuggled in via the back door and sold as farmed—and therefore legal—out the front. Debbie's team had found tiger skins for sale online in China, after which her e-mails informing the Dragon went unanswered.

On November 28, 2011, the World Bank held a meeting at its headquarters titled "One Year After the Tiger Summit—From Political Commitments to Action."[4] Keshav Varma remarked that "we can't be cute on this issue" of tiger trade, but he stopped there. Robert Zoellick mentioned that "demand for tigers and tiger products remains unacceptably high" but said nothing of the tiger farms that were stimulating that demand. Richard Damania, my partner in perpetrating what looked more and more like a crime, mentioned the "prestige consumption" that was continuing to make wild tigers worth vastly more dead than alive.

A few days later, an auction house in Beijing advertised more than four hundred bottles of tiger-bone wine on offer, with bids starting as high as $13,000 a case.[5] "I watched silently . . . , recalling that exactly one year earlier I had been listening to Prime Minister Wen Jiabao reaffirm his country's ban on such products at a global tiger summit in St. Petersburg," wrote the *Guardian*'s Jonathan Watts, who attended the auction. After a barrage of press coverage and public outrage, the Dragon stopped the auction at the last minute.[6]

Grace told me that auction houses in China were buying up pre-ban tiger-bone wine wherever they could find it. "They are now becoming collectibles," she said. "The same with rhino horns and carvings made from rhino horns. They are becoming a new asset class."

Right after Grace's comment, the *Wall Street Journal* ran a story about the phenomenon in January 2012. "With Chinese stocks falling, real-estate markets flat and bank deposits offering measly returns, Chinese investors have been looking for help in strange places," it read. "Besides traditional medicinal products, they are plowing money into art-based stock markets, homegrown liquors, mahogany furniture and jade, among other decidedly non-Western asset classes."[7] Banking—or at least speculating—on extinction.

Around that time, the Great Dane told me I must write this book. "For closure," he said. "And because you had an extraordinary front seat for all of it." He said I should call attention to the blood on our hands—his and mine, and those of our compatriots. "The ban wasn't the endgame," he said. "We all assumed it was. Everyone—including you and I—should be held to account."

And so I began to write.

11

SINO-US CAT FIGHT

Tiger meat for sale at 1-800-STEAKS.com?[1] *Not possible.* But there it was, under "exotic" offerings. Available pending approval by the US Department of Agriculture.

This cannot be happening. And if it is, it can't possibly be legal. Then again, a lot of what was legal regarding tigers in the United States didn't seem possible. Estimates put the number of US tigers between five thousand and twenty thousand—at least as many as in all the wilds of Asia, if not two, three, four times more—in a country that never had them in the wild. Nobody actually knew how many there were. If US laws allowed that many potentially man-eating pets to run around unaccounted for, then maybe they also permitted online sales of tiger tenderloin.

I rang Craig Hoover at the US Fish and Wildlife Service to find out. Craig had left his job as a federal wildlife inspector to join TRAF-FIC, where I delighted in working with him before he returned to the US government as a rising star in its CITES division.

"I can't believe my eyes," I said. "Did you know about this? Is it legal?"

"It's funny you should ask," Craig said. "I just got off the phone with Wan Ziming, who called from Beijing to ask the very same questions."

The Dragon was watching. Closely. Looking for evidence of America's hypocrisy as justification for legalizing tiger trade in China.

Craig confirmed that selling tiger meat, or any product even purported to come from a tiger, is illegal in the United States. Would Wan Ziming report that back to his bosses or take a screen shot and use it to argue that if the United States sells tiger commodities, then why shouldn't China?

"What about the thousands of undocumented tigers in this country?" I asked. "Doesn't that send the wrong message to China?"

Craig reeled off the standard American rationale, which goes something like this: "Yes, the United States may have as many tigers in private hands as China has in farms. But US law forbids sale of any tiger product, and we have no evidence that parts of US tigers enter international trade or in any way stimulate demand for products from wild tigers." *Never mind that we don't know how many US tigers there are, where they are, or what happens to them when they die.* If I were the Dragon, I would be shouting to the world: "Well, at least we know the whereabouts of *our* tigers."

"How do we know the bones and skins of US tigers don't enter trade?" I said.

"There's no evidence that happens," Craig said.

"Has any agency conducted undercover operations to confirm that?"

"No, because there's no evidence of illegal trade."

"But maybe there's not evidence because no one has looked for evidence."

Meanwhile, the Dragon continued to ask strategically chosen audiences, "Why should China reduce its captive tiger population when the United States isn't doing so?" More key people at CITES were echoing the question, including India's delegation.

Carole Baskin knows too much about America's tigers.[2] This became apparent one sunny Tampa day when she walked down the long dirt driveway from her Big Cat Rescue sanctuary and found its leopard-print mailbox filled with live snakes.

"Were they poisonous?" I asked.

"I don't know," she said. "I ran away screaming."

Another time, she opened the mailbox to an explosion of spiders. Then came the mail laced with white powder, which police later determined was cornstarch. "We don't get our mail in that box anymore," she said and laughed, which she often does, despite the fact that those who would silence her have gone as far as accusing her of murder.

I first corresponded with Carole when she asked if Big Cat Rescue could join the International Tiger Coalition. She came recommended by Adam Roberts, head of ITC member Born Free USA. "You may have read about her in *People* magazine," Adam said.[3] "She was falsely accused of murdering her husband and operates what is probably the finest sanctuary for tigers in the United States."

When I finally met Carole in person at the launch of the World Bank's tiger initiative in 2008, it was easy to see how people could mistake her for a femme fatale. But by the time I finally sat down with her in 2012 at the sanctuary, she had given up her bleached hair and realtor wear for flowing cat prints and granola sandals.

Big Cat Rescue sat amid fifty-five acres shaded by clusters of southern live oaks and palm trees edging a man-made lake only minutes from Tampa International Airport. It was home to 102 exotic cats, including thirteen tigers, contenting themselves in spacious, open-air enclosures, all with sun, shade, and an array of swings, tunnels, perches, pools, shelters, hiding spots, and new toys delivered at least once a week. They all loved catnip, anything sprayed with Obsession perfume, and any items they could "drown," Carole said. "Pumpkins, watermelons, cardboard boxes, and cardboard tubes are equally fun, as long as they can get them into a pool."

A bobcat brought Carole to tigers. She and former husband, Don Lewis, did well in Florida real estate, and they were at an auction in 1992 looking for llamas and goats to chow down on some overgrown property when a terrified bobcat on a leash appeared on stage. The man next to Carole began bidding. She asked him what he planned to do with a bobcat because she knew from rehabbing them at an animal rescue that they made vicious pets. "We're taxidermists," he said. "We'll just club him in the head and make him into a den decoration."

Carole started crying, and her husband started bidding. "We

probably paid more for that bobcat than anybody's ever paid for a bobcat in the history of bobcats," she said.

Bobcats are one-person animals, and Carole was this bobcat's person. Her husband wanted to be that person for another bobcat, which is how they ended up visiting a fur farm that had fifty-six bobcats and lynx. "Again I started crying, and Don says, 'How much do you want for every cat here?'" They agreed to overpay if the owners promised to stop killing cats.

The next year, they bought twenty-eight exotic cats from another fur farm under the same terms. Then twenty-two from a third. With help from Carole's father, mother, brother, and her daughter from a previous marriage, she and Don built a sanctuary. "It was like, 'If you build it, they will come,'" Carole said. Soon they were inundated with people asking them to take tigers, lions, cougars, leopards, lynx, and an array of other less common exotic cats.

One morning in 1997, Don kissed Carole good-bye and vanished. She fears he may have succumbed while pursuing his love of "treasure hunting" in dumpsters. In the ensuing years, she struggled to maintain what had become a $350,000-a-year operation on the $150,000-a-year allowance awarded by the court that froze their joint marital assets for six years before Don was declared dead.

In 2004, she married affable Howard Baskin, a lanky former banker. As we chatted on the screened-in patio of their streamside home not far from Big Cat Rescue, Howard told me that he'd known nothing of exotic cats before meeting Carole, but he loved turning around small businesses. "My initial focus was to make the woman I loved happy," he said.

The more Howard built up the sanctuary's donor base and bank account, the more time Carole had to look at the big picture of US tigers. And the more she nosed around, the more horrified she became. "When people first started coming to me with their tigers and lions, I thought this was unusual. Then I realized these big cats were everywhere—in backyards and basements and warehouses."

She learned that hundreds of tiger cubs were born each year for a commercial purpose that lasted only until they were twelve weeks old—cub petting. At shopping malls and county fairs across the country, people lined up to pay for playing and posing for photos with them. At the age of twelve weeks, they became too dangerous to be handled by the public, according to the US Department of Agriculture. Which meant the cub-petting industry needed a constant supply of infant tigers and to dispose of just as many retired toddlers.

Fortunately for the industry, the orphans still looked enough like oversized house cats to beguile buyers. "A year or two later, when the cubs have turned into five-hundred-pound tigers, their owners realize they can't handle them," Carole said. The next stop was too often a hell of small cages, chains, hunger, filth, and sometimes physical abuse. Well-meaning and not-so-benign tiger owners struggled to provide the amount of secured space, daily meat rations, and veterinary care needed to properly care for animals that grow to two to three times the weight and ten times the strength of a human, with teeth and claws like chef's knives.

Joan Byron-Marasek certainly meant well.[4] The former stage actress had lived quietly with her husband, Jan Marasek, for more than twenty years on their twelve wooded acres in Jackson Township, New Jersey, until state officials pounded at their door with a search warrant on January 29, 1999.[5] Two days before, police had shot a 431-pound tiger after it spent a day wandering through residential areas. Byron-Marasek said the big cat could not possibly have been one of the twenty-three tigers she was licensed to keep.[6] She continued her denial even after investigators found a hole in her fence with telltale tiger fur whose DNA matched the wandering cat's.[7]

According to the *New York Times*, Byron-Marasek left acting in 1976 after purchasing five eight-week-old tiger cubs and creating the Tigers Only Preservation Society. "It's a privilege, it's an honor, it's a God-given gift to be with these animals," she told reporter Joyce Wadler. "It's my mission to save these animals from extinction."

By 1999, she appeared to be in over her head, with seventeen adult tigers, five tiger cubs, and thirty large Anatolian shepherd dogs on her property. The tiger enclosures were thick with mud that smelled of urine and feces. The Maraseks reportedly fed the tigers rotting deer carcasses covered in flies and meat putrid from poor refrigeration. Patrick Thomas, curator of mammals for the Bronx Zoo, found the conditions "deplorable," calling her operation "the worst big-cat facility I have seen."

New Jersey officials first went to court to force Byron-Marasek to fortify her fencing.[8] When the state refused to renew her license to keep big cats, she went to court, where a judge ruled that her "unsanitary and rat-infested" facility should be closed.[9] Failed appeals went all the way to the New Jersey Supreme Court.[10] Finally, in 2003, a team of animal-welfare specialists packed up Byron-Marasek's tigers and transported them to the 102-acre Wild Animal Orphanage near San Antonio, Texas.[11]

"This is happening all over the country," Howard told me. There was the elderly Texas woman who died, leaving behind more than twenty orphaned tigers and cougars. Then there was the Mississippi contractor who had more than thirty tigers, cougars, and tiger-lion crossbreeds known as ligers. "The real estate crash hits, his construction business fails, and this guy moves seventy miles away to open a topless bar," Howard said. "He leaves his cats to starve."

The most infamous example occurred in October 2011 when Vietnam veteran Terry Thompson of Zanesville, Ohio, took his life after releasing his collection of fifty-six exotic animals, including eighteen tigers. Police gunned down all eighteen in the interest of public safety.[12]

"The day before Thompson shot himself, we got a call from a guy we think was him," Howard said.

"He was *very* upset," Carole said. "He was ratting out the rest of the industry saying, 'I hate what these people are doing.'"

People like Joe Schreibvogel, the wild man who ran the worst of the worst traveling cub-petting shows the Baskins ever encountered. Operating under at least eighteen different business names, Schreibvogel's crews would pull up in a semitruck at malls and fairs, set up a cluster of petting enclosures, and let long lines of people handle tiger cubs for hours. Videos show the cubs sick with projectile diarrhea, squealing in pain as their chafed, red bottoms are wiped for the umpteenth time. Sometimes the cubs became so sleep-deprived they would nod off while people repeatedly lifted and bounced them like human babies. In one video, a little girl asks if the cub is dead because it wouldn't wake up.[13] "Imagine how exhausted this cub has to be for it to be sound asleep while it's being dangled," Howard said.

Schreibvogel, who calls himself Joe Exotic, is a little bit country and a little bit Siegfried & Roy. He touts himself as "one of the world's leading experts in the care of big cats," despite being cited repeatedly for violations of the federal Animal Welfare Act.[14]

In 2009, Carole began tracking Schreibvogel's engagements and asking Big Cat Rescue supporters to share the inhumane facts of cub petting with parties booking his shows. Their protests generated torrents of e-mails and attracted a lot of media attention. Bookings were canceled. "The owners of hundreds of malls promised they would never have him back," Howard said. As the cancellations escalated, so did Schreibvogel's apparent hatred of Carole.

His Joe Exotic TV channel on YouTube broadcasts hour-long programs that feature an odd mix of his random ramblings, babes in bikinis, and rants about the Humane Society, the Global Federation of Animal Sanctuaries, *National Geographic*, and others opposed to his escapades. For a while, a frequent "guest" of the show was someone posing as a drunken Carole in skits such as "Carole Baskin: Sleeping with a Liger" and "Carole Baskin: Controlling the World."

In 2010, Howard received a call from an informant who said Schreibvogel had started using the name Big Cat Rescue Entertainment and a dead ringer for Big Cat Rescue's logo to market his cubpetting business. Soon Big Cat Rescue's phone began ringing with complaints about Carole's perceived hypocrisy. The Baskins sued Schreibvogel for trademark violations. He retaliated by suing them for defamation then tried to convince police that Carole had murdered her former husband.

In early 2013, the Baskins won a $1 million judgment in federal court against Schreibvogel for trademark and copyright violations.[15] They were doubtful he would ever pay, and Carole's daughter had nightmares about what he might do if he lost his tigers because of her mother. When CBS interviewed Schreibvogel after the Humane Society released a video of him punching tiger cubs in the face, he threatened a "small Waco" if anyone tried to shut him down.[16]

Even if Joe Exotic were forced to quit tigers, Carole believes there would still be many more than five thousand untracked tigers in private hands in the United States.

US tigers came as a surprise to me. They weren't even a blip on my radar until 2005, when the Dragon first brought them to my attention. But I was familiar with the US trade in tiger products, which had become an issue after the White House threatened trade sanctions against China.

Trade records showed China had exported more tiger products to the United States than any country besides Japan in 1991.[17] In 1996, a Chinese investigator for the Wildlife Conservation Society found "tiger-based" medicinal products "widely available" in New York City's Chinese medicine shops, grocery stores, and supermarkets.[18] From 1996 to 1997, TRAFFIC investigators found tiger products "common" in the Chinatowns of Atlanta, Los Angeles, New York, San Francisco, and Seattle.[19] This information prompted Congress to pass the Rhinoceros and Tiger Product Labeling Act of 1998, a federal law prohibiting import, export, and sale of products even *claiming* to contain tiger bone or rhino horn.[20]

The most compelling evidence of US tigers entering the black market surfaced in 1997 when an informant called US Fish and Wildlife Service special agent Tim Santel to report a group of people in the Midwest slaughtering tigers, leopards, and other big cats to sell their skins, meat, and body parts. An eighteen-month investigation amassed hundreds of recorded conversations and phone calls, eyewitness accounts, blood samples, shell casings, and a warehouse full of skins, bones, weapons, and stuffed tigers. Federal prosecutors charged one business and sixteen people in Arkansas, Florida, Illinois, Michigan, Missouri, and Oklahoma for crimes involving thirty-four tigers, eleven leopards, and one snow leopard. The defendants were animal exhibitors, taxidermists, collectors of hunting trophies, and an exotic-meat dealer. Eleven felony convictions resulted.[21]

It seemed to me that something more than Craig Hoover's reassurances was needed to prove US tigers weren't feeding demand for tiger parts and products. Which was why I used some of my budget at Save the Tiger Fund to contract TRAFFIC to investigate how many US tigers there were and what happened to them—and their body parts—when they died.

After a year of digging, TRAFFIC consultant Doug Williamson, a veteran of snooping around in the US bear trade, found no evidence of the skins or bones of US tigers entering international trade. However, he concluded that a confusion of laws with too many loopholes left "lax management" of US tigers that *could* provide a "drip-feed" of tiger parts to keep alive demand for the parts of wild tigers. He guesstimated that the United States was home to five thousand tigers.

Licensing and registration were inconsistent across jurisdictions and largely voluntary, making tracking of tiger births, whereabouts, and deaths impossible. Some deceased tigers were cremated. Burying them in pet cemeteries was prohibitively expensive, and burying them elsewhere was often prohibited. Perhaps hundreds died each year, yet no one could—or would—say what happened to their remains. Williamson found no evidence of tiger parts and products leaving the United States, but then no agency was on the lookout.[22] Just like bear gall bladders, tiger bones could be leaving the country for Asia in the luggage of anyone at any time.

A man with a Jersey accent called Big Cat Rescue in July 2011 to book a tour. With Carole. Alone. He didn't care how much it cost. Feeling uneasy, the staffer who took the call offered Howard instead. No, the man insisted, the tour had to be with Carole, and it had to be alone.

"I'm thinking this guy is an assassin," Carole said.

The man who flew down from New York City was in his sixties, long-legged, and slim, with tousled, graying-blond hair. Carole invited him into a golf cart and started the tour, stopping first at a female bobcat—one of the originals.

"I only want to see tigers," he said.

She set the brake and turned to look him in the eye. "Why are you here?"

He reached into his pocket and pulled out a list of names: Sultan, Sahib, Kismet, Bali, Burma, and three more. "I want to find these tigers."

He had last seen them fifteen years before. When they were cubs. Someone told him they were all dead. He wanted to know for sure.

Phil and his tall, slender wife, Kate, who asked that I not use their real names, had been working on Wall Street when they were invited in 1996 to see tiger cubs at the home of a friend's friend in New Jersey.[23]

"Have you ever been near a tiger or held a tiger in your arms?" Phil asked me when he and Kate recounted how they fell in love with eight infant tigers.

At first, the cubs nibbled at their Achilles tendons. As the cats grew, they graduated to knees. "We were charmed," Phil said. "Other than having house cats, we were completely devoid of anything to do with wildlife."

Phil and Kate drove down to see the cubs on weekends, stopping along the way to buy chicken, fresh straw, fencing—whatever their owner happened to need. The cubs were still somersaulting and cuddly when Phil and Kate left New York to take jobs in Hong Kong. They lost touch with the cubs' owner after a while. The last they heard, the eight had grown into a menagerie of twenty-four.

"Why so many?" I said.

"We didn't ask," Phil said. "And we don't know the cause of what happened in 1999." He wouldn't tell me the owner's name or what happened in 1999. All he would say was, "The tiger getting loose brought attention to it all." Then I knew the owner was the "Tiger Lady of Jackson Township"—Joan Byron-Marasek.

Someone Phil also would not name called him in June 2010 to tell him that the Wild Animal Orphanage (WAO), which had taken Byron-Marasek's tigers, had gone broke and that all of his beloved tigers were dead. Amid the ensuing scandal, legal wrangling, and scramble to find homes for WAO's 297 tigers, lions, cougars, bears, wolves, chimps, and baboons, no one would tell Phil the status of the former New Jersey cubs.[24] Which was why he sought out Carole. Painstaking research had led him to conclude that Big Cat Rescue was the top tiger sanctuary in the United States, so he was sure its founder could help him. Her response was more than he had hoped for.

"Carole immediately takes out her phone and calls WAO," Phil said. "They tell her some of the names on my list match the names of their cats. But she told me not to get too excited because a lot of tigers have Asian names."

Carole asked Phil if he had pictures of his tigers. Kate did. But they were taken when the tigers were cubs. "That's all right," Carole said. "The stripes on their heads are like fingerprints." And her daughter Jamie Veronica happened to be an expert at identifying them. Carole dispatched Jamie, with cub photos in hand, to Texas.

"We sat by the phone and waited for it to ring," Phil said. When it finally did, the news was good. Seven of the Byron-Marasek tigers were there. Six were among the eight Phil and Kate had known, though some had new names.

"Will you take them?" Phil asked Carole.

"We're full," she said, "and I don't want to be in the room if you ask Howard that question." Big Cat Rescue already had more than one hundred big cats to feed, not one free enclosure, and not one spare dollar to accommodate more.

"How much does it take to care for one tiger for a year?" Phil asked Howard.

"$10,000."

"If I pay to build new enclosures and take care of the $10,000 for each of them for the rest of their lives, will you take them?" Phil asked. Tigers live to be as old as twenty-five at Big Cat Rescue, which meant Phil and Kate would have to provide nearly $1 million, plus the costs of building new enclosures.

Howard agreed to take three. They would be siblings Amanda, Andre, and Arthur. "We picked the ones most in need for Carole,"

Phil said. "Andre had broken all four of his canines. Amanda had arthritis in her right rear leg." And they could not be separated from brother Arthur.

The other four went to a sanctuary in North Carolina that had ranked second in Phil's national analysis. It was also full, so Phil offered the same capital expansion and lifelong support. In all, he and Kate committed to ensure that the tiger cubs who had stolen their hearts could live out their old age playing, napping with full bellies, and receiving whatever medical care they might need—twilight years a lot of humans would envy.

In September 2011, after much hissing, roaring, and angry lunging, Amanda, Andre, and Arthur entered small black cages that were loaded into an air-conditioned trailer for the twenty-two-hour drive from Texas to Florida. They arrived in Tampa to five thousand square feet of adjoining open-air enclosures on prime lakeside property at Big Cat Rescue.

Under the generous shade of mature live oaks, there awaited houses for privacy, pools for hot days, grassy high points for surveying their new realm, logs to climb, a giant red ball, and enough space for jogging and playing tag. Amanda padded out of her travel cage and went straight to the pool for a drink. Andre exited and turned to lunge at the transport crew. Arthur leaped from cage to grass and immediately began exploring. Amanda hung onto her fear and anger for a while, but within hours the boys were contentedly rubbing against the wire fencing and each other.

"I thought that was pretty much the end of the project," Phil said. "That was the *beginning*. People say this rescue story is unbelievable. What's unbelievable is the captive-tiger problem in the United States."

"I just couldn't get the situation out of my mind," Phil said. And so he started talking about US tigers to anyone who would listen. "I felt like a Jehovah's Witness."

He hired a video production company to make short, high-quality spots on all the key issues "because people don't read." He showed them to New Jersey state senator Ray Lesniak, who said he would introduce a bill requiring registration and tracking of all privately owned tigers. Lesniak asked Phil to show his videos to nine other senators. When he did, "you could hear a pin drop," Phil said. In December 2011, the New Jersey Senate unanimously passed the bill.[25] Unfortunately, Governor Chris Christie vetoed it in August 2012, saying it should include other exotic pets besides tigers. And that's where things stalled.[26]

In the meantime, an attorney representing the foundation of *The Vampire Diaries* actor Ian Somerhalder called Carole. She wanted to know if anything could be done to help 550-pound Tony the Tiger, who had spent his life breathing diesel fumes in a cage next to a parking lot at a truck stop west of Baton Rouge, Louisiana.[27] Carole explained all that had been done over a decade—and was still being done—to try to free Tony from his roadside prison. "Actually," Carole said, "there's a much bigger problem we'd like your help on."

Carole described the whole out-of-control US tiger situation to the attorney. Somerhalder was interested in supporting a solution but only if it encouraged like-minded organizations to work together. Thus began the campaign to address "the big cat handling crisis" in America, led by a coalition of Big Cat Rescue, Born Free, the Humane Society, the Ian Somerhalder Foundation, the International Fund for Animal Welfare, and World Wildlife Fund.[28] Their proposed fix: end cub petting and ban private ownership and breeding of tigers and other big cats, with limited exemptions.

"There's no doubt in my mind that we're going to get this done," Carole told me. "It just makes sense. The time has come. And I don't think we can do anything about tigers in Asia until we solve this problem in the US."

"If we can get the law passed, then over the next twenty years, all the pet tigers will die out," Howard said, "Then, at last, we'll know for sure how many tigers are in America's backyards—zero."

If the United States were to ban private ownership of tigers, would China do the same? A we-will-if-you-will settlement between the two most powerful nations on earth may be the *only* way to force the Dragon's hand.

• • •

Phil and Kate told me their story at Big Cat Rescue on the eve of Thanksgiving 2012. While we were talking, Carole's daughter went shopping for fresh whole turkeys and large chunks of raw beef. Just before dusk, Howard walked us over to meet Carole, who arrived at the home of Amanda, Andre, and Arthur with a golf cart full of meat.

A keeper first tossed a turkey and a slab of beef over the fence to Andre, whose stripes draw distinct black check marks over each eye. He vectored in with his nose, grabbed the twenty-pound bird in his enormous fangless mouth and trotted off, like a house cat with a mouse, to lie in a patch of grass. He licked his prize all over before tearing off a wing and crunching it down, then a leg, then every bit of skin, meat and bone, all in under five minutes. He hurried back to make short work of several pounds of boneless beef. It was hard to tell whether Andre or Phil and Kate were more delighted.

"Astonishing!" Phil said.

"They *really* like their food," Kate said, not taking her eyes off Andre.

Arthur, distinguished by check marks over his eyes in the opposite direction of his brother's, took his feast in the same order—licking, tearing, crunching, and then chasing down the bird with beef.

Amanda, with butterfly-shaped markings above her eyes, jumped onto her back legs and roared as meat came flying her way. She then jealously dragged her prizes out of sight from her human audience.

"Amanda jumps for her food at every feeding," Phil said. "We think there may have been some periods of hunger."

As the day's light left us, Amanda was still enjoying her privacy. Her brothers carefully checked to make sure the other had not left a morsel uneaten, then they lay down in close proximity to carefully wash their faces with giant paws, licking each paw clean in turn.

It was too dark for anyone to see my tears of gratitude. I thanked Carole and Howard and Phil and Kate "for the cats," as Carole signs all of her correspondence.

12

HIDDEN IN PLAIN SIGHT

"We breed tigers. We also produce wines. There's a winery here. And we've started to create a hunting park," said chatty Zhu Yuqiang, who was likely in his forties, though his buzz-cut hair made him seem younger. On a blue-sky day in rural Hunan Province in South Central China, the entrepreneur smoked and smiled as he walked Ms. Yin, Mr. Yang, and their friend around the wooded grounds shared by Sanhong Biotechnology Company and Changsha Sanzhen Animal Artistic Specimens Company.[1] His visitors were in their thirties, well-dressed, and carrying iPhones—exactly the kind of city people he expected after they'd called for an appointment to see tiger products.

"Hunting is a high-class sport," Zhu said. "Even more so than golf. Many people have started to invest in this." He and his business partners had only just decided to add hunting to their offerings. "We will link these into a business chain"—hunting of captive tigers, processing tiger trophies for the "hunters," and selling an array of wildlife taxidermy to China's burgeoning luxury market. For the moment, though, tiger-bone wine was their focus.

A pack of guard dogs barked as the threesome strolled past a cement-block building locked behind a formidable metal fence topped with spirals of razor wire. The winery, Zhu said. Perhaps they could tour it during their next visit. The company's website showed pictures from inside—people in white lab coats fussing over bottles filled with amber, bronze, and reddish liquors. Sanhong's business plan for tiger-bone wine called for producing eight hundred thousand bottles a year, worth $160 million in revenues.

The trio of guests toured the taxidermy showroom featuring skins and stuffed tigers, ligers, Chinese pheasants, two pandas, a hippo, an Asian elephant, and a critically endangered Yangze crocodile. The pandas were selling for nearly $1 million, the tigers for around $300,000. The prices were the same whether the end product was a rug or the whole animal stuffed and mounted. An appraiser had valued the company's taxidermy stocks at more than $40 million. Zhu said someone from the Dragon's division of the State Forestry Administration told him, "If you can hold these things, hold them. They will increase in value in the future once there are less of these animals in the wild."

Just the government permit to transfer ownership of tiger skins costs more than $30,000, Zhu said. But the steep upfront costs are worthwhile. "Some rich businessmen who were born in the Year of the Tiger are willing to pay a fortune for a tiger skin," he said. "We choose our buyers carefully. We don't sell to just anyone."

Zhu tried to steer his guests' interest toward tiger-bone wine. Sanhong's sterile wine vats and fully automated bottling operation generated more than $325 million annually, half of which came from sales of its exclusive Quan Zhen Hu Jiu—Real Tiger Wine. He estimated the trademark's value alone at $16 million.

Sanhong had produced tiger-bone wine before the 1993 ban, Zhu said. The basis for its current production was a 2005 legal notification from the Dragon. Sanhong, like the Siberian Tiger Park near Harbin and the Xiongsen tiger and bear farm down south, had state permission for large-scale tiger-bone wine manufacturing, he said.

Zhu claimed that China's 1993 ban was "no problem" because Sanhong continued to "secure" its stockpile of tiger bones. Since the bones were steeping in wine, they weren't being sold per se. Nonetheless, none of the winemakers could advertise tiger bone as an ingredient. Not yet. There was a lot of international sensitivity, he said. Sanhong's tiger-bone wine business had had to be especially careful during the Beijing Olympics in 2008 and the 2010 Shanghai Expo.

"Now only two kinds of people drink our wine," Zhu said. "Government officials and rich businessmen." It was priced for exclusivity —from $300 to $1,600 a bottle. The most expensive was not only steeped with a tiger skeleton but enhanced with several ounces of ground tiger bone. He had distributors across China, he said. His distributor in eastern China was a buddy from his days in the People's Liberation Army. "In Beijing, we have a very powerful distributor," he said. "She wants to take over the whole North China market."

Ms. Yin and Mr. Yang repeatedly asked whether the making and selling of tiger-bone wine was legal. Zhu repeatedly reassured them it was, by permission from the State Forestry Administration. All was fine as long as "tiger bone" was not on the label and sales were restricted to exclusive circles.

"We and state forestry officials are very close," Zhu said. "If they want these wines, they just need to let us know. We send wines to all the ministries in Beijing before major holidays."

While Ms. Yin, Mr. Yang, and their friend were wrapping up undercover shopping forays in early 2013, the Skype icon on my Mac began jumping. It was a "Hiya" from Celtic warrior Debbie Banks.

ME: I was starting to worry you decided to stay in Scotland and give up tigers. Happy New Year!

DEBBIE: Got a bit of a bombshell.

ME: Okay, I'm strapped into my swivel chair.

DEBBIE: You know that Chinese pharmaceutical company's tiger-bone wine feasibility study we found online?

ME: You mean Sanhong Biotechnology Company?

DEBBIE: That's the one. Our investigators just met with an owner. It's not just a feasibility study. The company is in full-blown tiger-bone wine production.

ME: Do you have proof?

DEBBIE: Will do. The team's not out of the country yet.

ME: So what's the bottom line?

DEBBIE: There was never a ban! Sanhong, the Siberian Tiger Park, Xiongsen—they're all making tiger-bone wine. Because there's no bone *in* it—just skeletons steeped in wine—they get around the ban.

ME: So the ban was just smoke and mirrors.

DEBBIE: Pretty much. If anyone comes round to inspect, Sanhong can show they haven't technically sold any bones from their stockpiles. They just happen to store a lot of carcasses in vats of wine.

ME: Meanwhile, growing numbers of consumers in China are starting to use and then demand more tiger-bone wine. And the rich ones will want the best—made from the bones of wild tigers. But not necessarily to use. As an investment.

DEBBIE: That's right. They're banking on extinction.

A wise man named Bryan Christy, author of *The Lizard King: The True Crimes and Passions of the World's Greatest Reptile Smugglers*, once told me that expecting a bunch of conservationists to stop tiger trafficking was like expecting a bunch of botanists to stop the cocaine trade. We were *way* out of our depth. Basically living the parable of the blind men feeling the elephant, assuming the whole from the few confirmed facts we could get our hands on.

You might ask why so many experts and organizations committed to saving wild tigers stood by as the number of tigers on farms grew from a dozen in 1986 to six thousand by 2009. You may wonder why we didn't do more to intervene while the number was below one hundred in 1994 or when numbers climbed steeply at the dawn of the new millennium. Why hadn't we seen what was a straight-line progression toward domestication, commodification, and banking on extinction?

The New York Zoological Society, now known as the Wildlife Conservation Society, deserves credit for issuing a 1993 statement against tiger farming on the basis that (1) there was no evidence that legal trade in farmed tigers reduced illegal trade in wild tigers, (2) legal trade provided cover for illegal trade, (3) farmed tigers could not be turned into wild tigers, and (4) tiger farming's "only justification is as a business venture."[2]

There also was that one standout moment in 2007 when the fractious conservation community set aside its backstabbing jostle for funding and recognition to form an unprecedented alliance calling for an end to tiger farming. But for the most part we let tiger farming slide.

How the Dragon must have laughed as we missed what was hidden in plain sight. How I laugh at the memory of my belief that if I could just get the traditional Chinese community to disavow the use of tiger bones or the World (as represented by CITES) to disavow tiger farming or the World Bank to say it all made no economic sense, then wild tigers would be saved from catastrophic demand for their parts.

I missed clues as big as an army and as small as a word. I missed key connections between people, institutions, and geopolitics. I missed the underbelly of human nature at play.

I should have spent more time with Richard Harris, a friend from my long-ago days in Missoula. In his book *Wildlife Conservation in China*, he noted that "wild" in Chinese is associated with "unruliness" and "desolation." The concept of wildlife protection "rather than meaning protecting animals *in* the wild comes perilously close to meaning protecting animals *from* the wild," Rich wrote. So the tiger wasn't just "a drugstore capable of curing 100 ills," as described in a Chinese children's book he quoted, but a drugstore better off under human management.[3]

Mao Zedong sealed the deal on China's commitment to wildlife farming. "An economy without animal husbandry is an incomplete national economy," he said.[4] Work units were lauded for farming deer and other wild species to supply raw medicinal materials as early as the 1950s, when Mao also gave the People's Liberation Army (PLA) vital roles in the animal breeding and medicine manufacturing sectors.[5]

I had been too young to notice Premier Chou Enlai in 1972 giving delighted US First Lady Pat Nixon two pandas, the formidable embodiment of "soft power" that would be used by the Dragon decades later to quiet opposition to tiger farming.[6]

I didn't know that the PLA and China's Ministry of Public Health were uneasy with China signing on to CITES in 1981, seeing international trade controls as a threat to their pharmaceutical empire. The PLA was "implicated in protecting the smugglers of tiger bone and rhino horn," according to China scholars Michael Oksenberg and Elizabeth Economy.[7] One of the estimated twenty thousand companies owned by China's army until it was forced to divest in 1998 was Sanjiu Enterprise Group, China's largest manufacturer of traditional Chinese medicines.[8] In 2012, a PLA general was elected president of the Chinese Medical Association.[9] Around the same time, one of the Dragon's foreign consultants mentioned to me that she had seen "a lot of army types hanging around" the tiger farm near Harbin. And Zhou Weisen had repeatedly expressed gratitude for "technical cooperation" from the PLA's agriculture and animal husbandry university in developing his—China's largest—tiger farm.

I only belatedly realized that many members of the Dragon's staff had graduated from Northeast Forestry University, which was involved in developing China's first bear and tiger farms.[10] Confucian respect for teachers and allegiance to their teachings had been pillars of Chinese norms for centuries. The Dragon was likely made up of true believers seeking to protect wildlife *from* the wild and also duty-bound to carry out their mentors' dreams of turning tigers, rhinos, and bears into farm animals.

Perhaps most shocking of all, I missed the fact that my former employer had sent China the very tigers it used to start a tiger-farming industry. "You know WWF gave China those tigers, right?" Allan Thornton, head of the Environmental Investigation Agency's US office, asked me one day in late 2012.

"No way," I said.

"Ask George Schaller."

I didn't have to ask the iconic biologist/explorer. I only had to look at Appendix A of his 1993 book *The Last Panda*. In 1982, China was down to no more than two hundred wild tigers. The Dragon told George of plans to capture several of the country's last Siberian tigers for captive breeding. "To save the free-living tigers, the New York Zoological Society and WWF-Hong Kong coordinated a gift of eight tigers from United States zoos," George wrote. Eight Siberian tigers left US zoos for China in 1983. Three more followed in 1984. George would later regret helping when he realized these tigers were used to farm bones for medicine, further jeopardizing wild tigers.[11]

More importantly, I, like most of my peers, missed the ominous wording in China's wildlife protection law, which came into effect in 1989. In essence, the law gave the farming of tigers, rhinos, and bears top priority. "The state shall pursue a policy of . . . actively domesticating and breeding . . . wildlife, and rationally developing and utilizing wildlife resources. . . . Units and individuals that have made outstanding achievements in . . . the domestication and breeding of wildlife shall be awarded by the state," the law said—and still says as I write.[12] The 1993 State Council notification that most of the world had assumed banned tiger trade in China pertained only to tiger bone and did nothing to change the overriding national law that encouraged tiger farming and trade in tiger commodities.

"It is a *utilization* law," Grace told me in 2013. "It is *not* a protection law. The law is skewed, and the people who enforce it have become skewed."

While conservation A-listers rested easy in the perceived victory of China's 1993 ban, the Dragon had gone to work growing tiger farming from a start-up into an industry. No wonder the Dragon had been such a stickler over the years for only condemning *illegal* trade and *illegal* demand!

The Yin/Yang trio uncovered critical pieces of the puzzle. Once those pieces were snapped into place, the picture that was revealed was as shocking as it was obvious.

The team did not just randomly start shopping for tiger products in 2012. They found their marks on the State Forestry Administration's website. They followed an electronic trail to documents detailing a "wildlife utilization and marking system" launched in 2003. Under that scheme, 156 companies were permitted to "process" a category of protected species that included tigers. Within that group, six confirmed that they handled tiger products.

The Environmental Investigation Agency (EIA) had enough funding to investigate four. "These were businesses that were upfront and open," Debbie said. "They weren't shady operations down a back street." And every one involved a graduate of Northeast Forestry University. "They all had batch mates in the State Forestry Administration."

One business on the short list was Xiafeng Animal Specimen Factory, located in a city west of Shanghai. Owner Ning Gouqiang, a man of early middle age with squared wire-rim glasses and a crew cut, showed off a tiger in the freezer. In his office, he sat at a desk between a stuffed tiger and a table spread with a large, finely tanned tiger skin, complete with head, feet, tail, and a certificate from the Dragon stating: "This specimen is registered and can be traded within China."

"This was a female tiger," Ning told his guests. "Quite big for a female tiger. And also it is flawless." At first Ning said the tiger had died four months before, but the permit had been issued a year before. Then he said the tiger had come from one zoo, but the permit named another. He chafed as his guests pressed for the real story. "The certificate is here, you don't need to know more," he said. "It's like you ask a child trafficker, 'Who does the child belong to?'"

Ning said his company didn't buy skins from wild tigers but admitted to processing at least two for a government official. He claimed the Dragon had encouraged him to sell tiger skins because of the growing stockpile in farms and zoos.

The Dragon must have encouraged others too, given China's new taxidermy craze. "The market is booming and more and more people are buying taxidermy pieces to enrich their luxury art collections," Zhong Chunwei, co-owner of Beijing Northern Wildlife Taxidermy, was quoted as saying in the July 2012 issue of *NewsChina* magazine.

The number of registered taxidermy companies had risen dramatically, the Dragon's Wang Weisheng told the magazine. The first taxidermy championships were held in Beijing in March 2012. Wang Song from China's Academy of Sciences complained in the article that the fad had triggered a sharp increase in wildlife poaching and trafficking. "This has created a complete mess," he said.[13]

EIA investigators also found Beijing Longying Trading Ltd. through the State Forestry Administration website. Owner Yu Xiaojun boasted to Ms. Yin, Mr. Yang, and their friend that he had been a cofounder of the original Harbin tiger farm, helped arrange the infamous shipment of one hundred tigers from Thailand to the Hainan tiger farm, and was a schoolmate of the Dragon's Meng Xianlin at Northeast Forestry University. He claimed his business was licensed by the Dragon to breed tigers and process and sell tiger skins. Yu's goal was to one day have five hundred tigers, he said, because a "secret" 2005 State Forestry Administration notice announced that tiger farms with at least that many could sell bones.

EIA's team searched online and found mention of Notification 139, issued in 2005, as Yu had said, enabling "the pilot use of captive-bred tiger bone for medicine." After Debbie told me about it, I rooted around online for any tiger-bone winemakers with references to 2005, not expecting to find anything. Up popped Hengdaohezi Siberian Tiger Wine Company. Under a masthead featuring a wine bottle with a tiger logo, the text said the company began manufacturing "bone-strengthening wine" in 2005 with "resource advantages" from the nearby "Siberian tiger-breeding base"—the very farm I had visited in its infancy. Production capacity: nearly one million bottles per year.[14]

Lawyers in Beijing reviewed and confirmed what EIA had discovered. In essence, the Dragon had already started reopening tiger trade from farms by the time it announced to CITES in 2007 that China was "considering" lifting its 1993 ban and invited input on the decision.

The Dragon had ignored the entire twenty-year parade of threatened trade sanctions and UN-treaty dictates to shut down tiger trade and reduce demand for tiger products. In fact, the Dragon had done just the opposite. Even Premier Wen Jiabao's call at Vladimir Putin's tiger summit to end tiger trade had been ignored.

Suddenly everything the Dragon had done and said about tiger trade since 1993 looked and sounded different. What had at one time seemed to be awkward English became clever obfuscation. What had been taken for diplomatic rhetoric about China being *unable* to stop tiger farming became what it had actually been—declarations that the Dragon was *unwilling* to stop tiger farming. The world had been duped.

Of course, if I were the Dragon, I'd say, "You duped yourself. You saw and heard what you wanted to see and hear."

The pièce de résistance among the Yin/Yang discoveries was a 2009 article in the Chinese-language *Big Nature* magazine written by the Dragon's Wan Ziming. His subject: steps needed for China to once again use tiger bone as a commercial commodity.[15]

Wan wrote that the 2007 CITES decision against tiger farming could not be implemented because China's law mandated farming and use of endangered species. Furthermore, most of China's tiger farms were privately owned and licensed to legally speed-breed and "utilize" tigers. "If these industries do not violate the law, the government is not only unable to restrict their captive-breeding activities, it should actively consider advocating the use of captive-bred tigers," he wrote. *And indeed it is.*

Ignoring the fact that the mainstream TCM industry inside and outside China had repeatedly declared it no longer needed or wanted tiger bone, Wan argued that "tiger bone can help tens of millions of patients suffering from rheumatic pain." He offered China's control of legal ivory shipments from Africa as proof that tiger trade could be strictly regulated, though he failed to mention mounting evidence that China's illegal ivory market was triggering a renewed and escalating elephant slaughter in Africa and Asia.

Wan basically described every step of the Dragon's strategy we saw unfolding—and more. To reopen tiger trade, China must first "use diplomatic channels" to win advocates, especially among developing countries, he said. *Check*. China must actively participate in international forums about stopping *illegal* tiger trade, appearing "rational and restrained" but "fighting" for support of legal tiger trade. *Check*. China must enlist foreign and domestic "experts" and geopolitical support to overturn the 2007 CITES decision against tiger farming. *Check*. China must register its tiger farms under CITES, allowing them to sell tiger products internationally. *A goal apparently unchanged since 1992*. If CITES or any country sanctioned China for reopening domestic trade in farmed tiger products, the matter could be appealed in The Hague's International Court of Justice. *That is serious commitment to the commodification of tigers*. All the while, China must appear to be combating *illegal* tiger trade while continuing to mark and register farm stockpiles and setting up a "management system" for the "flow" of tiger bones from farm to factory to marketplace. *Check, check, check*.

Wan Ziming's manifesto explained why tiger farming was armtwisted off the agenda of Putin's 2010 summit. It also explained the answers I got when I asked World Wildlife Fund staff why they would not be taking issue with China's tiger farms at the 2013 CITES conference in Bangkok. "It's political," one said. "The message from our China office that's loud and clear is that tiger farming is *not* the issue," said another. *Verboten*.

I reread the 2010 TRAFFIC report that said all that needed to be said but remained unpublished.

> China is widely perceived as the destination for smuggling tiger products. . . . Even low levels of demand translate into a potential consumer base of millions of people. . . . New nontraditional types of consumption are growing. . . . This trade is centered on large and growing captive collections of tigers in China. . . . Farmed tigers are not acceptable because they perpetuate demand for tiger products, which runs contrary to international consensus to eliminate use. . . . Products from farmed animals are not perfect substitutes and lack the same status, thus perversely increasing demand for genuinely rare wild items.[16]

• • •

My Skype icon bounced again just before I packed for Bangkok. Debbie wanted to discuss strategy for releasing a report exposing the truth of the Dragon's deceit. She was drained from leading her international team of investigators and lawyers in triple-checking every detail. She was anxious about fire-breathing blowback.

> DEBBIE: This report will be about how China misled the international community. How it's in noncompliance with a United Nations treaty, warranting trade sanctions and global condemnation.
>
> ME: You have to get this out as soon as possible.
>
> DEBBIE: Should we go as far as saying, "We've all been duped"? That there never was a ban? That this is the biggest lie in the history of tiger conservation?
>
> ME: That *is* the story.
>
> DEBBIE: Let them try to deny it, in light of their official notifications, the taxidermists selling tiger skins with state-issued permits, and the manufacturing of tiger-bone wine.
>
> ME: This is one of the biggest geopolitical betrayals of all time.
>
> DEBBIE: Agree.

EIA's findings were released in a report entitled *Hidden in Plain Sight: China's Clandestine Tiger Trade* on February 26, 2013—five days before the CITES conference in Bangkok. "China Puts the 'Con' in Tiger Conservation" read the press release headline. "The stark contradiction between China's international posture supporting efforts to save the wild tiger and its inward-facing domestic policies, which stimulate demand and ultimately drive the poaching of wild tigers, represents one of the biggest cons ever perpetrated in the history of tiger conservation," Debbie was quoted as saying.[17]

"Report Reveals 'Secret' Tiger Trade in China," declared Australia's *ABC News.* "Species Under Threat as Ban on Sale of Body Parts Ignored," cried UK's *Daily Mirror.* "Tiger Bone Wine Trade Reveals China's Two-Faced Approach to Conservancy," accused *The Huffington Post.*[18]

The Dragon did not comment. At a Ministry of Foreign Affairs press conference in Beijing, a spokeswoman said only, "The Chinese government attaches great importance to the protection of endangered wildlife, including tigers."[19] No confirmation, no denial. *The Art of War.*

Then everything went strangely quiet.

13

THE EMPIRE STRIKES BACK

In the end, my promise to the Croc Farm Bear brought me full circle—back to Bangkok in 2013, some twenty years later. The sultry air in the city of ten million still carried that tantalizing mix of frangipani, stir-fry, and cacophony that first won my heart for Asia. There were more skyscrapers, but the golden temple spires still soared and canal boats still sold a profusion of fresh flowers and produce. The place was still teeming and alluring—a gridlock of candy-colored taxis, sooty concrete, ubiquitous massage parlors, and exuberant foliage. But the Croc Farm Bear was long dead, and every bit of progress I had championed in her honor seemed in jeopardy.

When she and I first met, some five thousand bears lived on farms in China. By 2013, that number was reportedly near twenty thousand, and neighboring countries had thousands more.[1] When I made my vow to her, China's single fledgling tiger farm had fewer than one hundred tigers. The last official admission said there were as many as six thousand tigers in an undisclosed number of farms. A new Chinese venture also had begun rhino farming, using more than one hundred African rhinos imported from South Africa as breeding stock.[2] Worse yet, there was an escalating bloodbath in Africa as poachers sought elephant ivory and rhino horn to sell into reawakened Asian markets.

Meanwhile, World Wildlife Fund (WWF), which had petitioned President Clinton in 1992 to punish China with economic sanctions for allowing domestic trade in tiger bone and rhino horn, had fallen all but mute. It had been joined in silence by other powerful organizations and governments once vehemently and vocally opposed to turning the King of the Jungle into a livestock commodity. The World (as represented by CITES) was beginning to feel a lot like the fictional town of Stepford, with precious few "wives" still speaking their minds.

The Bangkok CITES conference in March 2013 marked the treaty's fortieth anniversary. Its members now included 178 of Earth's 196 countries, and its international trade directives applied to nearly five thousand animal species and thirty thousand plant species.[3] Born in Washington, DC, in 1973 as a conservation treaty regulating trade, CITES was, in 2013, on the verge of becoming a *trade* treaty regulating conservation. That's what some CITES hands were saying. Yet another global force pivoting toward Asia.

At breakfast on the first morning, I read a *New York Times* feature about "white gold," the nickname Chinese speculators had given elephant ivory. "The Chinese hold the key to the elephant's future," African-elephant expert Iain Douglas-Hamilton was quoted as saying. "If things continue the way they are, many countries could lose their elephants altogether."[4] *And their wild tigers, rhinos, bears, and more.*

While registering at the Queen Surikit National Convention Center, I ran into one of Wang Weisheng's foreign advisors, who told me the Dragon had come prepared to "play hardball." The menu of priorities: reopen international trade in elephant ivory, rhino horn, and tiger products, while keeping trade in shark fin unregulated.

The pomp of the opening ceremony took place in a teak-paneled hall large enough to comfortably seat the meeting's estimated two thousand delegates and observers. The podium sat on an elevated stage set with life-size, white cutouts of a tiger, a rhino, and an elephant in a "forest" represented by a spring-green backdrop. "As if the treaty's flagships were already ghosts," I wrote in my notes.

We stood en masse for the arrival of Thailand's first female prime minister, Yingluck Shinawatra, while the national anthem played. In a prerecorded video address, Britain's Prince William welcomed us to the kingdom via Jumbotron. "What you decide in this room over the next two weeks could determine the fate of some of the world's most captivating species," he said. He spoke of the "shocking levels" of poaching of Africa's elephants and rhinos. "We must do more to combat this serious crime if we are to reverse the current alarming trends. If not, we could soon see some populations of these creatures—or even an entire species—disappear from the wild. We simply must not let this catastrophe unfold."[5]

Achim Steiner, eloquent head of the United Nations Environment Programme, took the podium to continue the drumbeat against the ongoing African slaughter. "The backdrop against which this meeting takes place should be a very serious wake-up call for all of us. Poached ivory is believed to be exchanged for money, weapons, and ammunition to support conflicts in the region." He called the crisis a "global crime."

"Illegal trade . . . increasingly involves organized crime syndicates and, in some cases, rebel militia" that threaten the stability of some African countries, said CITES Secretary-General John Scanlon in his Australian twang. "These criminals must be stopped."

Nothing about the demand driving it all.

What followed were two weeks of simultaneously interpreted, politely parliamentary nibbling around the edges of China eating the world. Great care was given to avoid mention of China, except in praise. The World (as represented by CITES) pivoted toward China, then bowed, and the Dragon seized the moment. The result was Orwellian absurdist theater that reminded me a lot of, well, Mao's China. During nine days of official proceedings, tiger farming would be mentioned just one time, and only in passing, during closing remarks. What was tacitly revealed about the Dragon's plans for tigers, however, was monumental.

• • •

Before the business of saving wildlife could begin, there was a skirmish over secret ballots. China and Japan wanted more of them, especially in decision-making about the ivory, fisheries, and timber they wanted to consume. The European Union wanted to limit secret voting. The procedural point was a tug-of-war between West and East, transparency and suppression, democracy and autocracy. China won the day, but only through a series of secret ballots.[6]

"China should be ashamed of itself," I overheard one CITES staffer say to another.

I felt obliged to act disappointed, but I was pleased. I'd ridden to the convention center in a tuk-tuk with a delegate from the Seychelles. "We need the secret ballot," he told me. "We want to vote for protections for sharks, but we have to abstain every time because our biggest donors are Japan and the European Union." I smiled knowing that secret ballots would allow little-guy nations to vote their conscience without fear of reprisals from their benefactors. I also smiled because the Dragon's behavior had sent chills up a lot of spines besides mine. (Sun Tzu: "One hundred victories in one hundred battles is *not* the most skillful.")

The protracted battle over secrecy delayed the business of wildlife by two days, nearly pushing tigers off the agenda entirely. I'd come to Bangkok certain that the new Environmental Investigation Agency findings would prompt a collective aha moment—and that the World (as represented by CITES) would rise up and set things right, at last.

I expected indignation and deep concern once CITES member countries grasped the fact that the Dragon never intended to comply with their 2007 decision against commodifying tigers. At the very least, I expected CITES members and formidable groups like WWF, TRAFFIC, and the Wildlife Conservation Society to publicly ask the Dragon to clarify whether China's laws did actually promote trade CITES sought to end. I truly thought EIA's report would be a game-changer. And I wasn't the only one. "Absolutely outstanding job," cat specialist and veteran tiger-trade investigator Kristin Nowell said in an e-mail about EIA's exposé. "I'm sorry I can't be there . . . to see the fallout."[7]

I figured many delegates hadn't found time to read EIA's findings in the avalanche of required reading before Bangkok. But I was sure that would change after EIA's lunchtime side event, which more than one hundred attendees squeezed into a small room to see and hear.

Debbie Banks let a video summary of the report do most of the talking.[8] It opened with hidden-camera footage of merchants in China showing off wine in tiger-shaped bottles, tiger skins, a tiger skull, and a tiger skeleton. Then it cut to a bloodied heap of tiger carcasses, limp without their bones, in a fridge at one of China's farms. Then to tigers pacing behind the iron bars of a farm's small cement cells. "The government of China has sent conflicting messages," a British actor's voice said. "They banned the use of tiger bone in medicine, but ever since they proactively encouraged the breeding and domestication of tigers."

A larger-than-life video Debbie, with a tiger-striped scarf swept around her neck, took over the narration. "We uncovered a system run by the State Forestry Administration of China that permits a legal trade in the skins of captive-bred tigers." More undercover footage showed Chinese traders offering to sell tigers skins with permits issued by State Forestry Administration and confirming the availability of tiger-bone wine—the latter a popular gift for winning favor from government officials, they said in Chinese with English subtitles. Then a cut to photos of an industrial bottling factory for tiger-bone wine tended by men and women in white coats.

The video ended with a young Indian woman named Shruti Suresh, a lawyer on Debbie's team, who said with penetrating, dark eyes, "Tigers continue to be poached for trade. Captive breeding and a *legal* trade in tiger parts is only worsening the situation for one of the most endangered species in the world. The international community *must* not accept any legal trade in tiger parts. A failure to act indicates implicit endorsement."

Real Debbie closed by underscoring the urgency to act. "Now is the time to send a very strong message from the international community calling for an end to the trade in tiger parts and products.

We're on a slippery slope. If we don't say something now—if we're all silent—then the assumption is that no one objects."

I wiped away tears, anticipating a standing ovation and calls for bold action or, at the very least, questions about EIA's findings. But after tepid applause, comments focused on US tigers, how easily tigers reproduce in captivity, and new seizures of tiger skins and bones in India and Nepal. None mentioned China.

My hope rebounded when I saw the flyer for a joint TRAFFIC/WWF press conference headlined "New Study Reveals Scale of Persistent Illegal Tiger Trade." I was sure they were going to validate or at least express concern about EIA's discoveries. I sat among the cameras, microphones, and scribbling reporters in the claustrophobic downstairs room reserved for press briefings, waiting for the moment.

Instead, TRAFFIC and WWF praised China for cracking down on online auction sites selling tiger products, then beat up on Thailand, Laos, and Vietnam for their tiny tiger farms. No mention of China farming some six thousand tigers or the government-licensed tiger-skin trade and rebooted tiger-bone wine manufacturing. "We're not saying any country is the villain," TRAFFIC's Steve Broad said.

I felt a bit saner the next day when Kristin Nowell e-mailed Debbie, copying key TRAFFIC and WWF colleagues: "Your investigation results are shocking and dismaying." Either China's permit system "is being widely abused . . . or the labeling and licensing system is being administered in an unaccountable fashion that would, in fact, appear to contravene China's laws."[9]

Kristin had come to the logical conclusion. She, however, was not with us in Stepford.

Stepford house rules remained in effect at a weekend meeting of the thirteen tiger-range countries called by the World Bank's loquacious Keshav Varma.

Several months earlier, Keshav had reportedly said he was fed up with being "lied to" and "blocked" by China's State Forestry Administration on tiger farming and had offered, on the floor of the 2012 CITES Standing Committee meeting, to provide $100,000 for a full assessment of the tiger-farming industry and its impact on wild tigers. Afterward, the Dragon was all over him "like flies on meat," said Debbie, who had witnessed the swarm. The Dragon later warned the World Bank against a repeat performance in Bangkok, according to one of Wang Weisheng's foreign advisors. Indeed, when Keshav's team arrived in Bangkok, they said they had come with a strict "listening brief."

Representatives of tiger countries and observers from the pro- and anti-farming camps filled every chair in the conference-center boardroom. Tiger-farm promoter Wang Weisheng sat next to wild-tiger champion S. P. Yadav, deputy inspector general of India's National Tiger Conservation Authority. Keshav presided like a Hindu master lecturing junior acolytes.

"I want you to tell us what's *really* happening on the ground—not just what is being planned," he said before calling on tiger-range countries in alphabetical order to report progress in implementing the Global Tiger Recovery Program. "Please, tell us what is going on with poaching."

One by one, presenters said precious little about whether tiger poaching and trafficking were up or down.

When it was China's turn, Wang Weisheng talked generically of "frontline action in the wild and in markets," the continued "rewilding" of that handful of South China tigers still in South Africa, and some $10 million earmarked for new tiger reserves and more—all for China's fewer than fifty remaining wild tigers. No mention of tiger farms.

Keshav intervened. There are two special issues "worth touching on" in China, he said.

I'm sure I wasn't alone in tensing for what came next. *Say "tiger farms"!*

"Rewilding and illegal trade and demand," Keshav said.

Illegal! What about legal?

"Reintroduction of the South China tiger is very difficult," Wang said. The plan was still to fly the "rewilded" ones home from South Africa, "but we need more research." *These tigers have been in South Africa for ten years. They might die of old age before they get a chance to fend for themselves in South China's shredded forests!*

As for trade, Wang said, "It is our firm position to fight illegal trade in tiger products." No one asked about legal trade.

The most surreal part of the day came after Vietnam's spokeswoman finished her presentation. "Captive breeding of tigers is a big issue," Keshav said. He wanted to know how Vietnam ensured that its captive tigers didn't enter trade or serve as laundering facilities for wild tigers. She said her country had only five facilities breeding tigers, including zoos, with less than ninety tigers, which were "not for commercial purposes."

"We should make sure these tigers are only for research and not for making wine and such," Keshav told Vietnam.

The charade was too much for Doug Hendrie of Education for Nature-Vietnam, who said in his deep American voice as he left the room, "Why isn't anyone here saying what's really going on?"

Time and again, Thailand and Vietnam took public blows more deserved by China. Thailand for elephant ivory, Vietnam for rhino horn. Not that they weren't guilty. They just weren't anywhere near *as* guilty.

Reports on ivory read like a crime novel.[10] In early 2012, heavily armed men invaded a park in northern Cameroon and slaughtered nearly three hundred elephants for their tusks. Afterward, the government sent in 150 soldiers to support park rangers. Two months later, poacher marksmen took out twenty-two elephants from a helicopter. In the fall, elephant poachers shot dead six park rangers during their morning prayers in one of Chad's national parks. Some of Africa's most notorious armed insurgents, including the Lord's Resistance Army, were poaching ivory to sell or barter for weapons and ammunition. Huge hauls of ivory had been stolen from government stockpiles. Military personnel were implicated in some countries. Between 2009 and 2011, law enforcement seized thirty-four large-scale illegal ivory shipments totaling sixty-one tons—a scale only transnational organized crime could move.

"Current levels of illegal killing of African elephants for their ivory may drive certain African elephant populations to extinction," the CITES Secretariat concluded.

Privately, no one disputed that China's out-of-control ivory market was the main driver of the ongoing slaughter of up to thirty thousand elephants a year. Undercover market surveys by the International Fund for Animal Welfare found "widespread abuse" of China's ivory control system and "large amounts of illegal ivory . . . for sale in shops, factories, and online."[11]

Profits from selling illegal ivory to China were providing "an un-traceable form of revenue funding extremist organizations such as Al-Shabaab, both in East Africa and potentially against the United States," Ian Sanders, founder of the Tsavo Trust, had told a US con-gressional hearing in November 2012. This prospect led him to ask, "Does this mean China . . . is potentially indirectly helping to fund international terrorism?"[12] Six months after the Bangkok CITES meeting, Al-Shabaab would take responsibility for a deadly attack on a Nairobi shopping mall, and NPR's Eleanor Beardsley would report that the group "is said to get nearly half its funding from the illegal ivory trade."[13]

But at the CITES conference in Bangkok, only Thailand was taking the heat on ivory trade. And, my sources told me, the Dragon was smiling. That was until day five.

For the first time ever, the rise in elephant poaching had been ex-amined in relation to household spending.[14] Julian Blanc, the Span-iard in charge of the CITES program tracking elephant deaths, told delegates that the new analysis had found that China was the only country where increases in household spending "strongly related" to upswings in elephant poaching. "This relationship only exists for China," Blanc said.

Kenya requested the floor. "The country identified is China, and the correlation needs to be taken seriously," said an impassioned Patrick Ormondi of the Kenya Wildlife Service. "We *must* reduce demand. If that happens, our law enforcement can work."

The Dragon's Wan Ziming countered by saying, in his heavy nasal voice, China was "very concerned" about the illegal killing of elephants, "but we would encourage elephant-range states to increase law enforcement to stop the supply of illegal ivory."

This was the standard merry-go-round between wildlife range and consuming countries: "Our people wouldn't buy it if your people didn't offer it for sale" versus "Our people wouldn't sell it if your people didn't offer a relative fortune to buy it."

The Democratic Republic of Congo said the issue had gone "beyond the control of law enforcement and armies. We are not dealing with mere poaching. We are dealing with international organized crime, and that needs an international response."

Chad said its elephants had been "decimated" to meet Asian demand. "We must find a way of getting these consumer countries to ban importation of ivory."

Then came a second blow for China, from TRAFFIC's Tom Milliken, who presented the latest findings from the CITES Elephant Ivory Trade Information System—ETIS.[15] I had not agreed with Tom's support for the one-off legal sales of African ivory to Japan and later to China, which stimulated this new round of elephant slaughter, but my respect for him shot up after what came next in Bangkok.

"Over the last three years, the Chinese market has been more heavily implicated in illicit trade in ivory than any other country," Tom's report concluded. "Since 2002, ETIS has identified the Chinese market as the key driver behind illicit trade in ivory." While China and Thailand were the two largest end-use markets, "China's illegal ivory trade has been about two-and-a-half times greater than Thailand's." Yet "kingpins" in China were not being arrested, he said. Forensic evidence wasn't even being collected.

The United States asked for the floor. In 1993, it might have demanded sanctions over such evidence. In 2013, it expressed "alarm."

The chair recognized a seething Wan Ziming. He noted that illegal ivory trade was a problem in many markets and said it was "regrettable that only some Asian countries" were identified in the ETIS report. He likened ivory trade to drug trafficking and said it was not fair or realistic to expect a country to be able to stop it. *Even an authoritarian state that stopped panda trafficking with the death penalty?* Furthermore, he said, "slandering and blaming" a particular country "is not helpful to international cooperation."

I walked up to Tom afterward to compliment his bravery. "Courage is a rare commodity these days," I said. "In fact, it seems close to extinction at CITES."

"Well, it was the truth," Tom said, "and I'm not afraid to say it."

"I'm just surprised you were *allowed* to say it," I said.

"Who's going to stop me?" he said.

On the last day of the conference, Tom waved me over. "You wanted to know when the Empire would strike back?" he said. "Well, it did." Thanks to the Dragon's behind-the-scenes maneuvering, Tom would no longer be presenting ETIS findings at CITES conferences.

That night, gunmen in Chad slaughtered more than eighty-five elephants. At least thirty were pregnant.

Vietnam served as chief scapegoat for the massive killing of African rhinos for their horns. Again, it wasn't that Vietnam was innocent. But it was not likely guilty at the same game-changing scale as China.

China had at least 1.5 million millionaires and a per capita GDP more than three times greater than Vietnam's.[16] The number of rhino-horn artifacts sold at auction in China had increased by more than 90 percent from 2010 to 2011, with an average price of $117,582 per piece.[17] According to the *Shanghai Daily*, local customs officials reported that seizures of smuggled wildlife contraband, including rhino horn, had doubled from 2011 to 2012.[18]

As with ivory, the facts of escalating rhino-horn trade read like an airport paperback. Poaching of African rhinos had risen from 13 animals in 2007 to more than 450 in 2012. An estimated 4,063 rhino horns left Africa illegally between 2009 and 2012. More than 100 horns had been stolen from Europe's museums and private collections. Or-

ganized criminal syndicates were in deep.[19] "Thai prostitutes, Irish
gangsters, Vietnamese diplomats, Chinese scientists . . . and recently an American rodeo star" were involved, according to the *New
York Times*.[20] Meanwhile, wild rhinos had round-the-clock guards.
When I visited Botswana in 2012, a reserve manager implored me
and other guests not to post our rhino pictures on Facebook for fear
poachers would discover the animals' whereabouts. Eight months
after the Bangkok CITES meeting, the Western black rhino would
be declared extinct.[21]

The Dragon was pleased as spiked punch that Vietnam was taking the heat, an inside source told me. "You have a mouse and an
elephant," a member of the African Rhino Specialist Group said
when I mentioned the inequity. "It's easier to step on the mouse." A
colleague advising Vietnam's delegation told me they were as angry as
the Dragon was chuffed—especially after they found out the Dragon
was brokering a deal to buy up South Africa's rhino-horn stockpiles.

South Africa made no secret of wanting to lift the ban on rhino-
horn trade. Its delegation hosted what amounted to a three-part sales
seminar over two catered lunches and a soirée pairing South African
wines and dim sum. The tone reminded me of 2007 when the Dragon
had "welcomed" input on whether to lift China's 1993 ban on tiger
trade. South Africa's rhetoric welcomed discourse too, but dissenting
opinions were brushed aside or met with hostility.

The rhino sellers' talking points also rang familiar:

"Bans don't work."

"We need to look at new strategies."

"This is a matter of national sovereignty."

"We're tired of Western ways of telling people what's good for
them."

It was Dragon consultant Hank Jenkins's signature spin. Through
it all, he sat at the back of every room, arms crossed over belly, oozing
self-satisfaction.

South Africa's sales team included government biologists, econo-

mists, a parliamentarian, a spokeswoman for the Professional Hunters Association, and a private rhino owner with a store of horns worth
a fortune. Their rhino-seller-in-chief was South Africa's minister of
water and environmental affairs, Edna Molewa, a stout black African
who projected her precise English like a Broadway diva. She spoke of
her country "bleeding" because of the "scourge" of rhino poaching.
"Criminals have started to steal our national heritage," she said. "We
need to put supply-and-demand concepts into the rhino space." And
in a bow to the Dragon: "Our policy is not to bash other countries.
Our policy is to engage them." *And whet more than a billion appetites
for rhino horn.*

Ron Orenstein of Humane Society International raised the issue
of the 121 rhinos from South Africa being used in China to start
rhino farming there. "What if rhino farming in China is stimulating
demand that would increase the poaching of South Africa's rhinos?"
he asked.

"It is our understanding from China that this was not the purpose," an official on Molewa's team said of the new rhino-farming
enterprise. "If it is, we will address it with China."

"Did they not read about the farm in *Time* magazine?" I wrote in
my notes. The 2011 article reported that the Dragon's Lu Xiaoping
had stood up at the 2010 CITES conference in Qatar and strongly
denied that China had plans to farm rhinos for their horns and to
rescind its 1993 ban to allow trade in those horns. Lu, the story said,
"now denies having said in Qatar that China had no intention of
farming rhinos for their horn and refuses to speak further on the
subject."[22]

Pelham Jones, head of South Africa's Private Rhino Owners Association (PROA), flew in with his wife just for the evening sales
event. The wiry businessman bounded to the stage to lament the current "poaching tsunami." He and his fellow private rhino owners, who
owned some five thousand rhinos on two hundred reserves, didn't
favor selling rhino horns for the money, he said. Rather, they favored
lifting the ban to protect "the world's natural heritage." He wanted
to stop *illegal* demand by "collapsing" *illegal* trade. He likened it to

the United States undercutting bootleggers by lifting Prohibition. He skipped the fact that there was a limitless supply of alcohol and only some twenty thousand wild rhinos in South Africa.

Tall, dignified Mavuso Msimang, the South African government's "rhino issue" manager, used charts and graphs to explain "rhinonomics" as if it were a science. Missing from his equations were market size (potentially over one billion), consumer preference for wild rhinos, and the wealthy Chinese investors banking on extinction.

"Some people might find this in poor taste, but we have to be realistic," Minister Molewa said in closing the presentations. She said that South Africa had identified a "trading partner" to buy its rhino horns should CITES grant permission at its next conference in 2016. There it was. The plan was to ask CITES to allow "limited" trade. Just like the "limited" trade in elephant ivory that had sparked insatiable demand in China.

"I'm not convinced," whispered Tanzanian Pratik Patel of African Wildlife Trust, who sat next to me during the evening presentation. He said that the South Africans had not consulted Tanzania on this approach that had implications in his country and others throughout the rhino's African range.

"I am confused and *desperately* unconvinced," Born Free CEO Will Travers said in his Queen's English during the evening question-and-answer session. "The only people who will be happy to hear what was said tonight will be poachers. Demand will grow, and poaching will undercut you at every turn. This is a huge risk you are contemplating unleashing on yourself and your neighboring countries."

South African MP Johnny de Lange flushed red and shouted back from the podium. "Crime syndicates thrive on prohibitions!"

"We may be on slippery ground," said a dispassionate Carlos Drews of WWF International. "We cannot totally anticipate what this might unleash, so WWF is not in a position to endorse what you are proposing."

Hank Jenkins finally stood up from his seat in the back of the room to make a comment. "You are now embarking on a bold venture," he said, speaking to South Africa's delegation like an Aussie life coach. "And you are brave to try new directions."

"It won't end with rhinos," warned Rishja Cota-Larson, founder of California-based Annamiticus. "They're coming for your lions too." She was right. Reports of lion-bone trade to China were way up.

In her evening farewell, Minister Molewa said, "We have not quite made a solid decision. We're trying to hear your thoughts and pick your minds."

The next morning, South Africa called a press conference at which Molewa again alluded to reopening rhino-horn trade. Some-one was creating demand for rhino horn, she said. However, there was "no linkage" between the legal shipments of African ivory to China and the current mass poaching of elephants, she said, con-tradicting the mountain of evidence presented to the contrary. Then she announced that South Africa would soon sign a memorandum of understanding on rhinos with China.

"The law of supply and demand best applies to normal goods," a Kenyan delegate commented from the audience. "Rhino horn isn't a normal good. I'm not sure if you have included this anomaly in your 'rhinonomics.'"

"The crime syndicates are popping champagne," Allan Thornton of EIA told Molewa.

South African economist Michael 't Sas-Rolfes reminded me of Prince William, though he was more than a decade older than the royal. He was a likeable guy, except for his adamant support for farm-ing and commodifying tigers, rhinos, and bears.

"Michael, I really want to understand your thinking," I told him as we settled in for lunch in a far corner of the conference center's noisy canteen. "I finally understand that China's laws never stopped mandating the farming and use of tigers, rhinos, and bears, so ex-plain to me how you think this will not lead to disaster in the wild."

"If you limit supply of a commodity and demand remains the same, then the price will go up," he said. Higher prices will entice suppliers. "CITES is good at limiting supply but not so good at limit-ing demand."

I agreed. Too many people thought CITES trade bans would be

automatically enforced and obeyed. And they were, to a surprising extent, for tigers, rhinos, and elephants—for a while. As a result, demand dropped and so did poaching, and wild populations began to recover. When China announced its domestic ban on trade in tiger bone and rhino horn in 1993, few imagined the Dragon would go full-speed ahead with farming tigers and eventually rhinos or that one day there would be astronomically wealthy Chinese investors banking on extinction. None of us dreamed the Dragon would purposely stimulate demand.

That was "a big cultural disconnect," Michael said. While CITES restricted supplies to save species in the wild, the Dragon went about producing more supplies in captivity to save *consumption*.

"That wouldn't be so bad if products from the wild weren't considered better," I said. "Bear farms have long produced enough bile to more than meet demand in China, perhaps even worldwide. Farmed bile is dirt cheap and easy to buy, yet poaching of wild bears for their gall bladders continues."

"The jury is still out on the effect farmed bear bile has on the market," Michael admitted. *On which planet?*

Michael argued that supplying demand with limited, controlled shipments of rhino horns from Africa and a bit of horn from rhino farms would satisfy China's appetite and allow Africa to keep the free-ranging rhinos on which its safari industry depended.

I recalled the words of Sean Willmore, who worked as a forest ranger in Tanzania. "People say you could kill every elephant in Africa and still not meet China's demand," he said. "In fact, poachers have told me legal markets help them."

I asked Michael if he or the Dragon had done any professional surveys to estimate the potential consumer base in China. "Do you know with any certainty how large the demand might be for tiger bone or rhino horn?" I said.

No, he said. He was convinced that demand could be limited to "strictly controlled medical use." At the same time, he acknowledged that wealthy Chinese investors were indeed buying up rhino horn, ivory, and tiger products as "tangible commodities." He called rhino horn "an analogue to gold" and tiger-bone wine "the Johnny Walker

Blue of TCM." Then he said, "If it's a mass market, all the rhinos will be gone. The only rhinos will be on farms."

"Exactly," I said.

"'Eaten by China' has long been a more famous saying than 'Made in China'" among wildlife conservationists. This is how Grace opened the blog entry she posted from Bangkok on China's Sina Weibo social-networking site, which had 368 million users at the time.[23]

Despite a new warning from the Dragon that she should "be careful," Grace was too distraught by what she saw unfolding to hold her tongue. She had come to Bangkok knowing CITES delegates would blame China for the elephant slaughter, she wrote. Market surveys confirmed that blame was deserved. But trade endangering wild tigers, rhinos, sharks, pangolins, and more was all "linked to demand from Chinese people." According to Kenya's government, "Every year 95 percent of those caught smuggling ivory out of Nairobi Airport are Chinese," she wrote. She confessed that, as a Chinese, she felt shame but also indignation:

> We have [Chinese] officials disregarding China's international role and image, turning a blind eye to wildlife in crisis, and finding all sorts of pretexts to shirk their responsibilities. . . . It is a handful of Chinese people . . . who have brought such disgrace and blame, but it is the country that must foot the bill. . . . Rejecting the consumption of wildlife is a matter for every Chinese person. . . . Our 5,000 years of civilization are brimming with knowledge and ethics on how to coexist with nature.

"I saw your blog," someone from the Dragon's team told her just before I found her.

"I don't care," she told me, with tears in her eyes. She had endured years of persecution and deprivation during the Cultural Revolution without a tear. What she saw her beloved homeland doing to wild nature was now breaking her heart.

•   •   •

Meng Xianlin, head of China's CITES office, sat alone finishing a blueberry muffin in the convention center's Starbucks when I walked up to his table for two.

"Hello, Dr. Meng," I said, with my best smile. "How are you?"

He didn't ask me to sit but didn't motion me away with a flapping hand as Wang Weisheng always did. He stood and asked me how I had been. I mentally noted the gray in his receding hair and the windbreaker that had replaced his signature bomber jacket. I told him I wanted to understand China's wildlife law. I hadn't understood before that the law never stopped encouraging domestication and use of wildlife, I said.

"Maybe the law will change," Meng said. Just before he had departed Beijing for Bangkok, the office of China's new president, Xi Jinping, had contacted his office seeking comment on a proposal from the Chinese People's Political Consultative Conference to remove the law's mandate to farm and consume wildlife.

That such a proposal had gone to the president's office for consideration was huge. That the president's office sought guidance from the Dragon probably meant it was DOA.

I told Meng I understood China was negotiating a deal to buy South Africa's rhino horn.

Meng said China's 1993 ban on trade in rhino horn and tiger bone remained in effect. *Standard Dragon dodge.*

"Yes, but China nonetheless has been negotiating to buy all of South Africa's rhino horn stocks," I said. "How would that work under the ban?"

Meng repeated that the 1993 ban remained in effect.

"I guess that means the ban would have to be lifted if China and South Africa get permission from CITES to trade rhino horn," I said.

Meng changed the subject to sharks and how China would never be able to control the trade in shark fins if sharks were listed on CITES. Then he excused himself.

I could hardly wait to tell Grace and Debbie that President Xi's office had received the Chinese-led proposal to eliminate the consumption mandate from China's wildlife law. But as I recounted my conversation with Meng, I suddenly understood the significance of all he'd said. "Oh my God," I said. "China wouldn't be making a bid to buy South Africa's unless it intended to lift the 1993 ban." The ban covered rhino horn *and* tiger bone. The Dragon would use South Africa's request for trade in rhino horn to convince the State Council that the ban should be lifted. "They're going for a twofer!"

Tigers nearly fell off the Bangkok agenda altogether. The discussion of Asian big cats was postponed again and again—into the second week of the conference, the final days, the final hours, and then, at last, the final minutes of an overtime session.

I was incredulous. China was production-farming tigers *and* licensing commercial trade in tiger skins and tiger-bone wine manufacturing. The handwriting was scrawled in giant Chinese characters across the wall, and the World that had said "no" to tiger farming in 2007 was turning a blind eye. John Sellar had retired, so he was not there to break the silence with some ballsy intervention on behalf of the CITES Secretariat.

The Dragon is not China! I wanted to stand up and scream into the UN hush. *The Dragon is just one division of one not-so-powerful ministry run by a bunch of middle-aged blokes married to an old-school mandate. Okay, they may have backing from the largest army in the world, but we're talking about the very survival of the King of the Jungle!*

The CITES Secretariat introduced the meager request that countries report to the 2014 Standing Committee meeting on efforts to stop trade in Asian big cats, including tigers. Otherwise, the matter would not be revisited until the next CITES conference in 2016. An irreversible catastrophe could take place during three years with no oversight.

India supported reporting in 2014, as well as "strict compliance" with all CITES measures to end "all trade" in tigers and their parts and products. This was not the vehement India of years past, but no one in the room missed the allusion to phasing out tiger farms.

The Dragon, speaking for China, argued for 2016.

As countries spoke to register their support for one option or the other, the chair abruptly ended the discussion. "We are simply out of time," he said.

No time for comments on the fact that the Dragon was allowing *legal* tiger trade and expansion of tiger farming after the CITES decision against both. No time for comments on how these activities were stimulating demand for the skins and bones of wild tigers. No time to hear Debbie's prepared intervention, which said,

> We have documented the licensed trade in the skins of captive-bred tigers in China. . . . These skins are accompanied by a government-issued permit that states: "The specimen is registered and can be traded within China." This perpetuates rather than eliminates demand. The skins of poached wild tigers, leopards, and snow leopards are also destined for China's legal market, as reported by poachers who have been commissioned to obtain them. We urge an end to *all* trade in *all* tigers and other Asian big cats from *all* sources.

The chair moved to a vote on whether there would be reporting on tigers in 2014 or 2016. *Please let it be 2014.*

The tally for 2014 came up on the Jumbotron: 64 in favor, 20 opposed, 28 abstentions.[24] CITES would revisit tigers in 2014. One more chance to rally the World before the Dragon went for a twofer in 2016.

It was a worrying victory, however. Half the tiger-range countries present had voted for 2016. The Dragon hadn't won the day, but it had enlisted more key comrades to support its long march toward bringing tiger-bone wine to a liquor store near you.

"Sprinkling gasoline on a fire" was how Steve Galster characterized the actions and inactions of CITES at its fortieth-anniversary conference. Steve's Bangkok-based group FREELAND joined with EIA and the Wildlife Protection Society of India (WPSI) to hold a reality-check press conference just as the meeting was winding down.[25] Steve opened by saying that the past two weeks had seen negotiations to reopen rhino-horn trade, zero progress in eliminating tiger farms, and discussions to continue "limited" ivory trade that proved impossible to limit. "It's like putting water on one side of a fire and sprinkling gasoline on the other."

WPSI's earnest young lawyer Avinash Basker said that "CITES is at risk of losing its relevance when it comes to tigers and rhinos and elephants."

EIA's formidable senior ivory-trade investigator Mary Rice said talk of so-called limited trade was "sabotaging" the CITES bans on elephant, rhino, and tiger trade. "Bans *do* work if they are implemented." Allowing some trade is like putting out an "open for business" sign to organized criminals, she said. "Trade *is* causing poaching. Demand-reduction strategies will never work if there are parallel, perverse policies promoting demand. . . . The key is to *stop stimulating demand*."

Their words got little press coverage amid the breaking news on sharks.

Secret ballots came back to bite the Dragon on sharks. Via secret votes, CITES approved regulating international trade in five shark species because of the devastating effects of finning to supply shark-fin soup at high-end Chinese banquets.[26] China and Japan tried twice at the last minute to reopen the shark debate, but secret ballots rejected further discussion.[27]

During closing remarks, one man found courage to at last mention tiger farming in official proceedings. Will Travers of Born Free, speaking on behalf of the 103 member organizations in the Species Survival Network, said that he had "witnessed a dramatic and impressive evolution of the treaty, in which the toughest conservation issues of our time [have been] tackled—crises in rhino horn and elephant ivory trade, the ongoing scourge of intensive tiger breeding, and now, the commercial trade in tree and fish species." That was it. That was the sole allusion to tiger farming during the fortieth anniversary of the UN treaty created to keep tigers and our planet's other most precious wild species from being traded to extinction.

In the meeting's final moments, CITES accepted South Africa's offer to host the 2016 conference in Johannesburg. That meant the worst-case scenario was likely a mere three years away. The World's next opportunity to weigh in on the Dragon's plans to commodify tigers, rhinos, and elephants would be as the official guest of a country that seemed keen to sell them out.

"Tigers got only fifteen minutes crammed in an extra session," I complained to Chris Shepherd, the intense Canadian veterinarian with an unrelenting passion for stopping wildlife trade, who was now deputy regional director for TRAFFIC Southeast Asia.[28] We were sitting amid the clanging bustle of a Denny's-like restaurant downstairs from the conference halls.

"That's fifteen minutes more than bears have gotten since the American black bear was listed," Chris said. His angry eyes held mine and did not blink.

"Pretty much," I said. "Not since Kyoto in 1992. My first CITES conference."

"Bear farms have never come up," he said. "Why not?"

"I've always wondered," I said.

Chris was leading the Bear Specialist Group's trade committee, and he refused to be silenced on the threat posed to wild bears by bile farming. "China is behind all of it," he said. Buyers were both Chinese and Korean, "but all the bear farms in Southeast Asia—with the exception of Vietnam—are Chinese-owned. Eighty percent of all the bear-bile products found in Malaysia are from farms in China. They say it on the packaging."

"But that's a blatant violation of CITES," I said.

Chris said China had around 20,000 bears in farms, while Vietnam had an estimated 6,000 and Laos another 4,800. "A lot of bear farms also have tigers, and a lot of tiger farms have bears." None of the bear farms he visited had facilities to breed bears, he said. "They're 100 percent wild-caught."

He talked about one farm in Myanmar where the cement was

blackened with bear blood. "Chinese like to have the bears brought out and killed in front of them so they know the parts they're buying are genuine," he said. "I've watched them bring out cubs and cut them open right there."

"How can you watch that?" I asked. "Doesn't it kill you?"

"It makes me want to kill the killers," he said. "I wish everyone in the world had to stand there and watch it. That might change a few things."

"So with all of this flagrant laundering and illegal trade, why *aren't* bear farms brought up at CITES?" I asked.

"No Asian country would bring up bears," Chris said, adding that "Big Brother"—aka the Dragon—"has squashed them."

I told him about the Croc Farm Bear. "I promised that bear I would make things better for her kind. I feel as if I've failed her."

Chris said he'd made a promise to a bear too. In Indonesia. "There was a sun bear at a zoo in Medan when I worked there. He was kept in a little crate. I used to go there and wrestle and play with him. He'd had his teeth knocked out with a sledgehammer, so I told the staff, 'Don't ever put him in with the other bears because he can't defend himself.' One day for fun, when I wasn't there, the staff put him in with the other bears. They bit his feet off. A friend of mine who worked there jumped in and just held him while he bled to death. I made the exact same commitment to that bear that you made. I couldn't help that bear, but I swore I would help others."

"So where are you in fulfilling your promise?" I said.

"I'm not anywhere near—not anywhere close," Chris said. However, he saw more and more Asians taking up the fight. "We're moving it all in the right direction. We just need more people and more resources. It will happen. The question is what will be left when we get there."

I thanked him for his dedication. As we prepared to leave, he said, "I read an article of yours a long time ago. I think it was called 'I Want to Eat Sun Bear.' That article inspired me to do what I do."

Full circle.

• • •

Revisiting the Samutprakarn Crocodile Farm had been on my Bangkok to-do list. I had wanted to tell the spirit of the Croc Farm Bear that I had tried mightily to fulfill my promise. I wanted her to know that much of the world knew about the plight of her kind but that getting the world to stop the madness was complicated. I wanted to confess to her that the Dragon had proven a far wilier foe than a former mall rat from Federal Way, Washington, could have anticipated.

After talking with Chris Shepherd, I knew that the Croc Farm Bear's legacy was in good hands, so I decided to forgo my visit to the Samutprakarn. I wanted to remember the Croc Farm Bear and myself as we had been when we met: she, alive, and I, young and utterly certain I could move the world for her.

14

HOPE FOR A TIGER SPRING

The disturbing realities in Bangkok followed me home. The day I landed back in the States, the *Washington Post* ran an article lauding "a new business model" for saving Africa's rhinos. The writers from the University of Virginia's business school showcased the "rhino-nomic" reasoning of South Africa's John Hume, owner of the world's largest private stockpile of rhino horn.[1]

I spent the next few days leaden with jet lag and a cold. Cocooned in my sunny flat with two needy tabbies and Kleenex stuffed up both sleeves, I told myself to rest, that there was time to regroup, to muster troops from I knew not where, to win back ground for tigers, rhinos, bears, and elephants from those banking on their extinction.

An e-mail with a leaked document attached splashed ice-cold reality in my face. It was a chipper update to South Africa's Private Rhino Owners Association about their government's three-part rhino sales pitch in Bangkok. "The many months of behind-the-scenes motivating . . . as well as some 'blood on the carpet,' has paid off!" wrote an ebullient Pelham Jones. "We have huge work ahead and many challenges, but we have crossed the Rubicon and have more international support than I imagined. With this turning point, let's hope to see . . . a rapid climb in rhino values!" *He wants the price on the head of every last rhino to skyrocket further!*

Jones shared results from a survey of South African's private rhino owners. Ninety-one percent supported lifting the ban on rhino-horn trade, while 97.5 percent supported "controlled" legal trade in rhino horn. They were nearly all-in for making a killing from selling their private holdings to the Dragon, regardless of the limitless demand their personal windfalls might unleash.[2]

South Africa already needed its army to protect wild rhinos from poachers. All of Africa's military forces combined could not stop the onslaught if poachers were given the opportunity to launder illicit rhino horn into a legal market made up of wealthy Chinese investors who were enamored with status symbols and desperate for a hedge against flaccid Chinese stock offerings, a cooling domestic real-estate market, and sinking gold prices.

As I read Pelham Jones's dispatch, something in that morning's *New York Times* came back to me, something about China's new president flying to Africa. I Googled President Xi Jinping's itinerary. After a stop in Moscow, the new leader's first international tour in March 2013 would take him to Tanzania, South Africa, and the Democratic Republic of Congo. The dots connected. There may not be another couple of years to thwart the Dragon's plan to reopen rhino-horn trade—and likely tiger trade with it. Not if that plan was about to be blessed by China's highest official.

I felt sick in that past-the-point-of-no-return way. The way I felt that Friday night three years before when I learned that both my parents were about to enter end-of-life care—a month before they were both gone from this life. *This can't be happening.*

I called my friend Rowena Watson at the State Department.

"It's happening," I said.

"What's happening?" she said.

"The Dragon is winning."

Rowena, a PhD in veterinary pathology and single mother of two gentlemen-in-the-making, caught me in freefall after my parents' deaths. But she had no time for all-is-lost outbursts. She told me to calm down and then write my concerns in a succinct e-mail with facts that she would forward up the chain of command, if possible, all the way to Secretary of State John Kerry.

So I summarized the issue and closed with these words: "I write in hope that the United States government can intervene in some manner so that the vested economic interests of a few individuals do not overtake the precautionary principle that has, until now, allowed the world to secure a future for wild rhinos, elephants, tigers, and other species at increasing risk of becoming nothing more than commercial commodities."[3]

The next day, the *Shanghai Daily* reported that two airline passengers had been arrested trying to smuggle ten African rhino horns and thirty-seven ivory products worth $800,000 into China through Shanghai's Pudong International Airport.[4]

News reports of Xi Jinping's stops in Russia, Tanzania, South Africa for a BRICS summit, and finally Congo were fawning as the second most powerful man on Earth stepped for the first time into global view with his famous-singer wife.[5] Fans back home in China thrilled at having an elegant First Lady—their own Michelle Obama.[6]

One picture showed South African president Jacob Zuma using two hands to shake the right hand of the much taller Chinese leader with thick, dark hair, a broad face, and wide shoulders, as he stepped onto the tarmac from his 747. China was South Africa's biggest trading partner. "It has been proposed that next year be heralded as the 'Year of South Africa in China,'" Zuma said, "and that 2015 be declared the 'Year of China in South Africa.'"[7] *And 2016 as the year South Africa sells out rhinos to China?*

On March 27, 2013, a week after I sent my note to the State Department, South Africa's Department of Environmental Affairs issued a press release announcing that a memorandum of understanding between South Africa and China on "rhino poaching" had been signed. The text contained some of the same code phrases for legalizing trade that Minister Edna Molewa had used in Bangkok. Theirs was a pledge of cooperation aimed at "curbing the current scourge" of rhino poaching.[8]

In a follow-up e-mail to the State Department, I underscored the worst part of it all. "China can only receive rhino horn from South

Africa if its 1993 ban on trade in rhino horn and tiger bone is lifted." The ban that China had decreed twenty years before. The ban that was announced as the president of the United States was considering trade sanctions because China's legal domestic trade threatened the survival of wild tigers and rhinos. The ban that, if lifted today, would trigger demand exponentially more lethal than the threat in 1993.[9]

Horrific news continued to break. At least 188 rhinos had been killed in South Africa during the first quarter of 2013, according to government officials. The spokesman for a group of South African landowners said he feared that as many as 1,000 rhinos might be poached by year's end. One game reserve had decided to inject pesticides and pink dye into its rhinos' horns as a deterrent to poachers and consumers.[10] Around the same time, thieves broke into the rhino-horn stockpile at another reserve and stole sixty-six horns with a reported value of $2.75 million.[11] In the United Kingdom, authorities announced a new DNA database for rhino horns in museums because of the spate of thefts from exhibits.[12] Meanwhile, India reported that it was deploying aerial drones to safeguard its rhinos from poachers.[13]

On the tiger front, poachers opened fire on police in Nepal in May 2013. Three were arrested with six tiger skins, nine tiger teeth, and nearly one hundred pounds of tiger bone destined for China.[14] Tiger poaching reached a seven-year high in India.[15] With regard to the apparently legal tiger trade in China that continued to stimulate demand and poaching, there was political silence. If I had been a tiger-farm investor, I would have seen the lack of protestation after EIA's revelations as a green light.

There was hopeful news too. Twin bills were in the works—in both the US Senate and House—that would ban private breeding and possession of tigers.[16] While Republicans and Democrats were divided on most issues, a poll found 81 percent of Republicans and 74 percent of Democrats in favor of taking US tigers out of private hands. The same poll found 75 percent of the American public in favor.[17]

News from China also was encouraging.

In May 2013, a video went viral—inside and outside China—of an animal handler at Wenling Zoo sitting on a cowering tiger tied down on top of a small metal platform. The handler bounced his full weight on the tiger's back, repeatedly slapping its head. Then a second handler began kicking it. Public outrage prompted local government officials to ask the zoo to apologize and improve its treatment of animals, according to the state-run news agency, which also reported that the two men and their boss had gone missing.[18]

A few days later, the media lit up with news that Li Bingbing, one of China's hottest young movie stars, was making a personal appeal to stop ivory and rhino-horn consumption. "Many years ago, I bought a bracelet made of ivory," she told the press. "But at that time, I had no idea that it was made of ivory or that it was connected to the mass killing of African elephants. People in China, many of them have no idea that the ivory is actually connected to the 'blood ivory' trade in Africa."[19] In a new WildAid video, Li stood in front of an elephant and said in Chinese, "There is a war in Africa you don't hear about in the news. A war that kills twenty-five thousand elephants a year—for ivory. A war that sponsors civil wars and criminal gangs, paid for with ivory. But this is a war we can stop, by simply saying no to ivory."[20]

Not long afterward, the Dragon held a press conference to deny that there was a connection between China's consumption of ivory and the slaughter of African elephants. Top officials told reporters that accusations of China eating the world's most rare and beloved wild species were "unprofessional" and "misleading." The defensive tone was unusual—perhaps a sign of worry over the growing number of Chinese voices not wanting the blood of tigers, rhinos, bears, and elephants on the hands of China, Chinese people, and Chinese culture.[21]

The same day, the New York Times carried a story headlined "Folk Remedy Extracted from Captive Bears Stirs Furor in China." The article recounted protesters in China wearing bear suits outside stores selling farmed bear bile. Hackers had brought down the website of a pharmaceutical company applying for a stock offering to finance expansion of its bear farm from four hundred to twelve hundred bears. After a supporter of the company told the media that bile milking was "natural, easy, and without pain," he was slammed by a "torrent of ridicule on social media." Lawyer Deborah Cao was quoted as calling these reactions in China part of "a bottom-up, grassroots movement—one that is contributing to an emerging civil society increasingly aware of individual rights and obligations, be it to humans or animals."[22]

Social scientist Mang Ping, a professor at Beijing's Central Institute of Socialism, headed the coalition lobbying to remove "domestication and use" from China's wildlife law. It was her group's proposal that had made it all the way to the office of President Xi Jinping prior to the Bangkok CITES meeting.

"If a wildlife protection law cannot guide people to protect wildlife and instead encourages people to excessive use and destruction of wildlife, then it should be amended as soon as possible," Mang said in China's *Legal Daily*. As is, the law directs China's wildlife protection authorities to protect commercial interests rather than wildlife. She said that the State Forestry Administration should be "reformed" into "a real wildlife protection agency."[23]

Meanwhile, Xie Yan, a researcher with the Chinese Academy of Sciences' Institute of Zoology, led a group with more than one hundred members calling for a new nature reserve law that would emphasize protecting wildlife *in* instead of *from* the wild.[24] Under existing regulations, she said, staff in most reserves had little incentive and few resources to stop poaching and illegal wildlife trade.

Weeks after the CITES conference had adjourned, Grace's "Eaten by China" blog post from Bangkok continued to resonate with Chinese netizens. It was retweeted on Sina Weibo more than two thousand times and received more than three hundred supportive comments.

"I share your feelings," said one respondent. "Every time my African colleagues ask about consumption of ivory and rhino horn, every time my Kazakhstan colleagues ask about demand for saiga antelope horn, every time my Myanmar colleagues tell me Chinese are cutting their virgin forests, every time my Indonesian colleagues mention the increase in tiger poaching linked to Chinese demand, my heart sinks!"

"China's use of wildlife is a massive industry that brings nothing to the nation but shame!" said another.

"Do we still have any 'face' left?" asked another.

The one person who posted a defense of China's wildlife consumption received an avalanche of backlash.

"We have to work with the like-minded from within China to influence policy," Grace told me. "There is no other way."

If anyone can find a way, it will be Tiger Lily. This is what she wrote to South Africa's rhino-selling environment minister Edna Molewa:

> I am Chinese and have been working on wildlife conservation issues in China for the past fifteen years. I have personally witnessed the price of ivory skyrocket and the demand exploding in China. The legal ivory market provides opportunities for illegal ivory trade and stimulates the desire for many people to make a quick profit in the illegal ivory trade. I have heard of cases where Chinese tour groups visiting South Africa emptied an entire store of ivory. . . . I hope the disastrous decisions to allow legal trade in ivory . . . to China can serve as warning for what might happen with rhinos if trade in rhino horn becomes legal in China.

On the same day that Grace sent me a copy of her letter to Minister Molewa, China's Olympic-medalist NBA star Yao Ming launched a campaign at the Westin Hotel in Beijing's financial district to discourage ivory and rhino-horn consumption. On a twelve-day "fact-finding" mission to Kenya and South Africa, Yao had reveled in the midst of wild elephants and rhinos but also came across the carcasses of five poached elephants and one poached rhino. "Poaching threatens livelihoods, education, and development in parts of Africa due to the insecurity it brings and loss of tourism revenue," he said in a press release. "No one who sees the results firsthand, as I did, would buy ivory or rhino horn. I believe when people in China know what's happening, they will do the right thing and say 'no' to these products."[25]

• • •

A couple of wild cards emerged to further inspire my hope for a Tiger Spring.

One was a man I'd never heard of until I read about him in a wacky story in the *New York Times*. He was a "poetry-loving" billionaire property developer named Huang Nubo, who'd offered a sheep farmer $7 million for his family's 116 square miles of property in the middle of Iceland's hinterlands. A former member of the Communist Party's propaganda machine, Huang claimed he wanted to build a golf resort for affluent Chinese craving tranquility in an unsullied place. Speculation buzzed over Huang's true motives. Rumors said he was part of a secret Chinese government plot to (1) establish an arctic military base, (2) exploit arctic oil reserves, and/or (3) stake a foothold in whatever uncharted opportunities might emerge from the melting ice cap.[26]

A few days later, I was chatting on the phone with my best male friend, Rand Rosenberg, who lives in Southern California and hangs out with the über-rich, Hollywood types, and rock stars. We hadn't spoken much since I'd introduced him to WildAid and he'd joined its board.

"I've started exchanging poetry with a Chinese billionaire," Rand said. "He's off climbing Mount Everest now. You might have heard of him. He's trying to buy Iceland."

"I just read about him," I said. "He's trying to build a military base there, right?"

"No, a golf course. The guy loves wild places. And he loves tigers and elephants and thinks stopping wildlife consumption is the most important thing. I met him when he joined WildAid's board. The first thing he did was write a check for $2 million."

I found Huang on YouTube in one of WildAid's videos.[27] This one featured five of China's top CEOs seated in front of a giant aquarium teaming with sharks.

"We must think about the future," one said.

"We must think globally and act locally," said another.

"We must make China proud."

"We must all say 'no' to shark-fin soup."

Huang told *Beijing Today* that he and his high-flying peers had once thought eating shark-fin soup was a must at business dinners. To not have it was to lose face. "When I look back, I feel ashamed," he said.[28]

Individuals like this will shape China's future and, perhaps more importantly, decide its status symbols. These princelings truly have it in their power to keep the King of the Jungle from the Dragon's mouth.

In fact, thanks to Huang and other business leaders, as well as celebrities in WildAid's demand-reduction campaign and thousands of young Chinese microbloggers, the popularity of shark-fin soup had plummeted. "People said it was impossible to change China, but the evidence we are now getting says consumption of shark-fin soup in China is down by 50 to 70 percent in the last two years," WildAid's Peter Knights told the press in October 2013.[29]

In December 2013, China's official news agency announced that the Central Committee and State Council had issued a directive barring Communist Party officials from eating shark-fin soup at official functions.[30]

The other dark horse worthy of mention came as a surprise to me. He was the last person I encountered the night before I departed Bangkok after the CITES conference. He was standing alone in the middle of the modest lobby of the apartment-style hotel we had shared for two weeks without once bumping into each other there.

"Dr. Meng, how are you?" I said to the man I had for twenty years thought of as China's Fonz and my nemesis.

"Yes, yes, hello," he said. "I am worried. We *cannot* regulate the shark trade. It is not possible. Not possible."

"I understand that regulating trade in shark fins will be very difficult," I said. But I didn't want to go there. "What about tigers?"

He shook his head. "Do not worry about tigers. Not necessary. I am against opening trade in tigers."

"Yes, but you're not in charge of tiger farms," I said.

"No need to worry about tigers," he repeated. "The next generation, they don't want to eat the wildlife. They wear Western clothes and eat Western food."

It's true that the generation that will supplant Meng's never had to numb itself against the deprivations and brutality of the Cultural Revolution as Meng and his colleagues did. Nor have they grown up memorizing Mao slogans or running with rifles and throwing grenades in PE. They tend to be more sensitive to cruelty and have more time and money to consider pet-keeping, animal welfare, and environmental protection. They also have far more exposure to the global perception of China eating the world, one beloved species at a time. Surely they, like the traditional Chinese medicine industry, will not want extinction's brand to be "Made in China."

"There's no need to worry about tigers," Meng said again. "Do not worry."

I didn't know whether Meng believed what he told me, but his eyes indicated he did. And he was born in the Year of the Tiger, which matters, according to Grace. I also sensed that, like me, he felt his central part in this story was ending. That the battle lines we'd drawn would not be those of our successors. I suddenly felt sad that he had given up his black-leather bomber jacket for the windbreaker favored by Chinese men of a certain age.

I shook his hand good-bye, knowing it was likely for the last time. As I walked toward the elevator, I thought that maybe—God and the Internet willing—tigers, rhinos, and bears might be spared the feedlot so that we humans might always have the privileged option of thrilling in their wildness—to unleash a bit of our own.

15

EPILOGUE

I've been accused of being a "panda lover" and a "dragon slayer"—both in the pocket of China's government and a China basher. I've been unduly lauded and also thrown under a bus or two. But this story isn't about me, nor is it about China. At its core, it is a story about how greed and well-meaning but outdated ideologies threaten to take from us iconic wild beings that guard our forests and the wildness of spirit that our higher selves long to meet.

Through it all, I've watched China rise from global whipping boy to Earth's second most powerful nation. Some of the people I've come to admire most in this "one wild and precious life"—as poet Mary Oliver so rightly termed it—are Chinese.[1] And I leave these pages with faith that the people of the People's Republic of China will insist that the Dragon desist from turning our shared world's most charismatic wild creatures into livestock.

"When I speak with Chinese people about these issues, I always use 'us,' 'we,' 'you,' and 'me,'" Grace told me. This choice of whether the world will have wild tigers, rhinos, bears, elephants, and more *is* a matter of us, we, you, and me. That fact is underscored by the US tiger problem, which is, in some ways, as monumental as China's.

How the US government proceeds with regard to America's tigers may well determine how China's government complies—or not—with the CITES decision to end tiger farming. Consider a quote from the *New York Times* in a June 2013 article about America's upset over China allowing NSA-leaker Edward Snowden to leave Hong Kong for refuge in Russia. After reiterating China's anger at the Obama administration over accusations of cyber-spying, a Ministry of Foreign Affairs spokeswoman said, "I'd like to advise these people to hold up a mirror, reflect, and take care of their own situation first."[2] The next month, a top official of the International Energy Agency said this about US leverage in China's decisions to mitigate climate change: "China, I think, is willing to take action if the US does."[3]

In November 2013, the United States crushed nearly six tons of confiscated elephant ivory in a public commitment to end the trade.[4] In January 2014, China followed suit. What would happen to China's tiger farms if the United States prohibited private ownership of tigers?[5]

Let us not lose the last wild tigers to a standoff between superpowers. Let us all, citizens and netizens of this one wild and precious world, encourage them to join together to save the royal court of the jungle and savanna from the feedlot and commodities market.

As I write these words, the slaughter in the wild continues. A news story out of Kenya says poaching of rhinos there doubled in 2013.[6] Are poachers stockpiling in anticipation of South Africa winning CITES approval to sell rhino horns to China and China lifting its 1993 ban?

An article on South Africa's *Times LIVE* website estimated South Africa's proposed sale of rhino horns to be worth more than $1 billion. Environment minister Edna Molewa "admitted the department did not know whether the proposed sale would curb poaching," the story said. "We do not know what would happen," she said. "All of us, as the whole world, we are travelling in uncharted seas. We don't know what is awaiting us there."[7]

Therein lies the danger. And here is some good news: Alejandro Nadal has joined the conversation about tiger farming. Nadal is a Mexican economics professor who is cochairing an international effort to understand the complicated economic forces causing unprecedented degradation of nature.[8] When I spoke with him in early 2014, he had reviewed 127 publications written about commodifying wildlife, many by people collaborating with the Dragon to promote tiger farming. "I don't want to be rude," Nadal told me, "but a lot of what has passed for economic analysis in favor of legalizing tiger trade is critically flawed and was theoretically discredited many years ago. Nearly all of the analyses show complete ignorance of game-changing factors at play. This is very dangerous." His bottom line: "Do not unleash forces you don't understand."[9]

The massive demand that will be unleashed on wild tigers and rhinos by even partially lifting China's 1993 ban can be likened in scope to the impact of sea-level rise on small island nations. They will be inundated and soon gone. Ditto for too many other wild species cherished by the world.

To "stop the bleeding," we must stop dangling the promise of supply that keeps demand alive and growing, only to make a handful of investors richer and our shared natural heritage irreversibly poorer.

President Barack Obama signed an executive order to combat wildlife trafficking on July 1, 2013. It reads, in part: "Poaching operations have expanded beyond small-scale, opportunistic actions to coordinated slaughter commissioned by armed and organized criminal syndicates. The survival of protected wildlife species such as elephants, rhinos, great apes, tigers, sharks, tuna, and turtles has beneficial economic, social, and environmental impacts that are important to all nations." The order established a presidential task force to produce a "National Strategy for Combating Wildlife Trafficking" that must include strategies to reduce consumer demand.[10]

That same month, the Dragon hosted a workshop in China on combating *illegal* tiger trade. People who attended reported that tiger farming was not on the agenda, although Hank Jenkins and company were there to advocate for lifting China's 1993 ban. When someone showed State Forestry Administration staff a recent photo of a tiger skin for sale with a permit from the agency, they admitted issuing the document. They said they were testing the impact of limited trade on wild tigers—a demand stimulus and a blatant snub of the CITES decision against commodifying tigers.

In March 2014, Chinese netizens raised their tweets in protest after police in the southern city of Zhanjiang uncovered "visual feasts" during which live tigers were electrocuted for the dining pleasure of wealthy businessmen.[11] Two months later, the Standing Committee of the National People's Congress ruled that under existing laws, knowingly buying or consuming animals poached from the wild was a crime.[12] The move was good news, but only so far as it went. "On one hand, the government says don't buy these products, but wildlife parks sell tiger wine and people think it must be okay," Grace told VICE News. "These parallel markets allow farmers to sell products from endangered species. It confuses the consumer and creates the possibility for people to traffic wild tigers."

Days later, the official Xinhau news agency published a series of photos under a headline touting the birth of "about 100" tigers at the Siberian Tiger Park—yet another outright contravention of the decision against tiger farming.[13]

Just when it looked as if CITES had become toothless on tigers, the Dragon's Wang Weisheng stated at the July 2014 Standing Committee meeting that China did not ban trade in tiger skins. A BBC story headlined "China 'Admits' Trading in Tiger Skins" ricocheted around the world.[14] "According to officials and participants at the CITES meeting, the admission from China followed the presentation of a report that gave details of how the Chinese government had allowed commercial trade in skins from captive tigers," the correspondent wrote.

The report released at the meeting was commissioned by the CITES Secretariat from the Cat Specialist Group and TRAFFIC. With regard to China's tiger farms, the report concluded: "It appears possible that tiger facilities are actually using or selling their tiger parts rather than holding them indefinitely and then periodically destroying them."[15] The report noted that most countries had followed

CITES' call to ban both domestic and international tiger trade, although the restrictions didn't seem to apply to farms. "In particular, China has systematically exercised internal trading privileges for companies dealing in big-cat skins and derivatives, produced mainly but not exclusively from captive breeding. It is not evident that any sale restrictions apply . . . nor how permitted sales are monitored and enforced." In other words, the report validated what investigators had been documenting for years and the Dragon had steadfastly refused to confirm or deny.

The Environmental Investigation Agency (EIA) asked the Standing Committee chair for the floor and confirmed that it had repeatedly, over many years, found tiger skins sold openly and legally in China. The Dragon said nothing.

In response, the Standing Committee asked CITES countries that allow legal trade in tiger parts and products (read: China) to report back on "what legal trade is allowed" and how it is policed to prevent illegal trade.[16] The committee also urged members to take steps to reduce the "growing use" of tiger parts and products as "luxury items."

Many observers expected China to object. Instead, the Dragon insisted that pet trade also be addressed—an apparent jab at the United States. I consider the latter good news because it provided fodder for a potential Sino-US agreement to eliminate the commodification of captive tigers at a time when the two countries were signing multiple pledges to fight global warming in tandem.

In another intriguing turn of events, the Dragon raced to volunteer itself as chair of an intersessional CITES working group charged with seeing that the Standing Committee's questions were answered. In the end, the fox was given charge of the henhouse. However, the hens included, among others, India, the United Kingdom, the United States, Born Free, EIA, the International Fund for Animal Welfare, and the Wildlife Protection Society of India—none of which were likely to allow the Dragon to use its position to let itself off the hook.

On another front, EIA formally requested that the US Department of the Interior revisit China's still-pending qualification in 1993 for US trade sanctions under the Pelly Amendment.[17] "The enclosed briefing provides information that confirms that the reasons for the certification of China under the Pelly Amendment continue to prevail and that China continues to diminish the effectiveness of CITES and other global tiger conservation agreements," said the letter, addressed to Interior Secretary Sally Jewell, and which was attached to more than thirty pages of evidence. "EIA requests that the information enclosed be taken into consideration as part of the ongoing periodic review of the existing certification of China for trade in tiger parts and products and that a determination be made that the reasons for certification of China continue to prevail."[18] Technically speaking, President Bill Clinton had left open business that the Obama administration was obliged by law to take up.

When I asked Secretary Jewell's office about how and when the Pelly charges would be revisited, in light of EIA's brief, I was told, "We will consult with the relevant authorities in China and work with other experts and entities to gather as much credible information as possible to inform our decision."

These responses from CITES and the United States were not the barn burners of yore, but, taken together, they meant the eyes of the world were again watching—at least for a while longer.

To underscore the growing menace at hand, a new analysis released in August 2014 found that from 2010 to 2012 poachers had killed some 100,000 elephants across Africa—"a huge spike in the continent's death rate," the Associated Press reported.[19] "The causation in my mind is clear," said the study's leader, George Wittemyer of Colorado State University. That cause: runaway demand in China.

Then, TRAFFIC's Chris Shepherd sent me a compilation of bear parts seized in illegal trade across Asia from 2000 to 2011. The contraband represented the deaths of "a minimum of 2,801" bears, said a press release.[20] "The number of seizures is a credit to the enforcement agencies, but they undoubtedly only stop a fraction of the overall trafficking because bear products are still widely and easily available across Asia," Chris said. Despite China's glut of farmed bears, demand for parts and products from wild bears was booming.

•   •   •

The time to stop this gamble is now. Any later will be too late. We, you, I—in the United States, China, and everywhere there is Internet connectivity—have the power to send, post, tweet, and video, via Facebook, Twitter, Tumblr, Renren, Sina Weibo, Youku, DianDian, and more a firm *no!* to the madness. When the buying, selling, and farming stop, the killing will too.

As China's very wise philosopher Lao Tzu said, "The journey of a thousand miles begins with a single step." Yours, mine, ours.

HOW YOU CAN HELP END TIGER TRADE

Please take action for wild tigers. While there's still time.

KEEP LEARNING

To follow this story, please go to JAMillsAuthor.com, where I'll post breaking news. You'll also find updates on the continuing efforts of the amazing people highlighted in this book. If you'd like to follow them directly, here are some links:

Big Cat Rescue
   bigcatrescue.org

Environmental Investigation Agency
   eia-international.org

FREELAND Foundation
   freeland.org

International Fund for Animal Welfare (on US tigers)
   ifaw.org/united-states/our-work/tigers/big-cats-captivity

International Fund for Animal Welfare (on China)
   ifaw.org/international/our-work/wildlife-trade/reducing-china's
      -wildlife-trade

WildAid (on China)
   wildaid.org/china

SAY NO TO TIGER TRADE

- Don't buy tiger products.

- Explain to friends, family, and acquaintances why you would never buy tiger products.

- If you see tigers or tiger products for sale internationally, notify WildLeaks (wildleaks.org), the first secure online platform to report wildlife crime around the world.

- If you see tigers or tiger products for sale in the United States, tell the US Fish and Wildlife Service Office of Law Enforcement (fws.gov/le/contact-us.html) or the relevant state wildlife agency (fws.gov/offices/statelinks.html). In Canada, contact Environment Canada (wildlife.enforcement@ec.gc.ca) or the appropriate provincial wildlife agency.

- Don't visit tiger "parks," tiger farms, temples that keep tigers, tiger-petting events, and the like. Most people and places engaged in legitimate efforts to preserve the wild tiger's gene pool, or care for rescued captive tigers, are accredited to do so. For example, in the United States, zoos engaged in professionally managed conservation-breeding programs are accredited by the Association of Zoos and Aquariums (aza.org/what-is-accreditation). The best US tiger sanctuaries are accredited by the Global Federation of Sanctuaries (sanctuaryfederation. org/gfas/for-sanctuaries). You also can recognize them by their efforts to inform the public about the needs of wild tigers and the necessity of stopping all tiger trade from all sources.

- Explain to your friends, family, and acquaintances why you would never pet tiger cubs or visit a tiger farm, tiger temple, or other places of this sort. Your story can be far more influential than any formal campaign because they know and trust you.

VOTE NO ON TIGER TRADE

You can have a voice and a vote about what happens to tigers at international, national, and state or provincial levels.

International Trade

Nearly every country in the world is now a member of CITES, the UN treaty on international trade in endangered species. Every member country has a voice and a vote. If you would like your country to act to end tiger trade, contact the appropriate government agency. In the United States, CITES falls under the jurisdiction of the Department of Interior (feedback@ios.doi.gov). In Canada, Environment Canada (enviroinfo@ec.gc.ca) handles CITES. Please encourage a strong stance against tiger farming and all trade in tiger parts and products from all sources.

If you'd like to communicate directly with China's government, write China's ambassador to your country. You'll be most influential if you communicate as a friend of China. Send letters to China's US ambassador via chinaemb_us@mfa.gov.cn and to China's Canadian ambassador at chinaemb_ca@mfa.gov.cn.

US Tigers

Captive tigers in the United States fall mainly under the jurisdiction of the US Department of Agriculture. Tell the USDA (agec@usda.gov) that tracking captive tigers from birth to disposal after death is essential for public safety and to ensure US tigers don't enter international trade and spur demand for parts and products from wild tigers.

Contact elected representatives from your state or province to register support for national, state, or provincial laws prohibiting private ownership of tigers.

START AN INTERNATIONAL CONVERSATION

If you'd like to start an international conversation about the necessity of ending tiger exploitation in China and the United States, you could do so through *chinadialogue* (chinadialogue.net), which publishes thoughtful discussions in Chinese and English to foster understanding on "urgent environmental challenges," including "species loss." The editors welcome ideas at ideas@chinadialogue.net, according to guidelines found at chinadialogue.net/static/get_involved.

You also might reach across the world by submitting letters or story tips about tiger trade to North American news outlets with Asia editions, such as *Time* magazine (ideas.time.com/submit-a-letter) and CNN (cnn.com/feedback), or China-based media with English editions, such as *China Daily* (editor@chinadailyusa.com) and CCTV (english.cntv.cn/special/application/contact).

To start an international petition for tigers and against tiger trade, consider working through Avaaz Foundation (avaaz.org/en), which offers the opportunity to reach millions of people worldwide.

SUPPORT THE WORK OF OTHERS

If you have the financial resources, helping to fund the tiger work of the organizations listed above will ensure that your money goes a long way and yields tangible results.

ACKNOWLEDGMENTS

John E. Southard said, "The only people with whom you should try to get even are those who have helped you." That's one of the most important truisms I've learned in writing this book. How I wish I could thank those people enough!

I owe special thanks to Jorgen Thomsen, aka the Great Dane, who gave me a front row seat to all the action. Without Chris Servheen's help, I would never have met the Bangkok bears or Jorgen.

Ashok Kumar, bless you for arranging my induction into the Cult of the Tiger. I hope that Fateh Singh Rathore is somewhere in the cosmos where he too can feel my gratitude.

I'm truly grateful to my agent, B. J. Robbins, for taking a risk on an untested author. She and I would not have met were it not for the generosity of best-selling author Maarten Troost, whom I met through his wonderful partner Sylvia Troost. And then there is my editor, Alexis Rizzuto, who not only bought a first-time author's work but also shaped this book to be so much more than it would have been without her. In many ways, she is my coauthor. I also feel enormous gratitude to the other talented people at Beacon Press who had a hand in making a book from my manuscript and then sending it out into the world.

My "writer-twin" cousin John Wood performed artful surgery on the manuscript when it came in too long. He is as gifted at editing as he is at writing.

I'm grateful to authors Scott Wallace and Bryan Christy for their invaluable guidance early on. I'll be forever indebted to Scott for advising me to "show not tell" and for introducing me to Sol Stein's ageless wisdom.

Thank you, He Who Walks with Tigers, Eric Ash, for lending your beautiful photo as cover art.

Bea von Watzdorf coached, cheered, and kept me sane. Stephanie Yates, my soul sister, saw me through with her love, empathy, and the filter that lets her see me as the person I would like to be. "Mama Bear" Mary Mills gave me the kind of validation that only a parent can give.

Many of the people I mention in these pages leave me in awe, so I will name them again because they deserve a standing ovation: Debbie Banks and her tiger team at the Environmental Investigation Agency; Carole and Howard Baskin and the Big Cat Rescue team; Mike Day; Grace Ge Gabriel and her International Fund for Animal Welfare China team; Steve Galster and his FREELAND team; Justin Gosling; Lixin Huang; Peter Knights and all at WildAid; Anil Manandhar and WWF Nepal's Terai Arc team; Kristin Nowell; Jill Robinson and her team at Animals Asia Foundation; John Sellar; Chris Shepherd; Valmik Thapar; Will Travers and the Species Survival Network; Steve Trent; Belinda Wright and her team at the Wildlife Protection Society of India; Jiang Zaizeng; Li Zhenji; "Phil and Kate"; and my unnamed sources in China.

The Hong Kong traditional Chinese medicine community, the American College of Traditional Chinese Medicine, the Bay Area Chinese community, the World Federation of Chinese Medicine Societies, the Council of Colleges of Acupuncture and Oriental Medicine, and the International Tiger Coalition deserve special recognition for their unprecedented efforts to stop tigers from being traded to extinction. I'm grateful for their partnership and courage.

I feel indebted to those who worked with me at TRAFFIC East Asia. Akiko Ishihara, Sue Kang, Hisako Kiyono, Sean Lam, Samuel Lee, Rob Parry-Jones, and Marcus Phipps are exceptional professionally and personally. Thanks also to Steve Broad for supporting and encouraging us all.

Last and far from least, I thank my husband, James Fuschetti, for supporting me in myriad ways and for diligently reading through all those painful early drafts.

NOTES

Chapter 1: *The Thrall of the Wild*

1. Jack Olsen, *Night of the Grizzlies* (Moose, WY: Homestead Publishing, 1996), 34–37, 110–75.
2. Stephen Herrero, *Bear Attacks: Their Causes and Avoidance* (Guilford, CT: Lyons Press, 1985), 58–60.
3. Geoffrey C. Ward, *Tiger-Wallahs: Encounters with the Men Who Tried to Save the Greatest of the Great Cats* (New York: HarperCollins, 1993), 107–21.
4. Valmik Thapar, *The Cult of the Tiger* (New Delhi: Oxford University Press, 2004), 1–6, 24–26.
5. Robert B. Marks, "Asian Tigers: The Real, the Symbolic, the Commodity," *Nature and Culture* 1, no. 1 (Spring 2006): 63–87.
6. "Tiger Is World's Favourite Animal," *Manchester (UK) Evening News*, December 6, 2004, http://www.manchestereveningnews.co.uk/news/greater-manchester-news/tiger-is-worlds-favourite-animal-1131562.

Chapter 2: *The Promise*

1. Unless otherwise noted, the references for bear trade information in this chapter are the following three documents: Judy Mills, "I Want to Eat Sun Bear," *International Wildlife* (January–February 1991): 38–43; Judy Mills, "Milking the Bear Trade," *International Wildlife* (May–June 1992): 38–45; Judy A. Mills and Christopher Servheen, *The Asian Trade in Bears and Bear Parts* (Washington, DC: World Wildlife Fund, 1991).
2. TRAFFIC stands for Trade Records Analysis of Flora and Fauna in Commerce. The organization now simply uses the name TRAFFIC.
3. UNdata, http://data.un.org/.

4. Paul Theroux, *Riding the Iron Rooster: By Train Through China* (Boston: Mariner Books, 2006), 317.

5. Kelly M. Brown, "Execution for Profit? A Constitutional Analysis of China's Practice of Harvesting Executed Prisoners' Organs," *Seton Hall Constitutional Law Journal* 6 (Summer 1996), http://heinonline.org/HOL /LandingPage?handle=hein.journals/shclj6&div=46&id=&page=.

Chapter 3: Finding the Man with the Keys

1. CITES is the acronym for the Convention on International Trade in Endangered Species of Wild Fauna and Flora. "What Is CITES?," http://www .cites.org/eng/.

2. *Summary Report of the Committee I Meeting*, Ninth Session, March 10, 1992, CITES Eighth Meeting of the Conference of the Parties, Kyoto, Japan, March 2–13, 1992, CoP8 Com. I 8.9 (Rev.), http://www.cites.org/sites /default/files/eng/cop/o8/E-Com-I.pdf.

3. *Summary Report of the Plenary Meeting*, Ninth Session, March 12, 1992, CITES Eighth Meeting of the Conference of the Parties, Kyoto, Japan, March 2–13, 1992, CoP8 Plen. 8.9 (Rev.), http://www.cites.org/sites/default /files/eng/cop/o8/E-Plen.pdf.

4. *Proposals to Register the First Commercial Captive Breeding Operation for an Appendix-I Animal Species*, CITES Eighth Meeting of the Conference of the Parties, Kyoto, Japan, March 2–13, 1992, CoP8 Doc. 8.39 (Rev.), http:// www.cites.org/sites/default/files/eng/cop/o8/doc/E-39.pdf.

5. *Summary Report of the Committee I Meeting*, Fourth Session, March 5, 1992, CITES Eighth Meeting of the Conference of the Parties, Kyoto, Japan, March 2–13, 1992, CoP8 Com. I 8.4, http://www.cites.org/sites/default /files/eng/cop/o8/E-Com-I.pdf.

6. "Efforts Grow to Save the Siberian Tiger," *Cat News*, no. 9 (September 1993): 4–5, http://www.catsg.org/. *Cat News* is the newsletter of the Cat Specialist Group, a component of the Species Survival Commission of the International Union for Conservation of Nature (IUCN).

7. Geoffrey C. Ward, *Tiger-Wallahs: Encounters with the Men Who Tried to Save the Greatest of the Great Cats* (New York: HarperCollins, 1993), 161–64.

8. "Poaching for Bones Threatens the World's Last Tigers," *Cat News*, no. 17 (September 1992): 2–3.

9. Peter Jackson, "The Cheshire Tiger?," *Cat News*, no. 17 (September 1992): 1.

10. Steve Charnovitz, "Environmental Trade Sanctions and the GATT: An Analysis of the Pelly Amendment on Foreign Environmental Practices," *American University Journal of International Law and Policy* 9, no. 3 (1994): 751–807, http://digitalcommons.wcl.american.edu/cgi/viewcontent.cgi? article=1474&context=auilr.

11. Esmond Martin, Lucy Vigne, and Crawford Allan, *On a Knife's Edge: The*

Rhinoceros Horn Trade in Yemen (Cambridge, UK: TRAFFIC International, 1997).

12. "Tiger Conservation Moves Again to Centre Stage," *Cat News*, no. 18 (March 1993): 2–3.

13. *Summary Report*, Twenty-ninth Meeting of the CITES Standing Committee, Washington, DC, March 1–5, 1993, http://www.cites.org/sites/default /files/eng/com/sc/29/E29-SumRep.pdf.

14. Government of the People's Republic of China, "Circular of the State Council on Banning the Trade of Rhinoceros Horn and Tiger Bone," May 29, 1993, http://english.7139.com/2609/08/52562.html.

15. "China Bans Tiger Bone and Puts Tiger Farm in Limbo," *Cat News*, no. 19 (September 1993): 3–4.

16. "Administration Moves to Halt International Trade in Tiger and Rhino Parts," US Department of the Interior, press release, June 9, 1993.

17. Judy A. Mills, "Asian Dedication to the Use of Bear Bile as Medicine," in *Proceedings of the First International Symposium on the Trade of Bear Parts for Medicinal Use*, ed. Debra Rose and Andrea Gaski (Washington, DC: TRAFFIC USA/World Wildlife Fund, 1995), http://www.traffic.org /proceedings/.

18. Judy A. Mills, *Market Under Cover: The Rhinoceros Horn Trade in South Korea* (Cambridge, UK: TRAFFIC International, 1993), http://www.rhinoresource center.com/index.php?s=1&act=pdfviewer&id=1338687960&folder=133.

19. "People's Republic of China, Taiwan CITES for Illegal Trade in Rhinos, Tigers," US Department of the Interior, press release, September 7, 1993.

20. *Summary Report*, Thirtieth Meeting of the CITES Standing Committee, Brussels, September 6–8, 1993, http://www.cites.org/sites/default/files/eng /com/sc/30/E30-SumRep.pdf.

21. Ibid.

22. Steven A. Holmes, "World Moratorium on Nuclear Tests Is Broken by China," *New York Times*, October 6, 1993, http://www.nytimes.com/1993 /10/06/world/world-moratorium-on-nuclear-tests-is-broken-by-china.html.

23. Kristin Nowell and Xu Ling, *Taming the Tiger Trade: China's Market for Wild and Captive Tiger Products Since the 1993 Domestic Trade Ban* (Hong Kong: TRAFFIC East Asia, 2007), https://portals.iucn.org/library /node/9157.

24. William Graham Sumner, *Folkways* (New York: Dover, 1906).

25. CITES Secretariat, *CITES Technical Assistance Delegation Report on Visits to the People's Republic of China, Taiwan and the Republic of Korea*, November 21–December 5, 1993 (Geneva, Switzerland: CITES Secretariat).

26. Jim Mann, "Clinton Presses China on Rights," *Los Angeles Times*, November 20, 1993, http://articles.latimes.com/1993-11-20/news/mn-58846_1_human -rights.

27. Rone Tempest, "China Knew US Political Bottom Line: Money Talks," *Los*

Angeles Times, March 28, 1994, http://articles.latimes.com/1994-05-28/news /mn-63198_1_human-rights.

28. "China Burns Confiscated Tiger Bones," Associated Press, January 13, 1994, http://www.apnewsarchive.com/1994/China-Burns-Confiscated-Tiger -Bones/id-ec8f114a0e4805674c77f795b854f085; "China: Rhino Horn, Tiger Bone Ban Has Cost US $230 Billion," Associated Press, February 5, 1994, http://www.apnewsarchive.com/1994/China-Rhino-Horn-Tiger-Bone-Ban -Has-Cost-Us-$230-Billion/id-a7e9f026e50141d63082ab2323030946.

29. James Gerstenzang, "US Will Impose Trade Sanctions Against Taiwan to Protect Wildlife," *Los Angeles Times*, April 12, 1994, http://articles.latimes .com/1994-04-12/news/mn-45173_1_trade-sanctions.

30. *Time*, cover issue, March 28, 1994.

31. William J. Clinton, "Letter to Congressional Leaders on Rhinoceros and Tiger Trade by China and Taiwan," April 11, 1994, http://www.gpo.gov /fdsys/pkg/WCPD-1994-04-18/pdf/WCPD-1994-04-18-Pg781.pdf.

32. James M. Broder and Jim Mann, "Clinton Reverses His Policy, Renews China Trade Status," *Los Angeles Times*, May 27, 1994, http://articles.latimes .com/1994-05-27/news/mn-62877_1_human-rights.

33. Judy A. Mills and Peter Jackson, *Killed for a Cure: A Review of the World-wide Trade in Tiger Bone* (Cambridge, UK: TRAFFIC International, 1994), https://portals.iucn.org/library/node/7114.

34. Philip J. Nyhus, Ronald Tilson, and Michael Hutchins, "Thirteen Thousand and Counting: How Growing Captive Tiger Populations Threaten Wild Tigers," in *Tigers of the World: The Science, Politics and Conservation of Panthera Tigris*, 2nd ed., ed. Ronald J. Tilson and Philip J. Nyhus (London: Academic Press/Elsevier, 2010), 223–38.

Chapter 4: Prescription Rewritten

1. Jonathan Czin, "Dragon-slayer or Panda-hugger? Chinese Perspectives on 'Responsible Stakeholder' Diplomacy," *Yale Journal of International Affairs* (Spring/Summer 2007): 101–12, http://yalejournal.org/wp-content /uploads/2011/01/072208czin.pdf.

2. Allan Thornton, in discussion with the author, October 2, 2012.

3. *Resolutions of the Conference of the Parties*, CITES Ninth Meeting of the Conference of the Parties, Fort Lauderdale, FL, November 7–18, 1994, "Conservation of and Trade in Tigers," Conf. 9.13, http://www.cites.org /sites/default/files/eng/cop/09/E9-Res.pdf.

4. Unless otherwise noted, information about Steve Galster comes from the author's personal experience or an interview in Washington, DC, November 12, 2012.

5. Unless otherwise noted, information about Mike Day comes from the author's personal experience, a telephone interview on October 11, 2013, or

from his book *Fight for the Tiger: One Man's Battle to Save the Wild Tiger from Extinction* (London: Headline Book Publishing, 1995), 309–83.

6. Ibid.

7. CITES Secretariat, *Traditional Medicine and CITES—A Discussion Paper on Traditional East Asian Medicine*, CITES Tenth Meeting of the Conference of the Parties, Harare, Zimbabwe, June 9–20, 1997, CoP10 Doc. 10.79 (Rev.) Annex, http://cites.org/sites/default/files/eng/cop/10/doc/E10-79t080.pdf.

8. J. A. Mills, *Rhinoceros Horn and Tiger Bone in China: An Investigation of Trade Since the 1993 Ban* (Cambridge, UK: TRAFFIC International, 1997).

9. Address by the president of the Republic of Zimbabwe, CDE R. G. Mugabe, Opening Speeches, CITES Tenth Meeting of the Conference of the Parties, Harare, Zimbabwe, June 9–20, 1997, http://www.cites.org/sites/default/files/eng/cop/10/E10-open.pdf.

10. Gerd Behrens, "In Africa, a Battle Rages on Ivory and Elephants," *New York Times*, June 11, 1997, http://www.nytimes.com/1997/06/11/opinion/11iht-edgerd.t.html.

11. "Traditional Medicines and CITES," Draft Resolution, CITES Tenth Meeting of the Conference of the Parties, Harare, Zimbabwe, June 9–20, 1997, CoP10 Doc. 10.79.1, http://cites.org/sites/default/files/eng/cop/10/doc/E10-79t080.pdf.

12. *Summary Report of the Committee II Meeting*, Eleventh Session, June 18, 1997, CITES Tenth Meeting of the Conference of the Parties, Harare, Zimbabwe, June 9–20, 1997, CoP10 Com. II 10.11 (Rev.), http://www.cites.org/sites/default/files/eng/cop/10/E10-ComII.pdf; *Resolutions of the Conference of the Parties*, "Traditional Medicines," Conf. 10.19, http://www.cites.org/sites/default/files/eng/cop/10/E10-Res.pdf.

13. Unless otherwise noted, information about Peter Knights comes from the author's personal experience or an interview in San Francisco on October 4, 2013.

14. Judy Mills, "Need for Further Research into Tiger Bone and Musk Substitutes Agreed," *TRAFFIC Dispatches*, April 1998, http://www.traffic.org/traffic-dispatches.

15. Unless otherwise noted, information about Lixin Huang comes from the author's personal experience or an interview in San Francisco on October 4, 2013.

16. World Wildlife Fund, *A Pilot Program to Increase Tiger Conservation Awareness in Traditional Chinese Medicine Communities in North America*, report to the National Fish and Wildlife Foundation, August 1998, https://www.panthera.org/sites/default/files/STF/1998-0093-066.pdf.

17. Steven Russell Galster and Karin Vaud Eliot, "Roaring Back: Anti-Poaching Strategies for the Russian Far East and the Comeback of the Amur Tiger,"

in *Riding the Tiger: Tiger Conservation in Human-Dominated Landscapes*, ed. John Seidensticker, Peter Jackson, and Sarah Christie (Cambridge, UK: Cambridge University Press, 1999), 230–42.

18. *Liquidating the Forests: Hardwood Flooring, Organized Crime, and the Last Siberian Tigers* (London: Environmental Investigation Agency, 2013), http:// eia-global.org/images/uploads/EIA_Liquidating_the_Forests.pdf.

19. CITES Secretariat, *Report of the CITES Tiger Missions Technical Team to the Forty-first Meeting of the CITES Standing Committee*, September/ October 1999.

20. Judy Mills, "Bear-Trade Stakeholders Find Common Ground in Korea," *TRAFFIC Dispatches*, February 2000, http://www.traffic.org/traffic -dispatches.

21. Fan Zhiyong and Song Yanling, "The Development of Bear Farming in China," in *Proceedings of the Third International Symposium on the Trade in Bear Parts* (Hong Kong: TRAFFIC East Asia, 2001), 100–109.

22. Grace Ge Gabriel, "A Bitter Medicine: The Use of Bear Bile in China," in *Proceedings of the Third International Symposium on the Trade in Bear Parts* (Hong Kong: TRAFFIC East Asia, 2001), 116–20.

23. "China Joins WWF Visions for Sustainable Future," World Wildlife Fund, press release, October 29, 1999.

24. "China Works to Balance Medicinal Wildlife Use and Conservation," Environmental News Service, October 29, 1999.

25. Judy Mills, "The Symbiotic Match of Traditional Medicine and Wildlife Conservation," presented at the International Conference on Traditional Chinese Medicine and Endangered Wildlife Conservation, Beijing, October 30–November 1, 1999.

Chapter 5: Intermission I—The Wild Ones

1. "The Eastern Himalayas' Terai Arc," *WWF Focus* 23, no. 4 (July/August 2001).

2. John Nielsen, "Preserving Nepal's Endangered Species," *Radio Expeditions*, NPR/National Geographic Society, June 18–20, 2001, http://www.npr.org /programs/re/archivesdate/2001/jun/20010618.nepal.html.

3. Belinda Wright, "Growing Up with the Tigers," presentation, TEDxBITS Goa, YouTube, February 12, 2012, http://www.youtube.com/watch?v=z9AI _uEw5bk.

4. Natasha Singer, "See the Last Clouded Leopard; See the Last Clouded Leopard Die; See the Last Clouded Leopard Skin in the Black Market; See a Pattern Here?," *Outside Magazine*, May 1, 2004, http://www.traffic.org /traffic-dispatches.

5. "What Is ASEAN-WEN?," Asean-WEN, http://www.asean-wen.org/index .php/about-us/what-is-asean-wen.

6. WildAid, http://www.wildaid.org/.

7. "China Bear Rescue," *Animals Asia*, http://www.animalsasia.com/index.php ?UID=97PHBYFBNQP7.

8. "Thai Deputy PM Charged over Export of 100 Tigers to China," *Global Times* (China), December 19, 2012, http://www.globaltimes.cn/content /751177.shtml.

9. Cao Desheng, "Thai Tigers Safe and Sound in Hainan," *China Daily*, May 13, 2004, http://www.chinadaily.com.cn/english/doc/2004-05/13/con tent_330516.htm.

10. "Tiger Park in NE China to Be Enlarged," China.org.cn, October 23, 2002, http://china.org.cn/english/travel/46561.htm; "From Snake Trapper to Wildlife Protector," *People's Daily* (China), September 10, 1999, http://english .peopledaily.com.cn/50years/celebrities/19990910C109.html.

11. Shaoni Bhattacharya, "Chinese Tigers Flown to Africa for Hunting Lessons," *New Scientist*, September 3, 2003, http://www.newscientist.com /article/dn4133-chinese-tigers-flown-to-africa-for-hunting-lessons.html.

12. Kenneth Howe, "Out of Africa, into Uncertainty," *Wall Street Journal*, September 4, 2003.

13. Tian Xiuzhen, "South China Tigers to Take Trip to South Africa," *China Daily*, September 23, 2014, http://www.chinadaily.com.cn/english/doc/2004 -09/23/content_376899.htm; Sridevi Pillai, "Spot the Tiger," *The Hindu*, June 5, 2005, http://www.hindu.com/mag/2005/06/05/stories/20050605000 90100.htm.

Chapter 6: Crouching Dragon Selling Tigers

1. *Summary Record*, Fifty-third Meeting of the CITES Standing Committee, Geneva, Switzerland, June 27–July 1, 2005, http://cites.org/sites/default /files/eng/com/sc/53/sum/E53-SumRec.pdf.

2. All quotes from *The Art of War* are taken from Sun Tzu, *The Art of War*, translated by Thomas Cleary (Boston: Shambhala Publications, 2005).

3. Zhang Jia, "To Allow the Use of Thirty Sets of Tiger Bones to Make Medicines in the First Year? Whether the Ban Should Be Lifted to Use Tiger Resources," Nanfang Daily Newspaper Group, July 29, 2005, in Chinese, http://business.sohu.com/20050729/n240204083.shtml.

4. Lynne Warren, "Panda, Inc.: What's Black and White and Adored All Over—and Can Cost a Zoo More Than Three Million Dollars a Year?," *National Geographic*, July 2006, http://ngm.nationalgeographic.com/2006/07 /panda/warren-text.

5. Unless otherwise noted, information about Debbie Banks comes from the author's personal experience and multiple interviews in Washington, DC, in October 2012.

6. Debbie Banks and Belinda Wright, *Skinning the Cat: Crime and Politics of the Big Cat Skin Trade* (London: Environmental Investigation Agency, 2006), http://www.wpsi-india.org/images/EIA-WPSI_Skinning_The_Cat.pdf.

7. WildFilmsIndia, "Tiger Attack: The Full Video & Behind the Attack!," YouTube, July 23, 2010, http://www.youtube.com/watch?v=Tokzdu_wTMo.

8. Sugita Katyal, "Tiger Future Not Burning Bright in India," Environmental News Network, March 28, 2005, http://www.enn.com/top_stories/article/1249.

9. "State Forestry Administration: News Reports on Abolishing the Ban on Trade in Tiger Bones Unsubstantiated," China News Service, October 8, 2005, http://www.smesc.gov.cn/.

10. Centers for Disease Control and Prevention, "SARS Basics Fact Sheet," http://www.cdc.gov/sars/about/fs-SARS.html.

11. Eswar Prasad and Isaac Sorkin, "Sky's the Limit? National and Global Implications of China's Reserve Accumulation," Brookings Institution, July 21, 2009, table 2, http://www.brookings.edu/research/articles/2009/07/21-chinas-reserve-prasad.

12. Ministry of Science and Technology, People's Republic of China, "China's Top Ten Medical Developments," *China Science and Technology Newsletter*, no. 355 (January 20, 2004), http://www.most.gov.cn/eng/newsletters/2004/200411/t20041130_17755.htm; Secretary General Li Zhenji, World Federation of Chinese Medicine Societies, in discussion with the author, September 21, 2006.

13. "The Dalai Lama Appeals to Save Wildlife," Wildlife Trust of India, October 23, 2005, http://www.wti.org.in/oldsite/archives/2005/10/23/the-dalai-lama-appeals-to-save-wildlife.

14. "Memorandum of Understanding Between the World Federation of Chinese Medicine Societies (WFCMS) & Save the Tiger Fund (STF) on Development of Traditional Chinese Medicine and Conservation of Endangered Species, Specifically Tigers," signed by all parties December 5, 2005.

15. Ying Zhu, *Two Billion Eyes: The Story of China Central Television* (New York: New Press, 2012), 240–44.

16. *One World, One Dream*, official website of the Beijing 2008 Olympic Games, http://en.beijing2008.cn/spirit/beijing2008/graphic/n214068253.shtml.

17. Wildlife Trust of India, "WTI Campaign at Amravati Kalachakra," Phayul.com, February 1, 2006, http://www.phayul.com/news/article.aspx?id=11727.

18. International Campaign for Tibet, "Tibetans Burn Wild Animal Skins in Tibet to Encourage Wildlife Preservation," Phayul.com, February 10, 2006, http://www.phayul.com/news/article.aspx?id=11801&t=1.

19. TA, "Tibetans Burn Fur to Protect Animals & Show Loyalty to the Da-lai Lama," YouTube, January 2006, http://www.youtube.com/watch?v= gt2ndeDa1kg.

20. "Tibetan Broadcasters Ordered to Wear Fur," *Radio Free Asia*, April 28, 2006, http://www.rfa.org/english/news/tibet_fur-20060428.html.

21. Debbie Banks and Belinda Wright, *Skinning the Cat: Crime and Politics of the Big Cat Skin Trade* (London: Environmental Investigation Agency, 2006), http://www.wpsi-india.org/images/EIA-WPSI_Skinning_The_Cat .pdf.

22. "China Tiger Farm Strapped for Cash," United Press International, August 14, 2006, http://www.upi.com/Top_News/2006/08/14/China-tiger-park -strapped-for-cash/UPI-69111155569156/.

23. Barun Mitra, "Sell the Tiger to Save It," *New York Times*, August 25, 2006, http://www.nytimes.com/2006/08/15/opinion/15mitra.html?_r=0.

24. Zhang Kejia, "National Ban Cannot Stop Tiger Bone Sales," *China Youth Daily*, August 25, 2006, in Chinese, http://zqb.cyol.com/node/2006-08/25 /zgqnb.htm.

25. Conservation International, International Fund for Animal Welfare, Save the Tiger Fund, TRAFFIC, Wildlife Conservation Society, and World Wide Fund For Nature, "Joint NGO Statement on China's New Regulation for Import and Export of Endangered Species of Wildlife," September 1, 2006.

26. Lixin Huang, letter to Premier Wen Jiabao, dated August 27, 2006.

27. Linda Krueger, in discussion with the author, October 2, 2006.

28. Wildlife Conservation Society, *Report of a Survey on Saiga Horn in Markets in China*, information document for CITES Fourteenth Conference of the Parties, http://www.cites.org/sites/default/files/common/cop/14/inf/E14i-14 .pdf.

29. Unless otherwise noted, the information in this passage comes from the author's personal experience and *Summary Record*, Fifty-fourth Meeting of the CITES Standing Committee, Geneva, Switzerland, October 2–6, 2006, http://cites.org/sites/default/files/eng/com/sc/54/E54-SumRec.pdf.

30. Information about Justin Gosling comes from the author's personal experience and an interview in Bangkok, Thailand, on March 13, 2013.

31. Fact sheet distributed by the delegation of the People's Republic of China at the Fifty-fourth Meeting of the CITES Standing Committee, Geneva, Switzerland, October 2–6, 2006.

Chapter 7: Tiger Lily and the Art of War

1. Information in this section is from the author's personal experience and from a segment on tiger farming broadcast by the UK's ITV News, April 20, 2007.

2. Jonathan Watts, "Bred for the Freezer: How Zoo Rears Tigers Like Battery

Hens," *Guardian* (UK), April 13, 2007, http://www.theguardian.com/world /2007/apr/13/animalwelfare.china.

3. "Administration Denies China's Tiger Bone Trade Had Been Eased," *People's Daily Online*, January 11, 2007, http://english.people.com.cn/200701/11 /eng20070111_339941.html.

4. "China's Tiger Farms Put Their Case," in *Tiger Conservation: It's Time to Think Outside the Box* (Lausanne, Switzerland: IWMC World Conservation Trust, April 2007), 13–15, http://www.iwmc.org/PDF/IWMCtiger.pdf.

5. Alister Doyle, "China Restaurant Served Banned Tiger Meat: CITES," Reuters, June 12, 2007, http://www.reuters.com/article/2007/06/12/us-tigers -idUSL1236495320070612.

6. "CITES: DNA Test Confirms Tiger Meat for Sale at Chinese Farm, International Tiger Coalition," PR Newswire, June 12, 2007, http://www .prnewswire.com/news-releases/dna-test-confirms-china-tiger-farm-selling -tiger-meat-58020927.html.

7. *Made in China: Farming Tigers to Extinction* (Yarmouth Port, MA: International Fund for Animal Welfare, 2007), http://www.ifaw.org/sites/default /files/Report%202007%20Made%20in%20China%20Farming%20tiger%20 to%20extinction.pdf.

8. Unless otherwise noted, information about Grace Ge Gabriel comes from the author's personal experience and multiple interviews in Washington, DC, during January and October 2012.

9. Grace Ge Gabriel, "Chu Chu's First Step to Freedom," undated blog post, International Fund for Animal Welfare, http://www.ifaw.org.

10. CITES Secretariat, *Report by the CITES Secretariat on Its Verification and Assessment Mission to China, 28 March–7 April 2007*, CITES Fourteenth Meeting of the Conference of the Parties, The Hague, Netherlands, June 3–15, 2007, CoP14 Doc. 52, Annex 7, http://cites.org/sites/default/files /common/cop/14/doc/E14-52A07.pdf.

11. *The Current Situation of Tiger Breeding and the Facing of Difficulties of the Guilin Xiongsen Tigers and Bears Mountain Village* [sic], CITES Fourteenth Meeting of the Conference of the Parties, The Hague, Netherlands, June 3–15, 2007, CoP14 Doc. 52, Annex 8, http://cites.org/sites/default/files /common/cop/14/doc/E14-52A08.pdf.

12. Brian Gratwicke et al., "The World Can't Have Wild Tigers and Eat Them, Too," *Conservation Biology* (October 18, 2007), http://onlinelibrary.wiley .com/doi/10.1111/j.1523-1739.2007.00802.x/full.

13. Brian Gratwicke et al., "Attitudes Toward Consumption and Conservation of Tigers in China," *PloS ONE* 3, no. 7 (July 2008): 222–23, http://www .plosone.org/article/info%3Adoi%2F10.1371%2Fjournal.pone.0002544.

14. "International Tiger Coalition Unveils Tiger Mosaic!" YouTube, June 7, 2007, http://www.youtube.com/watch?v=UPaKITMYaAs.

15. International Tiger Coalition, "End Tiger Trade," YouTube, May 25, 2007, http://www.youtube.com/watch?v=FG3-rSQH7pA.

16. Richard Black, "End of the Tiger Tale?," BBC News, June 13, 2007, http://news.bbc.co.uk/2/hi/science/nature/6745497.stm.

17. Delegation of the People's Republic of China, *Key Positions and General Introduction on Tiger Conservation in China*, distributed at CITES Fourteenth Meeting of the Conference of the Parties, The Hague, Netherlands, June 3–15, 2007.

18. *Summary Record of the Eleventh Session of Committee II*, June 12, 2007, CITES Fourteenth Meeting of the Conference of the Parties, The Hague, Netherlands, June 3–15, 2007, CoP14 Com. II Rep. 11 (Rev. 1), http://cites.org/sites/default/files/eng/cop/14/rep/E14-Com-II-Rep-11.pdf.

19. *Summary Record of the Thirteenth Session of Committee II*, June 13, 2007, CITES Fourteenth Meeting of the Conference of the Parties, The Hague, Netherlands, June 3–15, 2007, CoP 14 Com. II Rep. 13, http://cites.org/sites/default/files/eng/cop/14/rep/E14-Com-II-Rep-13.pdf; *Summary Record of the Fourteenth Session of Committee I*, June 13, 2007, CoP14 Com. I Rep. 14 (Rev. 1), http://cites.org/sites/default/files/eng/cop/14/rep/E14-Com-I-Rep-14.pdf.

20. *Summary Record of the Fourth Plenary Session*, June 14, 2007, CITES Fourteenth Meeting of the Conference of the Parties, The Hague, Netherlands, June 3–15, 2007, CoP14 Plen. 4 (Rev. 2), http://cites.org/sites/default/files/eng/cop/14/rep/E14-Plen-4.pdf.

Chapter 8: Off to See the Wizard

1. Wang Zhuoqiong, "China Tiger Trade Ban 'Won't Last Forever,'" *China Daily*, June 19, 2007, http://www.chinadaily.com.cn/cndy/2007-06/19/content_897158.htm.

2. Belinda Wright and Justin Gosling, "Workshop of Tiger Conservation Strategy Diary Notes," June 30–July 7, 2007, unpublished paper, in author's possession.

3. A.J.T. Johnsingh, "Summary of Our Visit to People's Republic of China," January 27–February 6, 2007, unpublished paper, in author's possession.

4. Kristin Nowell, "Tiger Farms and Pharmacies: The Central Importance of China's Trade Policy for Tiger Conservation," in *Tigers of the World: The Science, Politics and Conservation of Panthera Tigris*, 2nd ed., ed. Ronald J. Tilson and Philip J. Nyhus (London: Academic Press/Elsevier, 2010), 463–75.

5. Urs Breitenmoser, "International Workshop on Strategy for Tiger Conservation," summary report, Beijing, Guilin, and Harbin, July 2–8, 2007, http://

www.catsg.org/catsgportal/events-activities/02_reports/CatSG_Harbin_2007_Tiger_Workshop_Report_U_Breitenmoser.pdf.

6. Xinhua News Agency, "Official: Don't Be Squeamish About Tiger Bones," *China Daily*, July 8, 2007, http://www.chinadaily.com.cn/china/2007-07/08/content_912627.htm.

7. "Devouring Dragon, Disappearing Tigers: A Look at South China's Tiger Farms and Reserves," WikiLeaks Cable 07GUANGZHOU785, US Embassy in Beijing to US Department of State, July 2007, http://www.wikileaks.org/.

8. Li Zhenji, secretary general of World Federation of Chinese Medicine Societies, Beijing, January 23, 2008, in conversation with the author.

9. Zinta Lundborg, "Harrison Ford Works to Save the World, Gets Ant Named for Him," *Bloomberg*, November 8, 2010, http://www.bloomberg.com/news/2010-11-08/harrison-ford-works-to-save-the-world-gets-ant-named-for-him-interview.html.

10. "Lost There, Felt Here," Conservation International, video, http://www.conservation.org/fmg/pages/videoplayer.aspx?videoid=66.

11. *Investing in Life: The Critical Ecosystem Partnership Fund at 10* (Arlington, VA: Conservation International, 2010), http://www.cepf.net/Documents/CEPF_AnniversaryBK_English_web_with_Jacket.pdf.

12. Wildlife Conservation Society, "Tiger Futures: Mainstreaming Conservation in Large Landscapes," application for Global Environment Facility medium-sized project, May 15, 2008, http://www.thegef.org/gef/sites/thegef.org/files/gef_prj_docs/GEFProjectDocuments/M&E/TE/FY2012/World%20Bank/G003691/3691-P112108.pdf.

13. "Who We Are," Global Tiger Initiative, http://globaltigerinitiative.org/who-we-are.

14. Dana Milbank, "Indiana Jones and the Temple of Celebrity," *Washington Post*, June 10, 2008, http://www.washingtonpost.com/wp-dyn/content/article/2008/06/09/AR2008060902399.html.

15. CITES Management Authority of China, Response to Notification No. 2008/059, February 27, 2009, http://www.cites.org/sites/default/files/common/com/sc/58/E58-33A01.pdf.

16. Deepesh Shrestha, "For the Tiger, a Year Closer to Extinction," Phys.org, October 31, 2009, http://phys.org/news176194544.html.

17. Lincoln Tan, "Legalise Tiger Trade to Save Species, Economist Urges," *New Zealand Herald*, May 2, 2009, http://www.nzherald.co.nz/nz/news/article.cfm?c_id=1&objectid=10569890.

18. *Summary Record*, Fifty-eighth Meeting of the CITES Standing Committee, Geneva, Switzerland, July 6–10, 2009, http://cites.org/sites/default/files/eng/com/sc/58/sum/E58-SumRec.pdf.

19. Wildlife Conservation Society, "Dramatic Decline Found in Siberian

Tigers," *Science Daily*, November 24, 2009, http://www.sciencedaily.com /releases/2009/11/091124121429.htm.

20. "China's Tiger Farms," *New York Times*, February 18, 2010, http://www .nytimes.com/2010/02/19/opinion/19fri4.html.

Chapter 9: *The Vladimir Putin Show*

1. Endangered Species Import and Export Management Office of the People's Republic of China, *Comments on CoP15 Doc. 43.2*, brochure distributed at CITES Fifteenth Conference of the Parties, Doha, Qatar, March 13–25, 2010.

2. "China Expects Exports to Slow in 2011," *China Daily*, December 23, 2010, http://www.chinadaily.com.cn/china/2010-12/23/content_11742029.htm.

3. *Summary Record of the Seventh Session of Committee II*, March 18, 2010, CITES Fifteenth Meeting of the Conference of the Parties, Doha, Qatar, March 13–25, 2010, CoP15 Com. II Rec. 7 (Rev. 1), http://cites.org/sites /default/files/eng/cop/15/sum/E15-Com-II-Rec07.pdf; *Summary Record of the Eighth Session of Committee II*, March 18, 2010, CoP15 Com. II Rec. 8 (Rev. 1), http://cites.org/sites/default/files/eng/cop/15/sum/E15-Com-II -Rec08.pdf.

4. "The St. Petersburg Declaration on Tiger Conservation," Saint Petersburg, Russia, November 23, 2010, http://nationalzoo.si.edu/SCBI/WildTigers /pdfs/St_Petersburg_Declaration_English.pdf.

5. Kristin Nowell, Xu Ling, James Compton, Xu Hongfa, and Steven Broad, *Getting Off the Tiger: How China Can Eliminate Illicit Demand for Tiger Parts and Products and Deliver on Its Trade-related National Tiger Recovery Priorities*, TRAFFIC International, Cambridge, UK, November 2010 draft, unpublished paper.

6. Sabri Zain, e-mail to author, November 18, 2010, copied to Steven Broad and James Compton.

7. Endangered Species Import and Export Management Office of the People's Republic of China, *Comments on CoP15 Doc. 43.2*, brochure distributed at CITES Fifteenth Conference of the Parties, Doha, Qatar, March 13–25, 2010.

8. Global Tiger Initiative Secretariat, *Global Tiger Recovery Program: 2010–2022* (Washington, DC: World Bank, 2011), http://www.globaltigerinitiative .org/download/St_Petersburg/GTRP_Nov11_Final_Version_Eng.pdf.

9. Mark McDonald, "'Crisis Status' in South Korea After North Shells Island," *New York Times*, November 23, 2010, http://www.nytimes.com/2010/11/24 /world/asia/24korea.html?pagewanted=all.

10. "Chinese Student Decapitates Russian Woman," Agence France Presse, November 24, 2010, http://newsinfo.inquirer.net/breakingnews/world

/view/20101124-305018/Chinese-student-decapitates-woman-in-Russian
-university.

11. "International Tiger Conservation Forum, St. Petersburg," Global Tiger
Initiative, November 16, 2010, http://globaltigerinitiative.org/news/2010/11
/st-petersburg-tiger-summit.

12. "As Tiger Summit Closes in St. Petersburg, Conservationists Jubilant, Cau-
tiously Optimistic on Wild Tiger's Future," Global Tiger Initiative, December 7, 2010, http://globaltigerinitiative.org/news/2010/12/as-tiger-summit
-closes-in-st-petersburg-conservationists-jubilant-cautiously-optimistic
-on-wild-tigers-future.

13. Simon Montlake, "Leonardo DiCaprio Gives Russia's Tiger Summit a
Helping Hand," *Christian Science Monitor*, November 24, 2010, http://www
.csmonitor.com/World/Asia-South-Central/2010/1124/Leonardo-DiCaprio
-gives-Russia-s-tiger-summit-a-helping-hand.

14. Pauline Verheij, Kaitlyn-Elizabeth Foley, and Katalina Engel, *Reduced to
Skin and Bones: An Analysis of Tiger Seizures from 11 Tiger Range Countries
(2000–2010)* (Cambridge, UK: TRAFFIC International, 2010).

15. Jonathan Watts, "Putin May Be the Tiger's Champion, but China Will
Decide the Species' Future," *Guardian* (UK), November 23, 2010, http://
www.theguardian.com/environment/blog/2010/nov/23/putin-tiger-china
-premier-wen.

Chapter 10: Intermission II—In the Valley of the Shadow

1. "Complicated Grief," Mayo Clinic, http://www.mayoclinic.org/diseases
-conditions/complicated-grief/basics/definition/con-20032765.

2. Hannah Beech and Alex Perry, "Killing Fields: Africa's Rhinos Under
Threat," *Time*, June 13, 2011, http://content.time.com/time/magazine/article
/0,9171,2075283,00.html.

3. Doug Hendrie, in discussion with the author, November 4, 2011.

4. Video of "One Year After the Tiger Summit—From Political Commitments
to Action" can be seen at Frequency.com, http://www.frequency.com
/video/one-year-after-tiger-summit-entire/24813698.

5. "Chinese Auction Flaunts Tiger Trade Ban," International Fund for Animal Welfare, press release, December 1, 2011, http://www.prnewswire.com
/news-releases/chinese-auction-flaunts-tiger-trade-ban-134835848.html.

6. Jonathan Watts, "'It's Really Good Stuff': Undercover at a Chinese Tiger
Bone Wine Auction," *Guardian* (UK), December 6, 2011, http://www.the
guardian.com/environment/blog/2011/dec/06/china-tiger-bone-wine
-auction.

7. Dinny MacMahon, "Forget Stocks—Chinese Turn Bullish on Booze and
Caterpillar Fungus," *Wall Street Journal*, February 30, 2012, http://online
.wsj.com/news/articles/SB10001424052970203471004577142594203471950.

Chapter 11: Sino-US Cat Fight

1. Will Travers, "Lion Meat For Sale," *Born Free Blog*, March 24, 2009, http://www.bornfree.org.uk/blog/2009/03.

2. Nearly all of the information about Carole and Howard Baskin comes from interviews conducted in Tampa, Florida, November 19–20, 2012.

3. Pam Lambert, "Too Purrfect," *People*, December 7, 1998, http://www.people.com/people/archive/article/0,,20127008,00.html.

4. Susan Orlean, "The Lady and the Tigers," *New Yorker*, February 18, 2002, http://www.newyorker.com/magazine/2002/02/18/the-lady-and-the-tigers.

5. Ronald Smothers, "Mystery of Stray Tiger Leads Officials to a Preserve," *New York Times*, January 30, 1999, http://www.nytimes.com/1999/01/30/nyregion/mystery-of-stray-tiger-leads-officials-to-a-preserve.html.

6. Robert D. McFadden, "Tiger Mystery Still Unsolved in New Jersey," *New York Times*, January 31, 1999, http://www.nytimes.com/1999/01/31/nyregion/tiger-mystery-still-unsolved-in-new-jersey.html.

7. Joyce Wadler, "Defiant Defense of Big-Cat Preserve; 'Tiger Lady' Deflects Charges That One of Hers Ran Wild," *New York Times*, July 5, 1999, http://www.nytimes.com/1999/07/05/nyregion/defiant-defense-big-cat-preserve-tiger-lady-deflects-charges-that-one-hers-ran.html.

8. "Tiger Preserve's Owner Ordered to Make Repairs," *New York Times*, February 5, 1999, http://www.nytimes.com/1999/02/05/nyregion/metro-news-briefs-new-jersey-tiger-preserve-s-owner-ordered-to-make-repairs.html.

9. Ronald Smothers, "Tiger Camp Rebuffed on License; 26 Cats May Need a New Home," *New York Times*, April 27, 2000, http://www.nytimes.com/2000/04/27/nyregion/tiger-camp-rebuffed-on-license-26-cats-may-need-a-new-home.html.

10. Jayson Blair, "Two Dozen 400-Pound Tigers, Coming Soon, or Maybe Not," *New York Times*, March 31, 2002, http://www.nytimes.com/2002/03/31/nyregion/two-dozen-400-pound-tigers-coming-soon-or-maybe-not.html.

11. Iver Peterson, "Final Defeat for Tiger Lady Means End of Preserve," *New York Times*, November 11, 2003, http://www.nytimes.com/2003/11/11/nyregion/final-defeat-for-tiger-lady-means-end-of-preserve.html.

12. Greg Bishop and Timothy Williams, "Police Kill Dozens of Animals Freed on Ohio Reserve," *New York Times*, October 19, 2011, http://www.nytimes.com/2011/10/20/us/police-kill-dozens-of-animals-freed-from-ohio-preserve.html?pagewanted=all.

13. "HSUS Undercover Investigation Reveals Dead Tigers, Safety Threats at Oklahoma's GW Exotic Animal Park," Humane Society of the United States, press release, May 16, 2012, http://www.humanesociety.org/news/press_releases/2012/05/ok_exotics_investigation.html.

14. JoeExotic.com, http://www.joeexotic.com/.

15. "Big Cat Rescue Wins Legal Victory Against Tiger Cub Exploiter!," Big Cat

Rescue, February 9, 2013, http://bigcatrescue.org/today-at-big-cat-rescue -feb-9-2013-big-cat-rescue-wins/.

16. Armen Keteyian, "Alleged Abuse at GW Exotic Animal Park Seen on Tape," CBS News, May 16, 2012, http://www.cbsnews.com/news/alleged -abuse-at-gw-exotic-animal-park-seen-on-tape/.

17. Judy A. Mills and Peter Jackson, *Killed for a Cure: A Review of the Worldwide Trade in Tiger Bone* (Cambridge, UK: TRAFFIC International, 1994).

18. Dorene Bolze, Cheryl Chetkiewicz, Qiu Mingjiang, and Douglas Krakower, *The Availability of Tiger-Based Medicine Products and Public Awareness About the Threats to the Tiger in New York City's Chinese Communities* (New York: Wildlife Conservation Society, 1998), http://intranet -staging.wcs.org/Resources/Library/~/media/Files/Departments/WCS%20 Institute/wcswp12.ashx.

19. Andrea Gaski, *While Supplies Last: The Sale of Tiger and Other Endangered Species Medicines in North America* (Washington, DC: TRAFFIC North America, 1998).

20. 16 USC 5301-5306, Rhinoceros and Tiger Conservation Act of 1998, U.S. Fish and Wildlife Service, http://www.fws.gov/le/USStatutes/RhinoTiger .pdf.

21. "Eight Indicted in Illinois for Roles in Killing and Trafficking of Federally Protected Tigers and Leopards," US Fish & Wildlife Service, press release, May 1, 2002.

22. Douglas F. Williamson and Leigh A. Henry, *Paper Tigers? The Role of the US Captive Tiger Population in the Trade in Tiger Parts* (Washington, DC: TRAFFIC North America, 2008), https://www.wwf.or.jp/activities/lib/pdf _wildlife/conservation/papertiger0808.pdf.

23. Phil and Kate asked that their real names not be used. Information about them comes from an interview conducted in Tampa, Florida, November 20, 2012.

24. Seann Lenihann, "Ex Lab Caretaker Hopes to Save What Remains of Wild Animal Orphanage," *Animal People*, October 1, 2011, http://www .animalpeoplenews.org/anp/2011/10/01/ex-lab-caretaker-hopes-to-save-what -remains-of-wild-animal-orphanage.

25. Matt Freidman, "NJ Owners of Captive Tigers Face Further Restrictions under New Bill Passed by Senate," *Star-Ledger* (Newark, NJ), December 15, 2011, http://www.nj.com/news/index.ssf/2011/12/nj_captive_tigers_face _further.html.

26. "Christie Seeks Revisions to Tiger-Protection Law," Associated Press, October 5, 2012, http://www.northjersey.com/news/nation/christie-seeks -revisions-to-tiger-protection-law-1.342820.

27. Campbell Robertson, "A Tiger, a Truck Stop and a Pitched Legal Battle,"

New York Times, March 27, 2013, http://www.nytimes.com/2013/03/28/us
/truck-stop-tiger-in-louisiana-stirs-legal-battle.html.

28. "The Big Cat Handling Crisis," Big Cat Rescue, http://bigcatrescue.org/wp
-content/uploads/2011/01/FactsheetBigCatsHandling_rev.1.pdf.

Chapter 12: Hidden in Plain Sight

1. All of the information about the investigation by Ms. Yin, Mr. Yang, and
   their friend comes from the Environmental Investigation Agency. The investigators' real names have not been used for their protection. The results
   of their work can be found in *Hidden in Plain Sight: China's Clandestine
   Tiger Trade* (London: Environmental Investigation Agency, 2013), http://eia
   -international.org/wp-content/uploads/EIA-Hidden-in-Plain-Sight-med
   -res.pdf.

2. Wildlife Conservation Society, "The Commercial Use of Tiger Parts," *Cat
   News*, no. 18 (March 1993).

3. Richard B. Harris, *Wildlife Conservation in China: Preserving the Habitat of
   China's Wild West* (Armonk, NY: M. E. Sharpe, 2008), 59–61, 79.

4. "Tsoumakang Production Brigade Correctly Handles Forestry and Animal
   Husbandry Contradiction and Expands Sheep Raising," *Peking Review*,
   no. 31 (August 4, 1972), IRTR Cultural Revolution Archive, http://www
   .massline.org/PekingReview/.

5. *On work units*: Peter J. Li, "Enforcing Wildlife Protection in China: The
   Legislative and Political Solutions," *China Information*, March 2007,
   http://cin.sagepub.com/content/21/1/71.abstract; *on PLA roles*: Mao Zedong,
   "Proclamation of the People's Liberation Army, April 25, 1949," in *Selected
   Works of Mao Tse-Tung*, Marxists Internet Archive, https://www.marxists
   .org/reference/archive/mao/selected-works/volume-4/mswv4_62.htm.

6. Cui Tiankai, "Peace Through Pandas," *Washington Post*, December 1, 2013,
   http://www.washingtonpost.com/opinions/peace-through-pandas/2013
   /12/01/001a221c-5789-11e3-8304-caf30787c0a9_story.html.

7. Michael Oksenberg and Elizabeth Economy, "China's Accession to and
   Implementation of International Environmental Accords 1978–95," in *En-
   gaging Countries: Strengthening Compliance with International Accords*, ed.
   Edith Brown Weiss and Harold Karan Jacobson (Cambridge, MA: MIT
   Press, 1998).

8. "No Longer the Army's Business," *Economist*, May 6, 1999; Shirley A. Kan,
   "China's Military-Owned Businesses," CRS Report for Congress, Congressional Research Service, January 17, 2001, http://congressionalresearch.com
   /98-197/document.php.

9. Michael Woodhead, "Army General Is New President of Chinese Medical

Association," *China Medical News*, December 10, 2012, http://www.chinese
medicalnews.com/2012/12/army-general-is-new-president-of.html.

10. Richard B. Harris, *Wildlife Conservation in China: Preserving the Habitat of
China's Wild West* (Armonk, NY: M. E. Sharpe, 2008).

11. George Schaller, *The Last Panda* (Chicago: University of Chicago Press,
1994).

12. Law of the People's Republic of China on the Protection of Wildlife
(adopted on November 8, 1988), China.org.cn, http://www.china.org.cn
/english/environment/34349.htm.

13. Wang Yan, "The Stuff of Life," *NewsChina*, July 2012, http://www.news
chinamag.com/magazine/stuff-of-life.

14. This website was taken down after it was mentioned in *Hidden in Plain
Sight: China's Clandestine Tiger Trade* (London: Environmental Investigation Agency, 2013).

15. Wan Ziming, "Can Tiger Bones of Captive Bred Origins Be Used in Medicine?," *Big Nature* (China), in Chinese, February 2009.

16. Kristin Nowell, Xu Ling, James Compton, Xu Hongfa, and Steven Broad,
"Getting Off the Tiger: How China Can Eliminate Illicit Demand for Tiger
Parts and Products and Deliver on Its Trade-related National Tiger Recovery Priorities," TRAFFIC International, Cambridge, UK, November 2010
draft, unpublished paper.

17. "China Puts the 'Con' in Tiger Conservation," Environmental Investigation
Agency, press release for *Hidden in Plain Sight: China's Clandestine Tiger
Trade*, February 26, 2013, http://www.eia-international.org/china-puts-the
-con-in-tiger-conservation.

18. "Report Reveals 'Secret' Tiger Trade in China," ABC News (Australia),
February 27, 2013, http://www.abc.net.au/news/2013-02-26/an-china-tiger
-conservation-double-standard/4540604; Andrew Penmen, "China's Secret
Tiger Farms Revealed: Species under Threat as Ban on Sale of Body Parts
Ignored," *Daily Mirror*, February 26, 2013, http://www.mirror.co.uk/news
/world-news/chinas-secret-tiger-farms-revealed-1731268; Rachel Tepper,
"Tiger Bone Wine Trade Reveals China's Two-Faced Approach to Conservancy," *Huffington Post*, February 28, 2013, http://www.huffingtonpost
.com/2013/02/28/tiger-bone-wine-china_n_2782772.html.

19. "China Defends Record on Tiger Protection," Agence France Press, February 26, 2013, http://www.globalpost.com/dispatch/news/afp/130226/china
-defends-record-tiger-protection.

Chapter 13: The Empire Strikes Back

1. Andrew Jacobs, "Folk Remedy Extracted from Captive Bears Stirs Furor
in China," *New York Times*, May 21, 2013, http://www.nytimes.com/2013

/05/22/world/asia/chinese-bear-bile-farming-draws-charges-of-cruelty
.html?pagewanted=all.

2. Hannah Beech and Alex Perry, "Killing Fields: Africa's Rhinos Under Threat," *Time*, June 13, 2011, http://content.time.com/time/magazine/article /0,9171,2075283,00.html.

3. "Opening Statement by John E. Scanlon, Secretary-General of CITES, Bangkok, Thailand, 3 March 2013," CITES, http://www.cites.org/eng/news /sg/2013/20130303_cop16.php.

4. Dan Levin, "From Elephants' Mouths, an Illicit Trail to China," *New York Times*, March 1, 2013, http://www.nytimes.com/2013/03/02/world/asia/an -illicit-trail-of-african-ivory-to-china.html?pagewanted=all.

5. "HRH the Duke of Cambridge Prince William Address to the Sixteenth Conference of the CITES Parties," YouTube, posted March 2, 2013, http:// www.youtube.com/watch?v=ma4s74Dps04.

6. *Summary Record of the Second Plenary Session*, March 3, 2013, CITES Sixteenth Meeting of the Conference of the Parties, Bangkok, Thailand, March 3–14, 2013, CoP16 Plen. 2 (Rev. 1), http://www.cites.org/sites /default/files/common/cop/16/sum/E-CoP16-Plen-02.pdf; *Summary Record of the Third Plenary Session*, March 5, 2013, CoP 16 Plen. 3 (Rev. 1), http://www.cites.org/sites/default/files/common/cop/16/sum/E-CoP16-Plen -03.pdf; *Summary Record of the Fourth Plenary Session*, March 6, 2013, CoP16 Plen. 4, http://www.cites.org/sites/default/files/common/cop/16 /sum/E-CoP16-Plen-04.pdf.

7. Kristin Nowell, e-mail to Debbie Banks, March 4, 2013.

8. "Hidden in Plain Sight: China's Clandestine Tiger Trade," video summary of *Hidden in Plain Sight: China's Clandestine Tiger Trade* (London: Environmental Investigation Agency, 2013), Vimeo, n.d., http://vimeo.com /60444302.

9. Kristin Nowell, e-mail to Debbie Banks and copied to seventeen others, March 8, 2013.

10. CITES Secretariat, *Monitoring of Illegal Trade in Ivory and Other Elephant Specimens*, CITES Sixteenth Meeting of the Conference of the Parties, Bangkok, Thailand, March 3–14, 2013, CoP16 Doc. 53.2.1, http://www .cites.org/sites/default/files/eng/cop/16/doc/E-CoP16-53-02-01.pdf.

11. Grace G. Gabriel, Ning Hua, and Juan Wang, *Making a Killing: A 2011 Survey of Ivory Markets in China* (Yarmouth Port, MA: International Fund for Animal Welfare, 2012).

12. Ian J. Saunders, "Testimony for a Hearing of the US Senate and US House of Representatives International Conservation Caucus on the Global Poaching Crisis," November 15, 2012, http://iccfoundation.us/downloads /Hearing_Testimony_Saunders.pdf.

13. Eleanor Beardsley, "France Takes a Stand, Crushing Ivory Beneath the Eiffel Tower," National Public Radio, February 9, 2014, http://www.npr.org/2014/02/09/274075393/france-crushes-ivory-beneath-the-eiffel-tower.

14. CITES Secretariat, *Monitoring the Illegal Killing of Elephants*, CITES Sixteenth Meeting of the Conference of the Parties, Bangkok, Thailand, March 3–14, 2013, CoP16 Doc. 53.1, http://www.cites.org/sites/default/files/eng/cop/16/doc/E-CoP16-53-01.pdf.

15. TRAFFIC, *Monitoring of Illegal Trade in Ivory and Other Elephant Specimens*, CITES Sixteenth Meeting of the Conference of the Parties, Bangkok, Thailand, March 3–14, 2013, CoP16 Doc. 53.2.2 (Rev. 1), http://www.cites.org/sites/default/files/eng/cop/16/doc/E-CoP16-53-02-02.pdf.

16. Michael Barris, "China's Millionaires Multiply," *China Daily*, May 31, 2013, http://usa.chinadaily.com.cn/epaper/2013-05/31/content_16551648.htm; "GDP per Capita 2009–2013," World Bank, http://data.worldbank.org/indicator/NY.GDP.PCAP.CD.

17. China Auction Association newsletter, Spring 2012.

18. Zhao Wen, "Ivory, Rhino Horn Smuggling Rises," *Shanghai Daily*, March 21, 2013, http://www.shanghaidaily.com/metro/Ivory-rhino-horn-smuggling-rises/shdaily.shtml.

19. CITES Secretariat, *Rhinoceroses*, CITES Sixteenth Meeting of the Conference of the Parties, Bangkok, Thailand, March 3–14, 2013, CoP16 Doc. 54.2 (Rev. 1), http://www.cites.org/sites/default/files/eng/cop/16/doc/E-CoP16-54-02.pdf.

20. Jeffrey Gettleman, "Coveting Horns, Ruthless Smugglers' Rings Put Rhinos in the Cross Hairs," *New York Times*, December 31, 2012.

21. Denver Nicks, "Western Black Rhino Declared Extinct," *Time*, November 6, 2013, http://time.com/9446/western-black-rhino-declared-extinct/.

22. Hannah Beech, "Killing Fields: Africa's Rhinos under Threat," *Time*, June 13, 2011, http://content.time.com/time/magazine/article/0,9171,2075283,00.html.

23. Grace Gabriel, "My Angst over China's Role in the Endangered Wildlife Trade," *chinadialogue*, March 15, 2013, https://www.chinadialogue.net/blog/5802-My-angst-over-China-s-role-in-the-endangered-wildlife-trade/en.

24. *Summary Record of the Fourteenth Session of Committee II*, March 13, 2013, CITES Sixteenth Meeting of the Conference of the Parties, Bangkok, Thailand, March 3–14, 2013, CoP16 Com. II Rec. 14 (Rev. 1), http://www.cites.org/sites/default/files/common/cop/16/sum/E-CoP16-Com-II-Rec-14.pdf.

25. A video of the entire press conference ("Joint Press Conference – CITES CoP16, March 14, 2013") can be seen at http://vimeo.com/61788297.

26. *Summary Record of the Tenth Session of Committee I*, March 11, 2013, CITES Sixteenth Meeting of the Conference of the Parties, Bangkok,

Thailand, March 3–14, 2013, CoP16 Com. I Rec. 10, http://www.cites.org/sites/default/files/common/cop/16/sum/E-CoP16-Com-I-Rec-10.pdf; *Summary Record of the Eleventh Session of Committee I*, March 11, 2013, CoP16 Com I Rec. 11 (Rev. 1), http://www.cites.org/sites/default/files/common/cop/16/sum/E-CoP16-Com-I-Rec-11.pdf.

27. *Summary Record of the Seventh Plenary Session*, March 14, 2013, CITES Sixteenth Meeting of the Conference of the Parties, Bangkok, Thailand, March 3–14, 2013, CoP16 Plen. 7 (Rev. 1), http://www.cites.org/sites/default/files/common/cop/16/sum/E-CoP16-Plen-07.pdf.

28. Information about Chris Shepherd comes from an interview in Bangkok, Thailand, March 12, 2013.

Chapter 14: Hope for a Tiger Spring

1. Jared Harris and R. Edward Freeman, "A Business Model to Save the Black Rhino?," *Washington Post*, March 15, 2013, http://www.washingtonpost.com/business/a-business-model-to-save-the-black-rhino/2013/03/14/983f3194-8b4d-11e2-9f54-f3fdd70acad2_story.html.

2. Pelham Jones, "Update on CITES and the PROA Opinion Survey," undated PDF.

3. Author, e-mail to Rowena Watson, March 20, 2013.

4. Zhao Wen, "Ivory, Rhino Horn Smuggling Rises," *Shanghai Daily*, March 21, 2013, http://www.shanghaidaily.com/metro/Ivory-rhino-horn-smuggling-rises/shdaily.shtml.

5. George Obulutsa, "Xi Jinping Makes First Africa Visit as China Leader," *Independent* (UK), March 25, 2013, http://www.independent.ie/business/world/xi-jinping-makes-first-africa-visit-as-china-leader-29151423.html.

6. Jaime A. FlorCruz, "Charm Offensive: Peng Liyuan, China's Glamorous New First Lady," CNN.com, March 25, 2013, http://www.cnn.com/2013/03/23/world/asia/china-peng-liyuan-profile/.

7. Jacob Zuma, "Jacob Zuma's Remarks on Meeting with Xi Jinping," *PoliticsWeb*, March 26, 2013, http://www.politicsweb.co.za/.

8. Department of Environmental Affairs, Republic of South Africa, "Update on Rhino Poaching and Signing of MoU Between South Africa and the People's Republic of China," March 27, 2013, https://www.environment.gov.za/content/updaterhinopoaching_signingmoubetween_sa_china.

9. Author, e-mail to Rowena Watson, March 28, 2013.

10. David Smith, "South African Game Reserve Poisons Rhino's Horns to Prevent Poaching," *Guardian* (UK), April 4, 2013, http://www.theguardian.com/environment/2013/apr/04/rhino-horns-poisoned-poachers-protect.

11. Jon Herskovitz, "Safe Crackers Steal Nearly $3 Million in South Africa Rhino Horn," Reuters, April 6, 2013, http://www.reuters.com/.

12. Patrick Steel, "Rhino DNA Database Set Up to Prevent Thefts," *Muse-*

ums Journal, April 10, 2013, http://www.museumsassociation.org/museums
-journal/news/09042013-rhino-dna-database-set-up-to-prevent-thefts.

13. Subir Bhaumik, "India Deploys Drones to Save Rhinos in Assam State,"
BBC News India, April 9, 2013, http://www.reuters.com/article/2013/04/06
/us-safrica-rhinos-idUSBRE93503720130406.

14. Robin Des Bois, *On the Trail: Information and Analysis Bulletin on Animal
Poaching and Smuggling*, no. 1 (April 1–June 30, 2013), http://www.robin
desbois.org/english/animal/ON-THE-TRAIL-1.pdf.

15. Krishnendu Mukherjee, "Tiger Poaching in India Highest in Seven Years,"
Times of India, December 18, 2013, http://timesofindia.indiatimes.com
/home/environment/flora-fauna/Tiger-poaching-in-India-highest-in-seven
-years/articleshow/27554070.cms.

16. H.R. 1998—Big Cats and Public Safety Protection Act, http://beta.congress
.gov/bill/113th-congress/house-bill/1998; S. 1381—Big Cats and Public
Safety Protection Act, http://beta.congress.gov/bill/113th-congress/senate
-bill/1381.

17. "American Voters Support Nationwide Ban of Big Cat Private Ownership,"
International Fund for Animal Welfare, press release, October 7, 2013,
http://www.ifaw.org/international/news/american-voters-support-nation
-wide-ban-big-cat-private-ownership.

18. "China Zoos Asked to Apologize over Tiger Abuse Caught on Video," Associated Press, May 7, 2013, http://www.ctvnews.ca/world/china-zoos-asked
-to-apologize-over-tiger-abuse-caught-on-video-1.1270481.

19. Transcript of Li Bingbing video news release, United Nations Environment Programme, May 7, 2013, http://www.unmultimedia.org/tv/unifeed
/2013/05/unep-li-bingbing-poaching.

20. "Say No to Ivory and Rhino Horn PSA: 'War,' Featuring Li Bingbing,"
Shanghaiist, May 15, 2013, http://shanghaiist.com/2013/05/15/say_no_to
_ivory_and_rhino_horn_psa_war_li_bingbing.php; WildAid, "War," video
featuring Li Bingbing, YouTube.com, published May 14, 2013, http://www
.youtube.com/watch?v=ccRAHhBoUgM.

21. Bai Tiantian, "Experts Slam Wildlife Allegations," *Global Times* (China),
May 21, 2013, http://www.globaltimes.cn/content/783295.shtml.

22. Andrew Jacobs, "Folk Remedy Extracted from Captive Bears Stirs Furor in China," *New York Times*, May 21, 2013, http://www.nytimes.com
/2013/05/22/world/asia/chinese-bear-bile-farming-draws-charges-of-cruelty
.html?pagewanted=all.

23. "Mang Ping: Wild Animal Protection Ordinance Suspected of Encouraging Commercial Exploitation," *Legal Daily* (China), April 15, 2013, http://
www.legaldaily.com.cn/.

24. Zhang Chun, "Civil Society's Changing Role in the Chinese Political
System," *chinadialogue*, March 18, 2013, https://www.chinadialogue.net

/article/show/single/en/5804-Civil-society-s-changing-role-in-the-Chinese
-political-system.

25. WildAid, "Yao Ming Says No to Ivory and Rhino Horn," PR Newswire,
April 16, 2013, http://www.prnewswire.com/news-releases/yao-ming-says
-no-to-ivory-and-rhino-horn-203210741.html.

26. Andrew Higgins, "Teeing Off at the Edge of the Arctic? A Chinese Plan
Baffles Iceland," *New York Times*, March 22, 2013, http://www.nytimes.com
/2013/03/23/world/europe/iceland-baffled-by-chinese-plan-for-golf-resort
.html?pagewanted=all.

27. "Sharks," WildAid, http://www.wildaid.org/sharks.

28. Niu Chen, "PSA Lashes Out at Shark Trade," *Beijing Today*, August 3, 2012,
http://beijingtoday.com.cn/2012/08/psa-lashes-out-at-shark-trade/.

29. Simon Denyer, "In China, Victory for Wildlife Conservation as Citizens
Persuaded to Give Up Shark Fin Soup," *Washington Post*, October 19,
2014, http://www.washingtonpost.com/world/in-china-victory-for-wildlife
-conservation-as-citizens-persuaded-to-give-up-shark-fin-soup/2013/10/19
/e8181326-3646-11e3-89db-8002ba99b894_story.html.

30. J. T. Quigley, "No More Shark Fin Soup at CCP Banquets," *Diplomat*, December 9, 2013, http://thediplomat.com/2013/12/no-more-shark-fin-soup-at
-ccp-banquets/.

Chapter 15: Epilogue

1. Mary Oliver, "The Summer Day," *New and Selected Poems, Volume One*
(Boston: Beacon Press, 1992).

2. Jane Perlez and Chris Buckley, "China Brushes Aside US Warnings on
Snowden," *New York Times*, June 25, 2013, http://www.nytimes.com
/2013/06/26/world/asia/china-united-states-snowden.html.

3. Ben Geman, "IEA Official: Obama Plan Gives US Leverage in Climate
Talks with China," *Hill*, July 10, 2013, http://thehill.com/blogs/e2-wire
/e2-wire/310057-iea-official-white-house-plan-can-help-us-china-climate
-ties.

4. Bryan Christy, "Historic US Ivory Crush a Call to Global Action," *National
Geographic Daily News*, November 15, 2013, http://news.nationalgeographic
.com/news/2013/13/131115-united-states-ivory-crush-ivory-trafficking
-philippines-clinton-global-initiative-world/.

5. Simon Denyer, "China's First 'Ivory Crush' Signals It May Join Global Push
to Protect African Elephants," *Washington Post*, January 6, 2014, http://
www.washingtonpost.com/world/chinas-first-ivory-crush-signals-it-may
-join-global-push-to-protect-african-elephants/2014/01/06/267e432c-76d6
-11e3-b1c5-739e63e9c9a7_story.html.

6. Agence France Press, "Rhino Poaching in Kenya Doubled in 2013," *Huff-*

ington Post, February 27, 2014, http://www.huffingtonpost.com/2014/02/27
/rhino-poaching-kenya-2013_n_4868665.html.

7. Schalk Mouton, "SA Set to Sell Its Rhino Horn Pile," *Times Live* (South
Africa), July 3, 2013, http://www.timeslive.co.za/thetimes/2013/07/03/sa-set
-to-sell-its-rhino-horn-pile.

8. "TEMTI: Economic Perspectives on Global Sustainability," International Union for Conservation of Nature, http://www.iucn.org/news_home
page/news_by_date/?12643/TEMTI-Economic-Perspectives-on-Global
-Sustainability.

9. Alejandro Nadal, e-mail to the author, February 23, 2014.

10. Barack Obama, "Executive Order—Combating Wildlife Trafficking,"
White House, July 1, 2013, http://www.whitehouse.gov/the-press-office
/2013/07/01/executive-order-combating-wildlife-trafficking.

11. Agence France Press, "Some of China's Rich and Powerful Show Off Their
Social Status by Attending Ritual Tiger Killings," *Business Insider*, March
27, 2014, http://www.businessinsider.com/chinas-rich-and-powerful-show
-off-their-social-status-by-attending-ritual-tiger-killings-2014-3.

12. Kayla Ruble, "China Outlaws the Eating of Tiger Penis, Rhino Horn, and
Other Endangered Animal Products," *VICE News*, May 2, 2014, https://
news.vice.com/article/china-outlaws-the-eating-of-tiger-penis-rhino-horn
-and-other-endangered-animal-products.

13. "About 100 Cubs Expected to Be Born in NE China's Siberian Tiger
Garden," Xinhuanet.com, May 6, 2014, http://news.xinhuanet.com/english
/photo/2014-05/06/c_133313800_2.htm.

14. Navin Singh Khadka, "China 'Admits' Trading in Tiger Skins," BBC World
Service, July 12, 2014, http://www.bbc.com/news/world-asia-28258595.

15. Kristin Nowell and Natalia Pervushina, *Review of Implementation of Resolution Conf. 12.5 (Rev. CoP16) on Conservation of and Trade in Tigers and
Other Appendix-I Asian Big Cat Species*, report to the CITES Secretariat
for the sixty-fifth meeting of the Standing Committee, http://www.cites
.org/sites/default/files/eng/com/sc/65/E-SC65-38-A01_0.pdf.

16. CITES Secretariat, *Interpretation and Implementation of the Convention/
Species Trade and Conservation: Asian Big Cats*, Sixty-fifth meeting of the
Standing Committee, July 7–11, 2014, http://www.cites.org/sites/default
/files/eng/com/sc/65/com/E-SC65-Com-04.pdf.

17. Letter to US Secretary of the Interior Sally Jewell from Debbie Banks, head
of the Tiger Campaign, Environmental Investigation Agency, July 2, 2014.

18. E-mail to the author from the US Department of the Interior, July 22, 2014.

19. George Wittemyer et al., "Illegal Killing For Ivory Drives Global Decline
in African Elephants," *Proceedings of the National Academy of Sciences*,
August 18, 2014, http://www.pnas.org/content/early/2014/08/14/1403984
111.full.pdf+html?sid=ebfc205d-ea45-463a-9773-7efec0382a43; Jason Stra-

ziuso, "100,000 Elephants Killed in Africa, Study Finds," Associated Press, August 18, 2014, http://bigstory.ap.org/article/100000-elephants-killed -africa-study-finds.

20. Elizabeth A. Burgess, Sarah S. Stoner, and Kaitlyn-Elizabeth Foley, *Brought to Bear: An Analysis of Seizures Across Asia (2000–2011)* (Petaling Jaya, Selangor, Malaysia: TRAFFIC, 2014); TRAFFIC, "Parts of 2,800 Bears Seized in Asia over a 12-Year Period," press release, August 21, 2014, http://www.traffic.org/home/2014/8/21/parts-of-2800-bears-seized-in-asia -over-a-12-year-period.html.

INDEX

Africa, 59, 88, 91, 128. *See also* elephant
ivory trade; rhino horn trade and
farming; South Africa
African Rhino Specialist Group, 210
African Wildlife Trust, 212
Al-Shabaab, 207
American black bears, 12, 40–42, 43
American College of Traditional Chinese
Medicine, 72, 103
animal sanctuaries, 122–23, 172–74,
181, 182, 240. *See also* Big Cat
Rescue; private ownership of
exotic animals
Animals Asia Foundation, 89
Animal Welfare Act, 177
Art of War (Sun Tzu), 94, 100, 122, 125,
142, 160, 197
Asean WEN (Wildlife Enforcement
Network), 88
Asia: bear species native to, 12, 13;
petition to impose trade sanctions
against, 45; sponsorship to investigate
the Asian bear trade, 23. *See also*
specific countries
Asiatic black bear, 28, 29, 31, 33, 37,
122–23

Babbitt, Bruce, 46, 49
Bangkok bears, 11–17. *See also* bears

Bangkok CITES conference. *See* CITES
conference, Bangkok (2013)
Bangladesh, 120, 159, 162–63, 164
Banks, Debbie, 167, 168; dedication to
tigers, 100; EIA investigation, 95–97;
first experience seeing a wild tiger,
98–99; presentation on animal skins
trade, 100–101, 111, 203–4; tiger-bone
wine report, 187–88
Barkhor, Lhasa, 107
Basker, Avinash, 219
Baskin, Carole: campaign against Joe
Exotic, 177–78; sanctuary mission,
173–74; threats against, 172–73.
See also Big Cat Rescue
Baskin, Howard, 174, 176–77, 179, 181,
183–84. *See also* Big Cat Rescue
Bear Class Test Farm, 33–35
bear farming: absence of discussions on
at CITES, 220; authorized bear facilities in South Korea, 37; availability
of bear parts in shops, 27, 30; caging
of bears, 28; deception regarding
access to bile milking, 34–35; decline
in China's wild bear population, 25;
grassroots movement to end wildlife
consumption, 227–29, 231; illegality
of trade in bear bile, 29, 30; investigative trip to observe, 26; market